An Australian Army doctor in Viet Nam

Marshall Barr

ALLEN&UNWIN

First published in 2001

Allen & Unwin
83 Alexander Street
Crows Nest NSW 2065
Australia
Phone: (61 2) 8425 0100
Fax: (61 2) 9906 2218
Email: info@allenandunwin.com
Web: www.allenandunwin.com

National Library of Australia
Cataloguing-in-Publication entry:

Barr, Marshall.
Surgery, sand and Saigon tea: an Australian army doctor in Viet Nam.

Includes index.
ISBN 1 86508 463 8.

1. Vietnamese Conflict, 1961–1975 – Personal narratives, Australian. 2. Surgeons – Biography. I. Title.

959.7043092

Set in 11/13 pt Plantin Light by Midland Typesetters, Maryborough
Printed by South Wind Productions, Singapore

10 9 8 7 6 5 4 3 2

Foreword

At the end of World War II the communists and nationalists in Viet Nam combined to form a government for the whole country. But support in the South was weak and it enabled France to return to govern. After a bitter eight-year war the French were thrown out, and there was a separation of the North under Ho Chi Minh and the South, the Republic of Viet Nam, under Ngo Dinh Dim Diem. The communists now commenced an armed conflict against the Diem regime, which the USA, Australia, New Zealand and other Pacific countries saw as a threat not only to the South, but to the entire region. Initially only observers were sent to Viet Nam, then combat troops. The Diem government forces still had great difficulty holding back the strengthening Vietcong and North Vietnamese: the military assistance from America and its allies had to be increased.

Despite the increasing power of the army, navy and air forces, by 1967 there were serious doubts whether this war could be won. Major public protests developed in the US and in Australia, particularly with the introduction of National Service by ballot. In Vietnam, increasing numbers of serious illnesses and casualties threatened to overwhelm the small Australian medical units. It was into this climate that Major Marshall Barr volunteered for twelve months CMF full-time duty. His anaesthetic qualifications, experience and expertise came at a time of great need.

Marshall wanted to know what sort of a war it was and to this end went out on several combat missions. He worked hard, but he'd always enjoyed life and he took every opportunity to do this in many and varied ways. The time for any pleasures diminished however, with the unleashing of the massive Vietcong assault in the 'Tet offensive'.

The Field Ambulance was a wonderful unit which could be adapted to many roles. I was dismayed when it disappeared from the Australian Army. Basically a mobile evacuation unit, it had the capability of becoming static and, by adding a surgical team and nursing sisters, 8 Field Ambulance developed into 1 Australian Field Hospital in April 1968—a great unit working under difficulties.

It became obvious during the Tet offensive that the unit would need specialist reinforcements; there were none in the regular army, so a system was formed of volunteer surgical teams from the CMF. The Army was not particularly keen but there was no alternative and the system worked.

It was at this time that I arrived in Viet Nam to a unit under great stress. I was not well prepared. It did not help that my predecessor had left for Australia the day before I arrived and there was no surgical handover. But I hadn't reckoned on Marshall Barr who gave me a very good briefing and we immediately set to work on new casualties.

I realised what a tremendous support Marshall was going to be to me, not only for his anaesthetics but his initial management of casualties and resuscitation. He helped me in many ways to fit in with the team. He stimulated me to work harder and better than I thought possible. That was Marshall's great strength of personality. He carried the team along with him.

In this, the first major account by a member of the Australian medical services in Viet Nam, Marshall underrates himself. At times he was lighthearted but beneath this exterior was a serious commitment to do all he could for the wounded Australian soldier. When his twelve months of service was completed he left us a set of standards which we followed.

Colonel Donald Beard
AM, RFD, ED, RAAMC, Rtd

This book is dedicated to the memory of Mick Boyle,
truly my Great Friend.

Contents

List of illustrations

Preface

THE VIET NAM conflict was escalating rapidly when I volunteered for full-time duty with the Australian Citizen Military Forces. Never before having kept a diary of any sort, this seemed an appropriate time to start one.The length and the quality of entries from February 1967 to April 1968 vary considerably for reasons which are soon apparent. As well as reflective accounts of the day's activities, there are shakier recollections written the morning after and tired scribbles catching up on long periods of intense activity. As the first specialist anaesthetist to serve with the Australian Army in Viet Nam, I was granted many unique opportunities and confronted by many problems, culminating with the Tet offensive of February 1968. All were recorded in some fashion and this book is as correct as poor handwriting and fading memory permit. I have sought help with details of names and places, but responsibility for inaccuracies is mine.

In 1969 I began writing a sanitised account of these events. Happily this was not published and with the passage of time a franker portrayal can be given. It is still not the full picture. I have included very personal matters and descriptions or opinions which might be hurtful only where I feel they are needed to give important background or to explain key episodes.

While the build up to Tet and its unfolding have been examined many times, no one has told this particular story. Yet our small contribution has much of interest and some lessons to teach. My experiences differed markedly from many common perceptions of Viet Nam. On the military side, Australians should be aware how fragile their medical service really was and the huge reliance we placed on our American colleagues.

A view from the medical side of the bravery, the humour and the tragedies of the fighting men has certainly been worth recounting. More important to me, however, has been the opportunity to record something of the dedicated work of our own young soldiers in the finest tradition of the Medical Corps.

Acknowledgments

NEVILLE AND JOY Ripley's hospitality to a would-be author is not forgotten although it has taken 30 years to bear fruit. Mary, who uncomplainingly typed those first feeble drafts, continues to give me her love and uncritical support. My sister Alison Gregg urged me to produce the book and applied her literary skills to help make it readable.

I am grateful to the many who 'were there' and who helped fill information gaps. Very special thanks are due to Marie Boyle, and to Peter (Bruno) Davis who gave me the pick of his photographs and a greater gift—the Digger's viewpoint.

Brendan O'Keefe's excellent *Medicine at War* (Allen & Unwin 1994) was used extensively for checking names, dates and background information.

The photographs are acknowledged in their captions.

Prologue

'ARE YOU A chewing-gum chewer?'

'No, I'm a drinking drinker.'

The man in the aisle seat had the right idea. As our T-jet crossed the Darling Ranges I discarded the Spearmint and joined in his attack on the plane's stock of Red Label Johnnie Walker. The date was Monday 6 February 1967. I was flying eastward across Australia because the trains were fully booked. I was flying first class because the Army was paying, and it was paying because I was going to Viet Nam.

Several mini-bottles later, the air hostess in her TAA uniform had become sensationally beautiful, and Peter and I were the best of buddies. My new friend was clearly intelligent. He didn't agree with the mob opinion that volunteering for Viet Nam meant I was either stupid or mad. Peter was well up on current affairs, no doubt because of his foreign business interests. Indonesian militancy had by this time jolted Australians into awareness that geographically we were part of Southeast Asia. Peter was typical, I explained to him magnanimously, of the thousands who were trying to bridge the huge gaps in our knowledge and understanding of our neighbours.

The Scotch and our political discussions flowed on, interrupted only by a short pause during a refuelling stop at Adelaide. I remember the conversation as being remarkably profound, but probably we were just rehashing media-generated platitudes . . . the domino theory was more than theory; international communism had clearly shown its intention to take over the world; the free nations must unite; the UN had halted the Reds in Korea, and must do it again . . . firm military action, plus economic and educational aid; leadership, strong alliances, the spirit of humanity as well as political pragmatism—a great many of the world's problems were close to resolution when Peter and I parted at Melbourne.

Over the years, in more sober periods of reflection, I have come to accept that I was not simply out to do my bit against communist aggression—although I certainly did feel, and still do, that Australia's security was then genuinely at risk. Nor can I claim that I had a compelling urge to succour the sick and wounded soldiery. There was a kind of inevitability that I should be going to Viet Nam. Inborn military traits descending from earlier generations had skipped my peace-loving parents, but they were in me all right—stimulated by an assortment of events and influences over 30 years, and now leading me on this journey to a war.

Part I

‘Childhood shows the man’

One

MY FIRST CLEAR memories are fragmentary episodes from World War II, historical events mixed up with personal and family moments. In Brisbane we were a comfortably long way from the early campaigns in Europe and North Africa, and I have no firm recollections of those first two momentous years. But I vividly recall at the age of seven reading the huge newspaper headline, SINGAPORE SURRENDERS, and I have an exact picture in my mind of our mother's pale, strained face as she tried to explain to my sister Heather and me what had happened.

For a while the threat of bombs and Japanese invasion closed all the schools. This suited me, but my ex-schoolteacher mother most unfairly became active in the setting up of an alternative 'school', a small group of children illegally gathered in private homes to continue their education. Mother was much more in evidence than Dad, whose burdens at that time must have been fearful. In his thirties he had made the decision to leave a successful pharmaceutical practice in Perth to become a doctor. As he had no certificate in Latin, only Australia's newest medical school would accept his application, which was why the family had to move some two and a half thousand miles to Brisbane, on the other side of the continent.

Early in the morning he'd ride his bike the half mile to the top of Herston Road, to the medical school and the main Brisbane hospitals. At night and for most of the weekends he studied; during the vacations he worked as a representative for the pharmaceutical firm of May & Baker, calling on hospitals and doctors all over Queensland. The strain must have been appalling, with two young children, another on the way, minimal income, the family separated from friends and relatives, and caught in what looked to be a likely war zone. I was only aware in the vaguest possible way of all these matters. Two very specific things I do remember—his concern at the possible carnage if bombs fell on the closely grouped Brisbane public hospitals, and his return from a trip to North Queensland when he mimicked the train conductor: 'Next week I s'pose the train'll be full of little yeller fellers.' Sensitivity and tact were not his strongest points. Even I could see that my mother was not amused. But I had no idea just how close we were to invasion.

The first servicemen I remember were Americans, who suddenly appeared almost on our doorstep. Anti-aircraft guns and encampments were set up in Victoria Park, a great valley of tall trees, open grassy areas and belts of dense undergrowth, whose unfenced frontage ran the length of Herston Road. Our house on the opposite, elevated side thus looked out over unlimited greenery, and we local kids had a magnificent playground, to which were now added guns, searchlights and soldiers! I later recalled that Australian troops were stationed in Victoria Park, but my first memories are firmly fixed on the Americans. They wore caps at a rakish angle, and smartly pressed uniforms with ties puzzlingly tucked inside their shirts, a fashion I had never seen. They all seemed most friendly, offering us gum, which I didn't like, and cigarettes which I accepted and enjoyed, although I suspect I didn't inhale the smoke. They certainly were friendly towards many of the local girls, with whom they sometimes behaved oddly and very actively, and not always in the most secluded places in the park. I thought the condoms scattered about were discarded balloons until I brought one home. This was the second time I remember mother's normally calm features becoming white with anxiety. She snatched out a handkerchief and grabbed the thing from my hand. They were full of germs, she said; I must never touch one again . . .

I take an irrational pride in having personal memories of General Douglas MacArthur. When his headquarters for the South West Pacific Area was established in Brisbane, MacArthur and his family regularly attended St Anne's Presbyterian Church, to which I was unwillingly taken every Sunday. Without any real notion of his importance, I was impressed by the way members of the congregation would line each side of the broad church steps as he came out from the service, then stand back on the pavement while he and his entourage got into the waiting Chevrolet staff car with its starred General's pennant. That respectful, silent semicircle knew what I did not—for all practical purposes the future of Australia had been delivered into the hands of this one man.

Heather once reminded me that MacArthur's son had been in my Sunday School class. I don't remember him. I hated those dreary sessions, although I'm now grateful for having learnt fragments of the magnificent language of the King James Bible. Heather remained a committed Christian, and became the highly respected principal of the Presbyterian Ladies College in Perth. She possibly enjoyed those Sunday School sessions. Since she showed no interest in sport, guns, planes or any sort of fighting, as children we inhabited almost totally different worlds.

The ritual boredom of Sunday mornings did serve to make escape all the more pleasurable. *Rockfist Rogan RAF* was my favourite of the comic books, and I was soon devouring the wartime exploits of Biggles and Worrals. Planes became my passion. On Sunday afternoons Scottish Presbyterianism banned activities involving guns, water pistols, bows and arrows, and the slingshots we called shanghais; some unfortunates were confined indoors to read the Good Book. By comparison, my parents were positively indulgent. Glider-flying was accepted as a suitable pastime, and one of our gang had a model plane made of balsa wood and paper and powered by a rubber band. This was easily recognisable as a Westland Lysander, for some of us were becoming aviation experts. Shop windows regularly displayed new flying models to yearn for, while in the skies we could gaze at the real thing—every day more aircraft, and all of seductive shape and thrilling sound.

I remember most fondly the real Wirraways, growling, squat, efficient-looking trainers which continually buzzed over the city and suburbs. Sometimes they dived low to follow the winding Brisbane River just above the mast-tops of the freighters and ferries. If you were lucky, one might swoop down and fly along the street, the two-man crew waving to the ecstatic schoolboys below. It made you feel good to see Australian pilots flying Australian planes. Later I discovered they were actually American Harvards, made in Australia under licence and optimistically called 'fighter/trainers'. Later also I learned that RAAF crews in Rabaul had suicidally flown their Wirraways against the far faster, better armed and more manoeuvrable Japanese Zeros.

When our first proper fighters came they were all from America. The Tomahawks, Kittyhawks and twin-boomed Lockheed Lightnings were magnificent in their streamlining, their power and speed. I was taken as a treat to see a Kittyhawk on display in a public square, probably as part of a drive to sell war bonds. With its widespread wings bearing the Royal Australian Air Force roundels, its nose towering high, propeller blades gleaming, and the intricate detail of the undercarriage in perfect view from a small boy's height, this was the most beautiful thing I had ever seen.

At Kelvin Grove Primary School the classroom walls carried aircraft identification charts, and I could recognise every silhouette. Just once, I saw a real Japanese reconnaissance floatplane. We were at home, the air-raid sirens had sounded, and I was looking excitedly out of the shelter Dad had fashioned from the sunken concrete steps leading down to the footpath and Herston Road. The plane flew very high above scattered clouds, but its unusual features were instantly recognisable. I was delighted to think the war was coming to us at last.

Surprisingly few people know of the heavy bombing suffered by Australia's northern centres during the Japanese advance. The censors did well in hiding or minimising the devastation to Darwin, the attacks on Broome and Derby in Western Australia, and on Townsville in northern Queensland. But I knew something, probably from Dad's travels, and I knew the Japs sent reconnaissance planes before bombing a new target area. At last the guns and searchlights in the park would be in action! Alas for me, but not for Brisbane and its closely grouped hospitals, that solitary floatplane was to be my only sight of the enemy.

It must have been shortly afterwards that our parents took us down to the Brisbane River to see a remarkable spectacle—a line of aircraft carriers moored stem to stern along the wharves. I think there were no fewer than five, and to a small boy they were all massive. Hundreds of uniformed US sailors lined the flight decks and waved from portholes, hundreds more mingled with cheering civilians on the waterfront. The Brisbanites, parents as excited as children, were waving small American flags and getting sailors to sign their names along the white stripes. This mass rejoicing was a bit puzzling. I was amazed by the grandeur of those huge ships, it was interesting to see so many cheerful young sailors and we got a few autographs on my flag, but the amount of fuss seemed altogether excessive. Again I did not appreciate what the grownups were celebrating. This evidence of the military might of the United States was a near guarantee that our country was saved.

By 1944 I was following the progress of the war with a bit more insight. I kept a newspaper watch on the bombing of Germany and the invasion of Europe, and a closer eye on MacArthur's island-hopping advances in the Pacific. Hero-worshipping had swung from the Americans to the Australian Diggers. Magazines and books galore praised the mateship and heroism shown by our boys in their slouch hats, fighting the desert campaigns, on the Kokoda Track, and now in the jungle offensives.

In those years I also learnt for the first time something of their predecessors, when veterans came to talk to the school on Anzac Day. The simple ordinariness of these middle-aged men, their quiet dignity, and the way their voices trembled in speaking of lost companions, were uncommonly moving. Partly it was because we actually knew them or their families. This was in the country town of Miles, where Dad had become the solo doctor and where you knew everybody.

A few of the new generation of soldiers trickled back into this small community, wounded in body or mind. This was reality, very different from the tales of gallantry and high adventure. On the day Japan surrendered, I helped in keeping the small bell of the Miles Presbyterian Church triumphantly ringing. The feeling of relief and euphoria in just that one small town overwhelmed all martial ambitions. It would have been nice to have flown a Spitfire, but I was genuinely glad the fighting was over.

The family returned to Perth in 1948. There were two more of us than when we'd left—two more sisters, Alison and Janice, with no convincing interest in rugby, cricket, guns or planes. By this time the very poor vision in my right eye had been detected and assessed by specialists. It was due to a cataract I'd been born with and for which nothing worthwhile could be done. Goodbye to a career as fighter pilot. At Wesley College, instead of the Air Training Corps I joined the Army Cadet Unit, passing the medical by peering between my fingers when asked to cover the left eye.

If my parents doubted whether the continuing world unrest justified military training of fourteen-year-olds, they kept the doubts to themselves. But sisterly dismay was something to relish when I first brought home my .303 Lee Enfield. We were all issued with rifles, there being plenty left over from the war, and we treated our personal weapon with care and responsibility. I don't recall any pranks, dangerous behaviour or criminal misuse of a rifle anywhere in the Cadet Corps during those years. I do remember the smell of the oil, the tight feel of pulling through the 'four-b'-four' square of flannelette and the satisfaction of presenting a gleaming barrel for inspection.

We were drilled after school by a Regular Army NCO, a fatherly, uncomplicated sort of man, with no pretensions to cleverness or ambition. 'You will remember me, boys,' he said, 'because I am going to teach you to march.' Which he did, and I do remember him, although not his name—the soldier who transformed a bunch of schoolboys into a uniformed and disciplined body. When for the first time every drill movement sounded like a single rifle-shot, it was a moment of surpassing satisfaction. Another, even more unassuming instructor was Jim Gordon—a name I do recall, together with his quiet manner—the very antithesis of the typical warrant officer. Although he never mentioned it, he was also the holder of a Victoria Cross. We heard on the grapevine that under murderous fire in Syria he had charged a machine-gun post and killed four men with his bayonet.

I was strictly right-handed, so it was surprising to discover that, firing from the left shoulder with the .303, I was a good shot. The vision in my left eye proved to be exceptional. Using the Bren gun was more tricky: its foresight being offset and designed only for aiming with the right eye, it had to be fired from the right shoulder. I found a partial solution by using the left eye to make a rough calculation of distance and angle. I would then aim the first round at some feature just short of the butts, and use the resulting puff of dirt to adjust my line of sight. The next shots had a fair chance of hitting somewhere on the target. This one-eyedness continued to escape detection, and the strange disparity in results between the rifle and the Bren did not hamper my rate of promotion. In my last years at Wesley I captained the rifle team to some success, and was commissioned as a cadet lieutenant.

At medical school (Adelaide followed by Perth for our final year—we were the first clinical students of the Medical School of Western Australia), most of my friends were called up for National Service. By all accounts this was unutterably boring (except for a bloke called Barry Humphries, who they said nearly broke the instructors' hearts).

But the Korean War was over and there were better things to do at this stage than revisit school cadet drill, so I was happy to fail the eyesight test for the 'Nasho' medical. The examining doctor personally covered each eye with a card anyway. When a couple of years later I became a civilian medical examiner for the Army, we were instructed to fail as many as possible: the country could not afford the cost and didn't have sufficient instructors to cope with full conscription.

Meanwhile, I got on with study, graduated, did my resident jobs, and got married, which seemed like a good idea at the time. Rosemary Harris from Adelaide was slim and attractive, particularly in a pleated tennis skirt, and she was an outstanding amateur actress. Even to my callow, uncultured mind it was obvious she was destined for a career in the theatre. Though Roz and I were starry-eyed for a while, we were both far too young and too ambitious for the give and take of marriage. I fulfilled a promise to my father by joining his general practice, although I already knew anaesthesia was my real calling. The daytime workload was heavy, night and weekend calls in those days were frequent and expected. Roz joined the Playhouse Theatre repertory company as Rosemary Barr to avoid confusion with the well-known stage and film actress Rosemary Harris. Our lives were intense: my knowledge of plays classical and modern expanded rapidly, we had interesting friends and great parties. But our time together was too intermittent and too often spoiled by tiredness, mostly on my part.

After two years, I nearly broke my father's heart by rejecting his offer of a partnership and his unspoken dream of a Barr general practice dynasty. In 1962 I returned to the Royal Perth Hospital to train as a specialist anaesthetist, doing what I wanted and working even harder, postgraduate exams and research now added to the vast clinical burden of the anaesthetics registrar.

The early 1960s were years of disquiet. China was still menacing, Australian troops were helping the Brits in their fight against communist terrorists in Malaya, Soekarno was embarking on the expansion of Indonesia that led to 'confrontation'—and Indonesia was our nearest neighbour. The United States was escalating its involvement in South Viet Nam and asking for Australian help. I decided to join the Citizen Military Forces. Was it professional interest in casualty management, a need to boost my registrar's income, awareness that Roz and I were not as happy as we should be, an urge to be back in a uniform, a genuine sense of duty? I don't really know.

The Army certainly wanted doctors, especially those with resuscitation training and experience. For the eye-test this time I memorised the first three lines of the chart and that was good enough. With the temporary rank of captain, I joined the CMF Field Ambulance based at Fremantle.

Once I was back on a military path, the pace began to quicken. The unit was not very inspiring; at all levels there were many just seeing out their National Service, while the enthusiasts included one or two pompous amateurs play-acting a military role. But there were a few genuine soldiers and when the Field Ambulance exercised with troops training to fight I had a peculiar sense of belonging. The camaraderie, the traditions, the technology and expertise of an Army preparing for war, all felt exactly right. When a CMF infantry battalion in Perth suddenly needed a new medical officer, I jumped at the chance, without ever completing the exams to confirm my rank.

At this time, I believe, most Australians were convinced that a communist takeover of South Viet Nam would be both a threat to world stability and a danger to our own security. The communists had to be stopped, as they had been in Korea. The Australian Army Training Team in Viet Nam had already been considerably expanded. When the Americans decided to send in ground combat forces as well as advisers, Australia despatched the 1st Battalion, Royal Australian Regiment, in support of this new policy.

The Australian infantry in 1965 were small in numbers, but they were an elite. I was astounded at the quality of the Regular Army men attached to our CMF battalion in Perth and the level of skill they were creating among the part-timers. In their fitness, their bushcraft, their ability to move swiftly and quietly by day or night, their speed of reaction to any change in the situation, these men seemed the equals of fictional superfighters, and I was proud to be associated with them.

A bush training area was hidden in the ranges behind Perth where a most realistic Viet Cong village had been constructed. On weekend bivouacs and during the annual two-week camp, contact drills, ambushes and night assaults were repeatedly practised. My tasks were few. The hygiene and sanitary arrangements and the organisation of the Regimental Aid Post were all in the hands of Staff Sergeant Millhouse. In civilian life he was senior operating theatre technician at the Sir Charles Gairdner Hospital where I was now staff anaesthetist. (Even the hospital, named after a distinguished soldier, carried a subliminal call to arms.) In the CMF, Paddy Millhouse was a highly efficient military rogue, skilled in the art of controlling the medical officer, and making sure things ran to his own advantage. But they also ran smoothly, and the troops were all fighting fit in the truest sense.

Perhaps the fittest was Regimental Sergeant Major Bandy, ramrod straight and steely of eye, the only man in the battalion who could make Paddy Millhouse jump. He was a veteran of the Training Team, who at night would tell me tales of jungle combat and the delights of the Cercle Sportif in Saigon. Once on a night exercise, when he saw me shivering in the rain, miserable with a streaming cold, he produced a flask of fiery liquor. 'You know, RSM,' I said gratefully, 'if you had offered me the choice tonight of a woman or the brandy, I would still have taken the brandy.'

'Never let me hear you say that again, sir,' he grinned, 'you can get a drink any time.'

The Regular Army adjutant, Graeme Belleville, was my age, lived near us and was becoming a good mate. Graeme did not gladly tolerate fools; he hated pretension ('£1700 a year and they act as if they're on £5000') and he loathed hypocrisy, especially among politicians. But he loved the Army. He left the CMF battalion cheerfully and without fuss when posted to the Training Team in Viet Nam. A few weeks later he was dead—killed in an ambush on Highway 1, they said—and a young widow was quietly grieving.

In May 1966 the stakes were raised when the Australian Taskforce was sent to operate in Phuoc Tuy Province. This Taskforce consisted of two infantry battalions plus logistic support units, including medical cover provided by a much modified (meaning much reduced) Field Ambulance. This contribution of a few thousand men was piddling compared to America's commitment which was now in the hundreds of thousands, but it would soon use up Australia's limited military resources. Like the Americans, we chose a policy of one-year tours of duty. At that rate of rotation, medical officers were going to be in very short supply. It was no surprise when later in the year the proposition came—twelve months CMF full-time duty as specialist anaesthetist of the Field Surgical Team. I would have the temporary rank of major and a large say in my equipment.

I had now separated from Roz and was living at the hospital. Bob Elphick, the medical superintendent, was prepared to grant special war service leave with a guarantee of getting my job back. I had no dependants. Of various girlfriends in the wake of my separation the only serious one was involved with someone else in Melbourne. After a very few days' thought I said yes. Probably the decision had made itself when I heard that Graeme Belleville had been killed.

Part II

They're a weird bunch

Two

MELBOURNE WAS HAVING one of its heatwaves. The early afternoon temperature was 105°F (41°C), there was much talk of bushfires, and tempers were short. I was supposed to be on the transcontinental train, so the Army had no interest in me. 'Push off,' said the clerk at Albert Park Barracks, 'and don't turn up until Thursday morning.' Hardly a gracious, let alone grateful, welcome for a brave volunteer, but I was already on the payroll and a couple of days' paid holiday in civilian comfort was an inviting prospect. I booked into the Sheraton Motor Hotel in Spring Street. To be there without any postgraduate examination stress (the Royal Australasian College of Surgeons and its Faculty of Anaesthetists were nearby) gave added zest to this unexpected reprieve. I determined to make the time memorable.

Thanks to alcohol then and the passage of years since, the memories are blurred and episodic, like an old film ruined by poor projection. I recall great food at the Oriental Gourmet; great music at the Winston Charles, which used to be the Playboy; go-going to the deafening sound of the Clefs. Their keyboard player was my soon to be former brother-in-law Tweedy Harris, who bore me no grudge for walking out on his sister. It was little wonder—his attic flat was my introduction to the swinging sixties. He slept under a Union Jack bedspread and had, in close attendance, several nubile young groupies keen to help him with all manner of domestic duties.

Student songs with mates from medical school—'Nights upon the Torrens, we were doing Med. The students were all up, the nurses all in bed' . . . recovery periods with loving relatives . . . the opening night at St Martin's Theatre of 'The Devil's Advocate' still surprisingly clear—a pretentious introduction ('I have a message from Morrie West'), a disastrous play from a good book . . . backstage booze and hypocritical backslapping . . . theatre people partying on at the Sheraton . . . Judy Nunn from Perth, Ellie Ballantyne from Adelaide (both to pop up on British television 30 years later in the Australian soaps) . . .

What I recall in almost every particular is the Sheraton itself: the blissful relief to push through the double glass doors into its air-conditioned foyer, the vast room with wall to wall carpet and private bathroom. Months later, in the heat, sand and squalor of Vung Tau, the same scene kept coming back in exquisitely painful detail: the coolness and the quiet when all the revellers had gone, the huge bed, freshly ironed sheets, room service with chilled Great Western champagne. When she wept, for the first time I seriously faced the possibility of disablement or death. The thought of not seeing her again was awful beyond measure. Knowing the situation was ridiculously clichéd, we nevertheless filled the few hours with passion, even a desperate sort of fun.

This interlude, straight from a B grade movie, should have been followed by an immediate posting to a combat zone, with much heroic activity on my part. That script was binned when I reported on Thursday morning to M Block at Albert Park Barracks. I was delivered to Brigadier C M Gurner and Lieutenant Colonel Pretty of the Medical Directorate. Their welcome was flatteringly warm; I had no idea of the difficulties they were having in getting medical cover for the expanding Army in Viet Nam.

They handed me a sheaf of reports from the senior medical officer at Vung Tau. It was interesting, although curiously remote. 2 Field Ambulance were apparently relying heavily on the Americans. The SMO's main concerns seemed not to be battle casualties but a lack of supplies, undiagnosed fevers, venereal disease and malaria. The largest medical problem in war has always been sickness, not wounding, and Viet Nam was obviously no exception. From the telegraphic military language I tried to imagine the medical setup at Vung Tau, and failed totally. One good thing I learned was that my surgeon would be experienced. Major Ron Gregg had been there since September and would be staying to complete his twelve-month tour.

Several old Army hands had warned me to stand firm on rank and status. 'You're going as a specialist. Stick with that. Don't volunteer for any other duties.' I doubted I would follow that advice. The surgical work looked to be pretty intermittent and besides I enjoyed doctoring. I had happily retreated from the coughs and colds, aches and pains and neuroses of suburban general practice; treating genuinely sick and injured soldiers was a different matter. I had already enjoyed the comradeship and respect granted to a battalion medical officer, even in the part-time Army. When would we be going? The colonel and the brigadier were surprisingly vague. 'Unit's just getting together; all MOs to do military medicine and battle efficiency courses; no date yet . . . first get your equipment sorted out.' At last they said something definite: 'Transport this afternoon to Puckapunyal.'

Private Hill was an atrocious driver. After a jolting journey through the parched countryside north of Melbourne, he swung abruptly through the entrance gate and jerked the Landrover to a halt in front of some uninspiring huts. 'Headquarters 8 Field Ambulance, sir.' Puckapunyal was a camp much like every other military camp, but more disjointed than most. The Aboriginal word is said to mean 'the mountains of many winds'. More like a few low hills, and the units scattered over these dreary undulations had the feeling of isolated outposts.

My first impression of 8 Field Ambulance was that it was in chaos, the second was that nobody seemed too hurried or worried although it was now mid-February and I had expected to be in Viet Nam by the end of the month. The CO, Lieutenant Colonel Ralph Meyer, a small man with a rather blank preoccupied look behind his spectacles, was politely friendly. The unit had only been formed a few months, he said, and stores and staffing were far from complete. His interests were obviously more in administration than in medicine, although he had a Diploma of Tropical Medicine and Hygiene. He also wore a parachutist's badge. Fair enough, but you recognise a leader almost instantly, and I was disappointed.

Captain John Kelly, the quartermaster, was a small man too, rather rotund, radiating much more in the way of personality and bringing to mind a cheerful leprechaun. When I enquired about clothing issue, he spelt out some of his problems. He had indented for 120 pairs of GP boots and 52 had arrived—none my size, naturally. Of socks they had none at all. I did get jungle greens and a spare set of polyester trousers and he found me a service watch (non-maintainable). These watches were standard issue for Viet Nam service, made of plastic, waterproof and accurate. They were universally known as Mickey Mouse watches and were very good indeed. Mine lasted until I dropped it on a concrete helipad at Bien Hoa. He also got me some gold major's crowns from the RAASC Q Store and more impressively he persuaded the quartermaster of nearby 7RAR to supply me with a bush hat, which at that stage was a highly prized possession.

John seemed remarkably relaxed despite all the hassle. Over drinks in the Area Mess, I learned why no one was panicking. The earliest likely departure date for 8 Field Ambulance was said to be 12 April. Two further months of hanging around in Australia sounded a complete waste of time to me. I quizzed several administrative officers around the dinner table. None thought there was any hope I might be allowed to go sooner. I sank a good few beers and sulked off to bed.

Next day things improved somewhat. I spent the morning with Captain Wally Williams, the pharmacist, indenting for anaesthetic stores. Wally, like the CO and the quartermaster, was a Regular Army officer. He was knowledgeable and he was outspoken about the flawed system for medical stores, the result of a recent reorganisation. Behind his horn-rimmed glasses, the pharmacist wore the frown of a man who was under pressure. It was his responsibility to ensure adequate supplies of medical equipment as well as drugs. Failure or error could literally be fatal. With the shortage of Regular Army medical officers, he faced the prospect of dealing with prima donna specialists from teaching hospitals, part-timers who outranked him and who might insist on supplies way beyond the available military stocks. I was the first, and likely to be the most demanding for both equipment and drugs. Let me explain.

The standard anaesthetic procedure of the time was started ('induced' in medi-speak) with an intravenous injection of Pentothal (thiopentone) and continued ('maintained') using a mixture of nitrous oxide, oxygen and halothane from a Boyle machine. The patient breathed the gases through a face mask, or in more complicated cases via an endotracheal tube (ETT); this was put in place using a laryngoscope, a battery-operated torch with a curved metal blade which was slid over the tongue to look directly at the opening to the voice box (larynx). The basic skills needed were the ability to get needles into veins which might be hidden or constricted by shock, the ability to maintain an air-tight fit with the mask while supporting the jaw to keep the airway clear, and a degree of skill in using the laryngoscope and ETT, which is not always as simple as television hospital soaps may imply. Also required was the art rather than science of adjusting doses to keep the depth of anaesthesia at the Goldilocks level: not too little, not too much, but just right.

My minimum drug and equipment list therefore must include thiopentone, morphine or pethidine for analgesia, muscle relaxant drugs, both short and long acting, a large stock of syringes and needles, laryngoscopes with their bulbs and batteries, endotracheal tubes in a range of sizes, anaesthetic machines with cylinders of gases, wide bore corrugated delivery tubing ('elephant hose') plus connectors and valves, intravenous fluids and their plastic giving sets, large bore intravenous cannulae and apparatus to pump in the fluids in emergencies. Also needed were tubes and electric suction apparatus to empty the stomach and clear the airway of blood and vomit.

All these were basics. In addition I would need some specialised equipment such as nasal endotracheal tubes (to be passed through the nose to allow the surgeon room for operating around the mouth and throat), endobronchial tubes specifically for thoracic surgery, and breathing apparatus (ventilators) for post-operative intensive care. If our supplies failed for any reason, we must be able to give anaesthetics using agents and apparatus on the spot and not have to rely on gas cylinders. This meant going back as well to old-fashioned ether, ensuring a good supply of local and spinal anaesthetics and providing additional foot-operated suckers in case of power failure.

This list may seem daunting, but it was indeed minimal. My great interest at the time was anaesthesia in difficult situations, in the isolated outback or disaster scenarios—how to cope using limited agents and equipment. I was prepared to make do with just a few of the huge variety of available drugs and with almost no sophisticated monitoring equipment. During relaxant anaesthesia, with the breathing muscles paralysed, we would 'squeeze the bag' by hand rather than rely on a mechanical ventilator in the operating theatre. As Wally and I went through the requirements, his furrowed brow began to relax. The Army stocklists contained everything I wanted, including my favourite EMO (Epstein, Macintosh, Oxford) apparatus for ether/air anaesthesia. Some of the supplies I ordered were in fact never used, at least in my time.

Wally understood that professionally the situation I was heading for was a bit peculiar. The anaesthetist who set things up in Vung Tau, and whom I would be replacing, was Max Sloss. He had joined the Regular Army before completing his training in anaesthesia (subsequently he became a highly regarded specialist anaesthetist). I had known Max as an anaesthetics registrar in Perth and knew he was competent and safe, aware of his limitations. In Viet Nam he was developing the anaesthetic service with much reliance on backup from the nearby American military hospitals. Things were now moving on, however; the Australian facilities at Vung Tau were improving, and we would be expected to deal with more operations and more complicated cases.

The main theatre was equipped with two tables and two anaesthetic machines, yet our establishment was for only one surgeon and one anaesthetist. I had no idea what assistance I could look forward to, since the ability and experience in anaesthesia of my fellow medical officers (or indeed, apart from the CO, their identity) were totally unknown. For the bulk of the routine work I must use simple techniques which I could teach to others, supervising if necessary from the adjacent table. At least the unit pharmacist was clued up on the needs for safe anaesthesia. I was happy that Wally would lean heavily on the creaking system to ensure that the supplies all arrived, and on time.

In the afternoon, Lieutenant Ray Harvey, the bearer officer (that is, the Field Ambulance's junior administrative officer and general dogsbody), gave me a lesson in assembling the new field equipment. The design and quality of the one-man tents were leaps ahead of the old gear we had been given in the CMF. Better still, he took me to the mini-range for an introduction to two magnificent weapons. The medical officers were each to be issued with a 9mm Browning automatic pistol; although non-combatants, we would wear arms to protect ourselves and our patients. This was my first experience of a handgun. It had less kick and was more accurate than I'd imagined. Right-handed and left-eyed I managed to hit a beer can at 25 yards. But the new F1 sub-machine gun, like the Bren of my cadet days, had offset sights. I worked out a rough system—the target a thumb's breadth to the left of the magazine—with unimpressive results. Spraying from the hip, if a little extravagant in the use of ammunition, was more satisfying and much more effective. I knew which weapon I would prefer to use if called upon to fight.

Captain Morris Peacock turned up a couple of days later. He too had been an undergraduate at Lincoln College, and had qualified MB BS (Adelaide). He was young but already had tropical experience at Goroka in New Guinea and, thank God, he had done some anaesthetics. His wife was expecting their first baby on 13 April, the day after our proposed departure. Morrie was a very nice guy but I noted a couple of defects—he was embarrassingly fit and a tee-totaller. With amazing lack of forethought, it never occurred to me the great benefit I was to be granted by Morrie's healthy lifestyle. Nor did I realise how grateful I would be for his supportive friendship and his clinical skills. We clicked straight away; a communion of spirit comes when you meet a good doctor.

As CMF outsiders confronting a rigidly bureaucratic system, Morrie and I were able to indulge in a lot of mutual moaning. There seemed to be no information, little organisation and much inefficiency. By now I had met problems in the pay office. For allotments to wife (separated or divorced), which were compulsory, they wanted a marriage certificate, the number of Roz's bank account and a completed Form WF8A. Unfortunately the pay office only had stocks of Form WF8. Peremptory signals and mysterious multiple forms for signature followed me about for weeks, but Roz did get her money.

Morrie and I had dental checks by an Army dentist who had been at Puckapunyal for an incredible eight years and still seemed happy with his lot. We got crewcuts done by the Army hairdresser, and we gave each other vaccinations—first injections for cholera, plague and TAB, plus tetanus booster and smallpox revaccinations, all in 24 hours. This didn't contravene international regulations but was, to say the least, outside normal guidelines. We both got mighty sore arms, headache and fever, but at least it was all in one go; more importantly we would have the vaccinations completed if the powers that be suddenly decided on embarkation in early March rather than April. Morrie too was pretty gung-ho about that possibility—if he was going to miss the birth of his child it was better to do so by a month than by a couple of days. But neither of us was able to wangle exemption from the compulsory pre-Viet Nam training courses. On 17 February we were transported to Healesville.

Three

The School of Army Health, Healesville, was situated at the head of a magnificently green valley: a paradise after Puckapunyal, in both its environs and its proximity to Melbourne. Summerleigh Lodge, which had been built as a mountain resort, was a pleasant rambling building, with billiards, tennis court, swimming pool, and a golf course under construction. The living conditions were fine, but our lectures were conducted in drab, sweltering huts. Still headachey and irritable from Morrie's multiple injections, I soon concluded that the organisation of our six-week course on military medicine had taken talent of a remarkable sort.

The Director General of Medical Services took it upon himself to personally give many lectures on military surgery, including anaesthesia. He was the least competent lecturer I had ever faced, and his information was completely out of date. On the medical side we were subjected to weary hours on flies and faeces, tapeworms and heat stroke, fungal infections and battle fatigue. Some lecturers were actually good, notably physician Keith Fleming and ENT surgeon John Dunn, and some subjects were interesting, such as plague (which was still a threat in Southeast Asia), malaria and acoustic trauma. I would be hearing better today had I taken all of Colonel Dunn's advice on protecting the ears. We were also ferried to Melbourne teaching hospitals and to RAAF Laverton for specialist seminars which were frequently little better than the feeblest of our homegrown Army sessions.

What we needed to know from this whole course could easily have been provided in a fortnight. Even the compulsory drill each morning was of no value, the staff sergeant instructor being both inept and uninterested. At least four weeks were wasted in energy-sapping heat, with the dozen or so students becoming more and more aggravated and, in the Mess each night, more and more boozed—Captain Morris Peacock excepted.

In this unhappy environment Morrie and I began getting to know the odd mixture of CMF medical officers who were bound for Viet Nam, and odd they certainly seemed to be. Escaping to Adelaide on the first weekend gave us the chance to mull over our potential colleagues—potential because not all would be allocated to 8 Field Ambulance. We agreed that, whatever appointments were made, we could be landed with a pretty weird bunch.

Jack Blomley was fortyish, probably the oldest of the volunteers. He was a typical country GP, full of goodwill, entirely unacademic, gravel-voiced, overweight, an ex-Wallaby with a fund of stories about rugby tours to New Zealand and South Africa. He was an extraordinary mixture of the likeable and the irritating—friendly and tactless, jovial and boastful, concerned and self-centred. Tony Mooy, a bit younger, was a GP from Tamworth and almost a complete contrast. He was thin, lacking in confidence, with the simple warmth and open friendliness of a puppy. He had bursts of cheerful exuberance, but was nervous and excitable to an alarming degree. Peter Grainger was highly intelligent, but a loner, appearing remote and morose. He had trained in psychiatry and he viewed the behaviour of the rest of us with a forbidding countenance and uncomfortably piercing gaze. With his swarthy complexion and dark disposition, he was soon known as Black Pete. We had yet to discover the three subjects which could dispel his gloom. On religion, food or wine Pete would discourse expertly, displaying unexpected flashes of a dry humour. But that was in the future. For now, these three men were all worryingly peculiar and totally unmilitary. I remember few of the impressions made by the other course members. One was soon to be kicked out; the others went on different postings, where our paths would only intermittently cross.

When we learned it was indeed Captains Blomley, Mooy and Grainger who were destined to join us in 8 Field Ambulance, Morrie and I were less than ecstatic. There seemed a suspicious lack of modern all-round medical skills and of commonsense. Each day, indeed, seemed to bring more evidence that all three were a trifle crackers. Morrie, come to that, when the unbending military machine conflicted with his own strongly held ideas, began to display some peculiar episodes. My behaviour, naturally, was a model of consistency—mature, conscientious, stable and sober.

Towards the end of the course a professional arrived to join our gaggle of amateurs, and to profoundly affect the rest of my life. Michael Boyle, a bit too overweight and babyfaced to be called handsome, resembled in most other respects the super-talented hero of a 1930s novel. He was a Regular Army medical officer and a major at 30, newly posted as second in command of 8 Field Ambulance. He was an enthusiastic doctor with two years' tropical experience in New Guinea. An all-round sportsman, he had played rugby for the University of Queensland; he was gifted as a pianist and was a formidable card-player. He was manna from heaven. His sense of humour and his enjoyment of cigarettes, alcohol and the female of the species exactly matched my own. We both loved the Army and hated the incompetence of the course. We played tennis, golf and bridge, we smoked and drank a lot without getting maudlin, and we laughed at each other's jokes.

During the coming year I would learn many things from Mick, including a respect for malaria, a lasting love of gin and tonic, and sufficient card sense at poker to at least avoid being fleeced. In return I would teach him ways of giving simple, safe anaesthesia, along with some useful curses or quotations for difficult situations. I would also help him control the mood swings he'd inherited from his Irish forebears. We were to develop between us a sanity-saving philosophy, expressed often in comic banter, which made the impossible at least tolerable. Within a few months we would often instinctively know the other's thoughts.

This is a feebly inadequate attempt to describe the start of a friendship which endured for more than 30 years and was the best thing to come from my year in Viet Nam. If Mick were alive today he would enjoy the flattery but tell me to cut down on the bullshit. Hardly a day goes by, though, when I don't think of him.

Mick's arrival meant that my friendship with Morrie, also so immediate and so quick to grow, now had to plateau out. There were too many differences for us to become the three musketeers. Morrie was younger and less cynical and he was bright-eyed with enthusiasm for impending fatherhood. I had failed at my marriage, and Mick's was in trouble despite three adored children. Morrie was happy to join us in pontoon and poker, but he would not be a participant in any carousing. Rank too had some influence, less in the status it carried than in the responsibilities. It may be immodest but it's the truth that very early on I had the feeling that morale in 8 Field Ambulance was going to depend a good deal on Majors Boyle and Barr.

Towards the end of our time at Healesville, a series of lectures were due to be given by Army psychiatrists. We feared the worst.

Psychiatrists, being notoriously a bit dotty themselves, are suspected of making diagnoses by recognising their own symptoms. In fact, we got some sensible, practical advice, with a good leavening of humour. We learned how to cope with a range of problems from the alcoholic warrant officer to the nineteen-year-old with battle fatigue. Our distinguished teachers performed brief playlets to illustrate the technique of the indirect interview ('You say your wife is the cause of it all?'), and how to manage the inquisitive pest at a social function ('Interesting that you should wonder if he is homosexual'). They certainly helped to raise the value of the course, which ground to its end in late March. Brimful with knowledge on infectious diseases, heatstroke, mine injuries and latrines, we still faced fourteen days in the bush before departure for Viet Nam. All ranks, including medical officers, had to complete the battle efficiency course.

First, though, the Easter weekend, and I persuaded an RAAF nurse I had met at Laverton to come with me, touring the Victorian high country through Mt Beauty and the Bogong High Plains. I hired a Holden and we camped overnight in appropriated Army equipment. The weather was cold, but sunny, the scenery magnificent. Helene and I had a great time, if not as great as I had hoped. Back at Puckapunyal my brightened spirits were obvious. Mick's eyes widened in interest, but I confessed to separate sleeping bags. He grinned in sympathy.

The many winds of Puckapunyal were uninvitingly chilly in the training area of Scrub Hill as we struggled to get our newly issued field equipment off the trucks. Jeers and catcalls met us from a large group of infantrymen also about to be made battle efficient prior to embarkation for Viet Nam. They were soon silenced by the NCOs conducting the course. These rugged, efficient sergeants and corporals had handled similar groups of officers before and were undaunted by our motley appearance. We were formed into the most unlikely section of infantry in the history of the Australian Army—six doctors, a Catering Corps major, a lieutenant of the Intelligence Corps and a dentist.

Jim Walton of the Catering Corps was appointed our fearless leader and told to get us in line and to attention. The instructors were superb, their attitude beautifully balanced between respect for rank and amusement at our bumbling inefficiency. By the end of the first day we were tired and hungry, but our least experienced members had learned some of the elements of soldiering in the bush. In the fading light we set up lightweight weatherproof 'hoochies' and inflated our air mattresses. We each had a tiny collapsible stove heated by small cakes of a smokeless fuel called hexamine. The 24-hour ration packs were broached and strange concoctions prepared in metal dixies. All of us ate greedily except Black Pete, who stared moodily at his baked beans and tinned sausages, mournfully reciting details of the French menu in his favourite restaurant.

I woke about midnight with the sensation that I was lying on a ridge pole; of the three longitudinal compartments in my mattress only the middle one had remained airtight. Jack Blomley appeared, teeth chattering, to announce it was my turn for guard duty. For two hours I sat quietly on the perimeter of our section area. It was pitch dark and very cold. The wind had dropped, but the gum leaves still rustled overhead and around me twigs cracked with astonishing loudness as bush creatures went about their nocturnal business. A dozen companions were sleeping within 50 yards of me, yet I had rarely felt more physically lonely. The worst facing me was the roar of an NCO instructor as I drew on a furtive cigarette. In Viet Nam, for lonely guards, death stalked in the night. It was another of those times when you are suddenly gripped by awareness of a frightening reality. I shivered.

At dawn our cold stiff limbs were unsympathetically mobilised for a mile run followed by joint-cracking 'contact and ambush' drills. This was merely a warm-up to a program of increasingly strenuous physical activity. F Troop, as the soldiers had immediately dubbed us from a current TV comedy, galloped about the countryside, dug latrines, threw grenades and built barbed wire barricades. We also achieved varying degrees of proficiency with the pistol, the self-loading rifle and the F1 sub-machine gun. I had a head start with the hand gun and the F1, thanks to Ray Harvey. Now I handled the clean lines of the SLR with an almost sensuous pleasure. Intimate control of such power and accuracy brought an exultation of which neither Hippocrates nor the Australian Medical Association would approve. It is probably fortunate that I never experienced the psychological effect of firing at a man rather than a target. On the firing range, however, F Troop outshot the Diggers, which gave a nice boost to our morale.

Before leaving Scrub Hill we were required to cover five miles [eight kilometres] in full kit in one hour. This sounds easy, but it is not; intermittent jogging is necessary as well as a very brisk marching pace, and 'full kit' means a very heavy load. Mick and I stayed together. He put his mind strictly into neutral; I concentrated on girls I had known or wished to know, particularly in the biblical sense. We staggered in, strap-chafed, aching of foot and close to exhaustion, in 57 minutes. This was followed by a fully clad 50-yard swim in the camp's Olympic-size pool. A few weeks earlier, in the Victorian heatwave, it would have been refreshing. That was then; this was now. I made a reasonably graceful shallow dive. The icy water viciously penetrated the jungle greens and I gasped involuntarily before regaining the surface. Vocal cords slammed together in acute laryngeal spasm, not relaxing even after my head broke free of the surface. Waterlogged lungs screamed silently. Drowning seemed imminent, despite safety officers at the poolside. After an eternity, I was able to cough; spluttering and retching, I returned to the pool a ration of its chlorinated contents and wheezed and floundered my way to the far end. I dragged myself out, blue with cold and anoxia, reflecting bitterly on the Army's notion of acclimatisation for Viet Nam. Seen in retrospect, what I had was cold-induced asthma, a condition which did not trouble me again for ten years.

Surviving participants were now switched to a training area called Trentham. This was much more rugged, almost mountainous, terrain. We cursed and panted for three days as fiendish instructors pushed us through obstacle courses, jungle patrolling exercises and night manoeuvres. On the second night, volunteers were called to go into the nearby town of Gisborne and give blood. Mick and I reckoned that where there was a Red Cross blood-letting there would be females, and indeed we found a tall, vivacious divorcee who daintily shook the bottles as they filled with our life fluid. We had immediate rapport, but she was heading back to Melbourne.

Switching to a goal more attainable, we persuaded the NCO driver that all donors were in medical need of fluid replacement at the pub. Some fast drinking followed with a group of sergeants who were most appreciative of our concern and most amused at our obvious failure with the Red Cross. Later we discovered that one of the pathology lab staff sergeants had long before established proprietorial rights.

Two days later F Troop disbanded. We returned to Puckapunyal fitter probably than we were ever to be again. I don't believe I have used any of those painfully acquired battle efficiency skills, but the course was an experience not to be missed.

8 Field Ambulance now *was* in a state of chaos. The CO and advance party had gone already, and had left a million and one details of equipment and medical documentation still to be sorted out. All the remaining stores were checked. The medical officers worked into the

night vaccinating the troops and completing their International Health Certificates. Mick did his second-in-command stuff, pushing all officers and NCOs with his trademark mixture—beaming approval when things went right, roaring displeasure at laziness, ice-cold anger at inefficiency.

Our personal weapons, the 9mm pistols, were issued, signed for and immediately put into bundles wrapped in hessian—fat use if we were shot at on arrival! Each of us packed a trunk with personal belongings, which went away with the pistols. I got my blood group, O Pos, engraved on my dog tag. We collected new Bags Travelling Universal, the kitbags to accompany us on the plane. We were invited to Drinks for Officers in the Sergeants Mess. We got the last batches of medical documents sorted and signed. Suddenly the whirl of activity ceased. People vanished on pre-embarkation leave and Mick and I descended on Melbourne.

The autumn sun shone. The Sheraton was welcoming. Friends and relatives bombarded us with hospitality. My anaesthetist mate John Marum produced nurses from the Childrens Hospital. They were good fun but disinclined to offer themselves completely to warrior heroes. It was our last day. 'If I'm a-gonna cross the ocean, give me a girl in my arms tonight.' I telephoned. She argued: we had said our goodbyes, it would be a mistake; but she came. Next door in the early hours we heard sounds of revelry. Mick had found a student midwife who was now swigging champagne, singing and pelting chicken bones at innocent passers-by. 'The insatiable Israelite', he called her.

Four

THE MAIN PARTY of 8 Field Ambulance departed on 15 April 1967, travelling on the overnight train to Sydney, then by bus to Kingsford Smith Airport. Sixty-five of us boarded a chartered DC6B for the flight to Darwin. The word was that we would then be put on a Boeing 707 to Viet Nam. This was going to war in some style. Safely in the air, we learned that there would be an overnight stop in Darwin, then we'd proceed in an RAAF Hercules. So we had not spent our last night in Oz after all. Mick and I directed our attention to the two air hostesses.

Michelle and Lurline were terrific. Coping with a planeload of men all heading to war, just parted from their wives and sweethearts, was no easy task. Emotions were running very high. These girls were true professionals. They had a genuine smile and a friendly word for everyone, and they expertly dodged the few halfhearted passes. More importantly, they agreed to join Mick and me for a drink on our last night in Australia. 'But they'll never allow you out,' they said.

Darwin Transit Camp was a few miles out of town. As forecast by Lurline, we were transferred there immediately to be incarcerated till the morning, with no exceptions. The Army did not intend to risk any soldier being absent from the Hercules flight. By a most remarkable and happy coincidence, the Regular Army major in charge of movements had been at Wesley College with me in Perth. I persuaded him, on school's honour, that Mick and I had friends to see in town, which was perfectly true, and that we would guarantee to be back in time for the Hercules' departure. We showered and shaved and quietly departed to the Darwin Hotel.

It was a textbook tropical evening, pleasantly warm with the regulation breeze swaying the palms. The girls were even better out of uniform, tall, slim and tanned in shimmering summer dresses. We progressed from a patio meal to the inside bar. After everyone else had gone to bed, we just helped ourselves to Bacardi and tonics. Then to the upstairs lounge, a tiny portable radio and dancing, slow and close. A damn sight better than the transit camp. Those soft, comforting girls were perfect for two grateful soldiers, a bit lonely and a bit frightened. About 3 a.m. they conjured coffee and toast from the sleeping hotel and kissed us farewell. I arranged to meet Michelle at Falls Creek in July 1968. At the time, I meant it.

The RAAF woke us at 0500 hours. Bacon and eggs went down surprisingly well. Last night had been more talking and cuddling than boozing. In time-honoured Service fashion we then stood around while nothing whatsoever happened. At 0700 hours the transport arrived. A nod of thanks to my school chum chalking our names on his list, a short drive and we were straight aboard the Hercules.

These Lockheed C130s were being used to bring wounded Diggers home and there had been a lot of unfavourable media publicity about the aircraft—too slow, too uncomfortable and the four engines too noisy. No-one, they said, could sleep in a Hercules. I clambered on to a pile of kitbags, put in earplugs, and curled up. After less than an hour's sleep in the camp and with a residue of rum in my bloodstream, I crashed out immediately.

Four hours later I regained consciousness and was able to take an interest in the surroundings. The most remarkable feature of the Hercules, despite the dozens of soldiers and their baggage, was spaciousness. With its high ceiling and tiny portholes, the belly of the aircraft resembled a large cavern. I had slept, comfortably slanted on my nest of kitbags, on the upward sloping floor to the rear of the fuselage. We were flying smoothly and the earplugs solved the problem of noise. The Royal Australian Air Force now provided an excellent lunch: ham salad, bread and cheese, an orange and a cold carton of milk. What they did not provide was permission to smoke. Oh for a Peter Stuyvesant!

At 3 p.m. Central Time the Hercules was over Vung Tau airfield, circling; a DC3 had blown a tyre on the runway, someone said. Through the porthole a patch of muddy sea, mangroves and sand; a jumble of huge, low buildings; helicopters and planes in revetments; a Caribou taxiing toward a broad macadam runway. And then we were on Vietnamese soil.

Nobody shot at us when we stepped from the aircraft; the heat and dust were enemy enough. Our disembarkation point was next to a ramshackle shelter, just a flat tin roof supported by rough wooden posts. No flooring, no seating, no facilities, and no other buildings.

What a desolate, miserable place. Were we being hidden from spying eyes or simply kept out of the way while we were processed?

Sun-blasted and already dripping with sweat, we crowded under the shelter. Our welcome was a couple of cans of lukewarm soft drink and a demand that we produce all our bank notes. A representative from the Army Pay Office exchanged Australian dollars for small, multicoloured Military Payment Certificates. These were the standard currency for US and Australian servicemen in Viet Nam. The MPCs looked like children's play money. I climbed aboard the waiting Landrover, unable to shake off a growing sense of unreality.

The driver whisked us the half mile from our shanty 'terminal' to the massive complex of airfield buildings, skirted around them and drove us smartly past the US sentries at the main gate. As we jolted along the narrow roads into Vung Tau town I tried to sort out some first impressions. It all seemed oddly Lilliputian. Along the outer streets there were just a few people, all very small. Nobody was hurrying. The adults, most in white shirts, black trousers and flat conical hats, ignored our progress. The children, many naked, paid us more attention. Some smiled broadly, shouting and waving, others glowered and deliberately turned their backs.

With increasing traffic came a happier atmosphere, a bustling toy-town. There were pushbikes and tricycles, puttering Honda mini-bikes and raucous motor scooters—all of them capable of transporting entire families, parents and two or three children all on the one machine. Small bug-like Renault taxis competed for fares with Lambretta three-wheeler minicabs. We even passed a small sulky, drawn by a pint-sized horse in decorative harness.

The dwellings were small too. Many were poor shacks made from scrap bits of timber and flattened tin, with palm fronds as the roof. Others were more solid: squat boxes of wood or rough cement roofed by orange tiles. Each had its complement of half-clad children, chickens, dogs—and a TV antenna.

I suddenly lost interest in sightseeing when we hit the stench from the market streets, a sickly sweetness which banished any more thoughts of a toy-town. I was tired and irritable from the flight, the heat and humidity, and the sudden exposure to strange surroundings. The smell of overripe fruit and drains was almost overpowering. What was particularly irksome was to discover that we were on a detour. The driver thought the new arrivals might like a sightseeing trip through Vung Tau before heading for the base. In this he was very wrong. We were sitting in a stunned sort of silence, only half taking in the utter foreignness of this country. What we really wanted to see was what comfort and facilities would be offered us in our new home within 1 Australian Logistic Support Group.

At last the driver turned eastwards, away from the stench and out of the town. From a swampy depression, the road suddenly swung upwards, past an Australian sentry post and over a rise, the first of a succession of semi-vegetated sand dunes. An untidy mixture of elongated huts and battered khaki tents were scattered on dune tops and in the hollows between. In the distance lay a murky, wind-chopped sea. The Landrover, whining in low gear, churned along a sand track past a few of the huts, climbed a small hill of sand and halted beside a row of particularly dilapidated tents. A gale force wind tore at the flapping nylon and canvas. We dismounted as the wind hurled sand into our clothes, our hair and our eyes. With an ill-concealed smirk the driver announced we had arrived at the officers' lines of 8 Field Ambulance.

Half a dozen officers appeared and escorted us into the worst looking tent, which proved to be the Officers Mess. With considerable sympathy the veterans poured beer down our parched and eager throats. Intelligent conversation was beyond me. I ate some sort of meal in a complete daze, and was shown to a tent and a bed. Before crawling under the mosquito net I wrote in my diary: 'This place will take some getting used to.'

Part III

Surgery, swans and Saigon tea

Five

Tuesday 18 April 1967

Viet Nam was an infinitely better place after ten hours sleep. There was no wind; the sand remained docilely underfoot. The South China Sea was blue and it sparkled in the morning sunlight as we clumped down the rough wooden steps from the Officers Mess to the Admin section of the Field Ambulance Unit.

Next to the Orderly Room tent was a truck with an air-conditioned office on the back, something I had never seen before. The commanding officer of the outgoing 2 Field Ambulance gave his briefing from this lofty perch. We stood in a half circle like new boys at school being lectured, with Lieutenant Colonel Bill Rodgers as the headmaster. The sun climbed. We tried to ignore the heat, and the noise from trucks, workshops, generators and low-flying aircraft. I took in about half of what was said.

The CO had some large maps and charts to summarise the setup we were inheriting: our position in relation to neighbouring units, the 'Dustoff' helicopter casualty evacuation system, our hospital facilities, the tie-up with the Americans—particularly 36 Evacuation Hospital at Vung Tau airfield and 24 and 93 Evac Hospitals 50 miles (80 kilometres) northwest at Long Binh. These three between them had the specialist surgical cover we needed: ophthalmology, ENT, orthopaedics, neurosurgery and chest surgery. In all of these we could provide emergency and basic care only, but we were well set up for our general surgical role. Rodgers had been battling to get decent equipment and was understandably proud of his air-conditioned operating theatre.

This emphasis on the surgical facilities would obviously suit me, but I listened a bit uneasily. Although Rodgers' presentation was expert, it raised some worrying questions. *Should* the commanding officer have air-conditioning ahead of ward patients? Why weren't

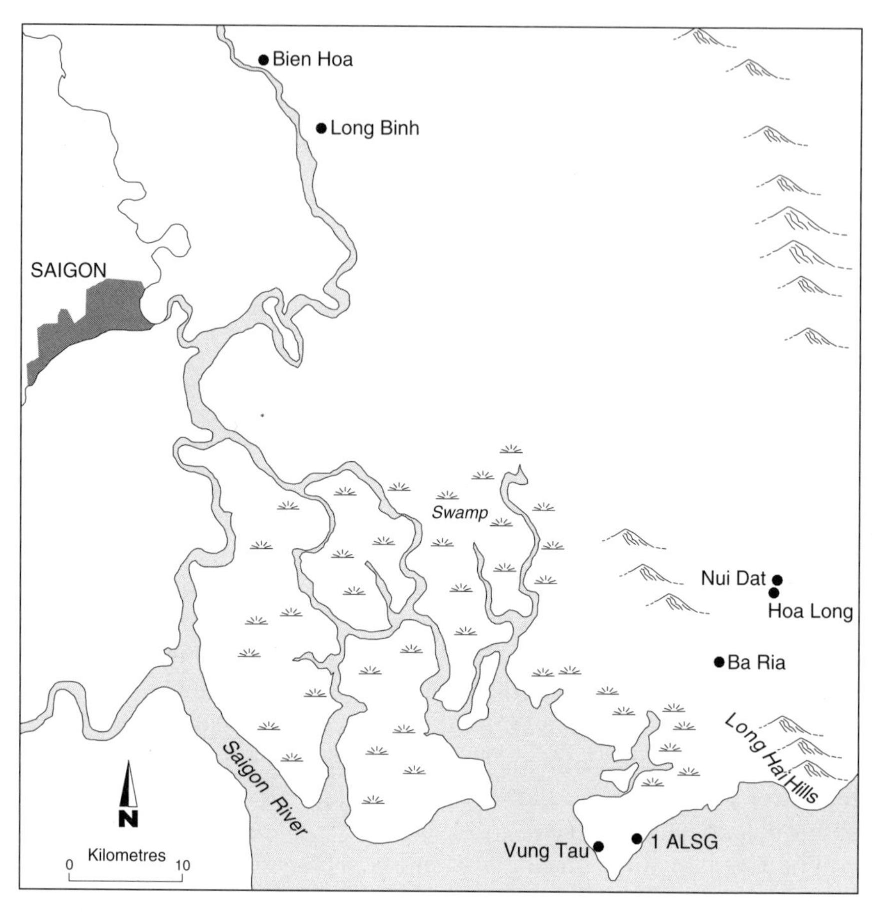

A few places I would get to know during my time in Viet Nam.

the systems for medical care as clearly defined as those for major surgery? Why, after twelve months on the site, was accommodation still so poor? The weatherbeaten tentage on the dunes behind us was an embarrassing eyesore. Maybe this was unfair; I did have much to learn about local difficulties with material and manpower. Mick muttered a few epithets. Rodgers had disappointed him too, particularly on medical management. But Mick was disappearing at once to Nui Dat, to get the feel of the Forward Medical Detachment. No experienced ally for me, then, as I set off with the others on our introductory tour, trying to sort out what was what and how we would cope with the changeover.

Our title of 'Ambulance' was a complete misnomer. The transport of casualties (apart from not infrequent traffic accidents in the town) was entirely by helicopter. What 8 Field Ambulance was about to take over was a static field hospital of some 65 beds, the major medical component of 1 Australian Logistic Support Group (1ALSG). The Forward Medical Detachment was with the Task Force 20 miles inland at Nui Dat. Here at Vung Tau the actual hospital facilities, casualty reception, theatre, wards, outpatients, dental clinic and path lab were by now in Kingstrand prefabricated aluminium huts. The rest was still tented—Orderly Room, Quartermaster's Store, Medical Store, living quarters, latrines, the chapel, everything—an untidy jumble of faded canvas in all shapes and sizes. Metal containers were dotted around, half buried in the sand, stores still without a home. It was not an edifying sight.

As the morning grew hotter and more humid our tour became more and more depressing. The personnel seemed as forlorn as their tentage and hardware. A few of the unit's soldiers wore rolled up sleeves and jungle green trousers; most were bare-chested and in shorts, with khaki socks turned down to the ankles. They trudged around in morose fashion, GP boots sinking deep in the sand. Those we talked to obviously just wanted to go home.

The officers' dining tent was a large marquee of roof and supporting poles only; it was too hot for sides, being set in the wide depression of deep sand between the hospital and the Diggers' lines. Lunch featured much sand, the wind having now got up. I sat next to Major Laurie Doyle of the Army's 161 Reconnaissance Flight whose chopper was parked just 100 yards away. This splendid man completely restored my spirits by offering me a quick 'area familiarisation' flight before he returned to Nui Dat. Thus it happened that the new anaesthetist's first visit to the hospital helipad was not to receive casualties but to have a joyride, my first flight in a helicopter.

The two-seater Sioux Possum, the standard mount of 161 Recce, seemed to me a little beauty: the surge and lift were exhilarating, and the all-round bubble canopy gave a magnificent view. As we rose, Bill Rodgers' map of the unit and its surroundings became actuality. Between the Field Ambulance and the sea were Composite Ordnance and the Engineers' field workshops, the more ordered buildings of 1ALSG headquarters were just to the north and a mile away in a haze was the US airfield where we had landed yesterday.

'The Long Hai Hills,' said Laurie, pointing to a dark mass in the northeast distance. 'Full of VC.'

On the beach were sunbathers and swimmers, out to sea there were sampans and junks and at least a dozen big ships; as we swung south and west we could see they were queuing around the Vung Tau peninsula. 'Waiting to go up-river to Saigon,' Laurie said, answering my unspoken question. We continued our right-hand circuit, over the hill of the southern headland, along the palm-lined seafront of Vung Tau township, across cluttered markets and shacks, then back to the sand dunes and Kingstrand huts. I thanked Laurie profusely, ducked low under the whirling rotor blades, trotted to the edge of the helipad, turned and gave a thumbs-up. The Possum eased forward, tilting then lifting, and a blast of wind and sand caught me full in the face. Lesson one learned—turn your back immediately you have signalled OK to the pilot. I rescued my bush hat and some semblance of dignity, then headed along the path to the hospital, eyes down to avoid the grinning faces at the windows.

My interest in the path's construction was not totally feigned. It was a raised sand causeway carrying twin tracks of pierced steel planking. The 'sleepers' supporting the planking were ten foot (3 metre) sections of pipe sunk in the sand but almost completely exposed at the sides. A little beyond the exposed pipe ends, on each side, ran a fence of steel spikes connected by two strands of barbed wire. These were obviously provided to discourage any shortcuts to or from the Diggers' lines; GP boots would soon have eroded the embankments of sand. The construction seemed a bit makeshift for the transporting of serious casualties. A sudden giving way or a stretcher bearer's stumble could have serious consequences. Second mental note—check if there were any problems with litter parties from the Dustoffs.

Once safely past the witnesses to my amateur performance on the helipad, I strode up to the Mess feeling very pleased with myself. Only 24 hours in-country and I had been up in a Possum. It was an opportunity which few of those jeering onlookers would have—or even most members of the Officers Mess. A lot of advantages come with rank.

The Officers Mess was a big tent supported chiefly by two large poles about ten feet apart. From the high ridge this formed, the drooping canvas roof sloped down to a rectangular framework of uprights which were the basis of the 'walls'. These were mostly open, as in the dining tent, but could offer some protection—there were two sections of shoulder-high plywood panelling with open space above them for ventilation; elsewhere there were canvas flaps all around.

Looking east from the Officers Mess, April 1967.

These flaps were furled, because of the heat, except at the northeast corner. Here they were firmly fixed, providing a rear wall for the makeshift small bar guarding a large refrigerator.

Untidy guy ropes surrounded the whole tent, attached to iron spikes thrust at varying angles into the sand. A low wall of sandbags gave the south side some protection from the elements, while another sandbag wall jutted out a few yards to the rear, marking the edge of the path from the officers' tents. Its main function was probably to prevent revellers from impaling themselves on a spike or falling down the dune on their way to bed.

The floorboards of the Mess were irregular and distinctly tilted by erosion of the underlying sand. Most of the rough boards had a hessian type of carpeting but it was rarely visible because of the covering of sand. This was supplied almost continuously by the wind and in intermittent dollops from the boots of all arrivals. The furniture consisted of a dozen or so inadequately cushioned cane chairs and a few low tables, all having seen better days. Outside were a rusting 44 gallon drum serving as a rubbish bin, and several empty food and drink cartons. In short, the Officers Mess was a most unlovely place.

It did, however, have a view. Perched on the seaward edge of the sand dune, it looked down on the whole of the Field Ambulance Unit, then across the engineering units to the sea some 500 yards away. The vast levelled area south of the Engineers was occupied by the Composite Ordnance Unit, a giant's playground of stores, machinery and vehicles. Further south, on this first day, twin-rotor Chinook helicopters were going down, then up again lifting loads in a sling which trailed rearwards as the huge aircraft tilted forward and away. They were using St Kilda Pad, I was told, one of the many features I had not observed in my brief Possum flight. But there in the northeast were the Long Hai Hills, across the bay where the curve of Vung Tau peninsula merged into the mainland, a dark and forbidding range falling abruptly to the sea. The view to the west behind the Mess was not so spectacular. Immediately to the rear were the double line of officers' tents and a few hundred yards away the neater buildings of 1ALSG clustered on their much bigger and better vegetated sand dune. Much further, beyond the unseen town of Vung Tau, was a tall green-covered hill bristling with radio and radar antennae. How could I have missed noticing that? The Great Observer!

Coming back to 'home', I tried to put in place the main elements of the Field Ambulance, which had become a confused blur by the end of our morning tour. The flight of rickety wooden steps went down the side of our forty foot dune to the Orderly Room, Quartermaster's Store and Medical Store. Between these Admin tents, churned-up vehicle tracks snaked back to the graded main 1ALSG thoroughfare. Opposite, and facing them across a sparsely gravelled access area, were the new buildings of the hospital itself—six Kingstrand aluminium huts which partially enclosed a square of struggling lawn with a flagpole still flying the 2 Field Ambulance flag. The long low huts housed, first, outpatients on the left, then the medical and surgical wards. The two furthest Kingstrands formed a continuous line because the gap between them was a roofed passageway. On the right was the surgical ward and on the left were casualty reception and the operating theatre. The dubious planking causeway led from this passageway across the sandy depression behind the hospital to the elevated helipad. Foreshortened on its black asphalt, you could just make out the large red cross on a white painted square. Vampire Pad was its call-sign, but nobody seemed to know who had invented the name.

The large natural hollow to the right of the causeway was used as an open air theatre. An ungainly, tall wooden edifice tilted gently in the shifting sand. This, they said, served as both a movie screen and a narrow stage. The lines of the Diggers' tents lay on the ridge above.

The southeast view—looking across the dining tents to 33 Dental Unit and Vampire Pad.

On the near side of the hollow, the kitchen and dining tents were behind the hospital buildings. Closer to us were the sergeants' lines, then our own tents, ablutions and latrines. Behind our lines, in the depression below HQ 1ALSG, a large parking area separated an elongated green tent which was the interdenominational chapel from the wooden huts of the Pay Office and the Field Postal Unit.

There was a pattern to be discerned in the priorities for upgrading accommodation: the administrative staff at 1ALSG looked to be doing fairly well, as did the hospital patients, but pay and mail also came high on the list.

I spent a quiet afternoon finding and sorting out my personal gear, then went back to the Mess for beer, followed by a lousy dinner, a lousy movie in the sandy hollow and more beer. A late-arriving guest in the Mess was Colonel George Warfe. From the respect shown by the Regular Army officers he was a man of some importance, although he seemed a bit old to be in a war theatre. He was full of stories of New Guinea, Korea and Malaya. He revealed nothing about Viet Nam except a wristband given to him by the Montagnards, the hill people. I had no idea what his job was. He was unashamedly gung-ho. He hated flak jackets and helmets. 'They clutter up the Digger and take the adventure out of war,' he said.

Not enemy action, but a burning tyre dump! The view from the ridge where the Diggers' lines stood; the Kingstrand hospital buildings are in the middle ground and the Officers Mess is on the hill opposite. (Photo: P. Davis)

Nobody else was much interested in the veteran colonel's stories. The new medical officers had sloped off to bed; those we were relieving seemed reluctant to talk about the war or anything associated with Viet Nam. Their answers to my eager questions were terse and uninterested. Vung Tau had never been attacked. The town was scarcely worth a visit. There had been no rain for five months. Only in conversation about home or their experiences on R&R was there a spark of animation. They were all pleasant and obviously capable, just oddly lethargic and withdrawn. They had served their year and wanted out. The Diggers, as always, had a phrase for it—they were 'switched off'. What these short-timers did not want was adventure, even reminders of adventure. Someone commented that it was just as well we were out of mortar range of the Long Hai Hills. In the moonlight, as I stumbled to the tent I was sharing with dentist Ron Benyon, the hills looked bloody close. I felt a flicker of schoolboy excitement. I wanted to see some action, enough to test my behaviour under fire—without, of course, actually getting hurt.

Six

19–22 APRIL 1967

It was a requirement that all Australians in the Logistic Support Group be armed, which gave continual and convincing evidence that there was a war on. The Diggers carried F1s, the drivers SLRs and the officers wore their pistols, ours having arrived safe in their thick hessian wrapping. Your personal weapon stayed with you wherever you went, although in the operating theatre and in the Mess they were hung up rather than actually worn. At first it was distinctly odd to see the weapons hanging alongside stethoscopes on hospital walls and soldiers carrying their arms between the wards, even to the latrines and ablution blocks. In a few days I was accepting it as normal.

For those first few days the lethargy of the old hands was matched by a sluggishness on our part as we slowly adjusted to the strangeness, the heat and humidity, the sand, the primitive living conditions. After a disturbed, uncomfortable night on a sand-filled bed we woke feeling sweaty and jaded. Water was limited at this time of year, the end of the dry season. It was delivered by truck to our ablutions block behind the tents. Our showers were canvas bags filled (when possible) from buckets, then raised to the ceiling with a rope and pulley. The adjacent latrine offered neither privacy nor comfort for a few minutes' quiet contemplation. It was a standard Army three-holer—sawn-off fuel drums over a pit. The wooden seat was never free from gritty sand.

An excellent guide to initial acclimatisation was the volume of urine one produced. It took a few days for the sweating to diminish and the bladder output to increase. Ironically, on our arrival a new officers' urinal was provided. It was another standard Army device, the pissaphone, a simple large metal funnel soldered to a drain pipe sunk deep in the sand. Later, to make allowances for the arrival of the nurses, we moved the urinal somewhat further from the Mess. Tony Mooy helped supervise the construction of an improved triangular wall of hessian around the new pissaphone, which thereafter was known as the Tamworth Triangular Toilet.

The changeover of staff from 2 to 8 Field Ambulance unit-wide was in one way or another heavy going. People seemed either to have left early, with business unfinished, or to be staying on so long that eventually they were in the way. The CO, John Frewen the adjutant and John Kelly the quartermaster were working flat out on administrative details. Wally Williams kept his pharmacy staff going till midnight sorting out the American replenishment system and creating order from a huge jumble of crates loaded with equipment, instruments, dressings and drugs. He discovered a cache of flammable anaesthetics—cans of ether, bottles of ethyl chloride and chloroform, cylinders of cyclopropane—all hidden in a Conex hut half buried in the sand without any warning notice. This was no joke. Cyclopropane in particular is highly explosive. I had never entertained the idea of using it in Viet Nam. We got the other agents safely stored and sent the cyclopropane back to the American Medical Supply depot. Lieutenant John Purser, who had replaced my firearms instructor as bearer officer, suffered the harassment and excessive workload the most junior officer has to expect. There were numerous complaints both from the NCOs and Diggers about to depart and from their replacements; the biggest moans meant that an expected replacement had failed to arrive.

For the doctors, during those early days of slowly improving urine output, things were very quiet. With a doubling up of most of the medical officer staff, we had the time but not the expertise (nor in truth any great keenness) to assist our pressured administrative colleagues.

I stuck with Max Sloss. He seemed to me less affected than most by the switched-off syndrome. He had always been a big, slow-moving and slow-speaking man, reserved and genial. Now clumping around the sand dunes in sweat-streaked shirt, baggy shorts and heavy boots, he was more than happy to discourse at length on the equipment, the surgeon and the problems he had faced. His burden of responsibility had been a lonely one. With another anaesthetist now on the scene the intense pressure was relieved. Routine operating had been stopped to allow a smoother handover. We checked the theatre stores together and the systems for handling emergencies. Each day, as no emergencies came and his departure date grew closer, Max's smile grew broader.

On my third day, Max took me to meet my opposite number in 36 Evacuation Hospital at Vung Tau airfield. It had rained a little the night before, breaking the drought and settling the sand. Although the Landrover ride was more comfortable, it was still stinking hot and now even more humid. We took a back road which wound behind the sandhills through an unfertile tract with just a few struggling rice patches adjoining poor shanties.

The one substantial piece of architecture along this back road was a tall, forbidding French fort, built in modern times but now derelict and eerily incongruous—Beau Geste stranded in the mid-twentieth century. The Vietnamese, combining expedience with unsubtle symbolism, were using the site as a massive rubbish dump. This ghostly pile, defeated and now degraded by the stinking smoke of burning refuse, was a discomforting reminder that Vung Tau, so apparently peaceful, had seen much bloody violence. Remembering, too, the gruesome pictures shown in CMF training of French vehicles ambushed by the Viet Minh, I fervently hoped Max knew what he was doing in taking this unpopulated route.

It was difficult to know how dangerous Vung Tau was. The consensus seemed to be that it was full of Viet Cong but that they wanted no incidents: like the forces of the US and its allies, the communist soldiers were using the area as a rest and recreation centre too. It was a weird thing to accept. Max's blissful unconcern was apparently justified: we arrived safely at the heavily defended airfield and I breathed a little easier.

Compared to our small hospital in the sand dunes, 36 Evac was a big establishment. However, it was just one small part of the gigantic American medical system in Viet Nam. I never got to understand exactly what constituted an Evacuation Hospital or a Field or a Surgical Hospital, as the Americans I asked seemed pretty vague about it. They did know about their own place though. 36 Evacuation Hospital had 400 beds, maintained at 45 per cent availability for emergencies, and a staff of more than 20 medical officers and 40 nurses. It consisted of many permanent-looking, air-conditioned Quonset huts—long, low half cylinders with curved, corrugated roofs—which were squashed together by the congestion of buildings clustered inside the airfield perimeter. The sides of the huts were protected by sandbag walls, while the roofed walkways between offered protection only from the midday sun and from vertical downpours. There was no sea view, but no sand either, and the immediate scenery was excellent. Despite the uniform of drab green shirt and trousers, most of the nursing staff were indisputably female.

36 Evac's helicopter pad, codenamed Cotton Gauze, was almost at the door of the tunnel-like triage hut. The operating theatre ran at right angles to Triage, another long air-conditioned tunnel with a row of six fully equipped operating tables. In addition to general surgeons they had specialists in eyes, ENT and orthopaedics. Compared to our one surgeon, the strength at 36 Evac never fell below three trained surgical teams. They even had physiotherapists for post-operative rehabilitation.

The atmosphere differed completely from that at 8 Field Ambulance. Weapons were absolutely forbidden, which was difficult when we had to wear our Brownings at all times. The choice was between bringing a driver especially to stay with our weapons in the Landrover or finding a secure niche in 36 Evac. (Very secure! Our 9mm pistols were highly prized by the Americans, and had an incredible bargaining power on the black market.) The US staff dressed more smartly, as well they might with the benefits of air-conditioning and no sand. There were no ill-matched shirts and shorts and certainly no bare chests, yet discipline and respect for rank were much less in evidence.

The chief of surgery was a very youthful looking major, Bob MacLean, babyfaced, breezy and jovial. The specialist anesthesiologist was Captain Robert Watson, who was slim, softly spoken and much more intense. They were both instantly likeable and most generous in their welcome, personally escorting me on the obligatory 'ten cent tour'. There was much to be admired, particularly the first class X-ray equipment, pathology laboratory and excellent field anaesthesia machines.

As with us, though, there was little going on and all the operating tables stood idle. You can't learn much unless something is happening. Like MacArthur I promised to return, and Max and I headed back in time for lunch.

By a coincidence two more American medical officers were in the Mess. These were Colonels Harry Dangerfield and Don Hunter from the Walter Reed Army Institute of Research in Saigon, who had come to talk infectious diseases with Bill Rodgers. We would meet again in strange times and places, and I have never encountered two more gentlemanly or delightful companions.

In the afternoon I gave my first anaesthetic since early February. The patient was a Viet Cong prisoner named Toi with shrapnel wounds in buttock and leg. All Max's systems, his equipment and his assistants worked well. The enemy patient was treated by the surgeon and all the theatre staff with some curiosity but with courtesy and respect. He was very thin, but otherwise fit. We could not communicate since he admitted to no English or French and I certainly had no Vietnamese. He resignedly accepted my preliminary checking of his chest, heart, pulse, and blood pressure and then, obviously worried, the intravenous needle and the thiopentone.

Ron Gregg, the surgeon staying on after eight months with 2 Field Ambulance, had kept fairly clear of me until now, preferring to drink and chat with his mates. When I commented about the lack of surgical activity, he muttered that hard work would come soon enough. Ron was tired, homesick and depressed by the gradual departure of his comrades. He was a country-style general surgeon of the old school, a great admirer of Max, and naturally suspicious of the newcomer from a teaching hospital. It was an unlikely start to what would become a most harmonious relationship. His relief was almost palpable when he saw that I was not a demanding, technically inadequate academic. I was equally glad to see that my surgeon was quick and competent. Nothing was said, nor needed to be.

In the evening, while we watched the flashes of naval guns shelling the Long Hai Hills, Ron opened up a bit with some coarse jokes, but he was back to being maudlin and disconsolate by the time he went to bed.

Next morning my familiarisation programme continued with a visit to Nui Dat. An American Iroquois gunship arrived at Vampire Pad. Into it piled the CO, Harry Dangerfield, Don Hunter and George Warfe, the four sitting in a comfortable row on the padded seat between the M60 gunners on each side. I, as a lowly major, sat on the metal floor between the colonels and the pilots. The machine-gunners were commendably and worryingly vigilant, their eyes constantly traversing the tracks, swamps and jungle below. With no seatbelt I spent the journey gazing through the open sides next to the guns, my interest increasing each time the Huey banked. It was my second chopper trip, and I was not yet blasé.

The Australian Task Force at Nui Dat occupied a disused rubber plantation. It was cool under the rubber trees but everything was coated in red dust. Our ears were pounded by the 105mm howitzers of the Australian and New Zealand gunners, and the greater concussion of supporting American heavy artillery. We were taken on a lightning tour of the 5th and 6th infantry battalions (5 and 6 RAR), whose sandbagged tents and huts were dotted among the trees.

Wherever we stopped for a briefing, the officers treated George Warfe with an almost religious deference.

The brigadier gave us a few minutes in his heavily fortified HQ, mainly to complain about a signal that there would be no Dustoff helicopter that day. There was nothing Ralph Meyer or I could do about this. We were entirely in the hands of the Americans and the RAAF for helicopter support.

The brigadier's concern, rightly, was to ensure the best possible treatment for every casualty from his command. Everyone around us was very alert and very professional. Nui Dat had been mortared recently, their tour was finishing and they wanted to get home in one piece. Our ride round the perimeter became very speedy at the sites favoured by snipers.

A patrol brought in a blindfolded VC prisoner. In this environment self-consciousness about the pistol on my left hip was soon gone. There was no time, though, to get used to this seriously warlike atmosphere or to take in anything but the briefest impressions of the Task Force setup. No time for more than a few words with Mick. An advance party from 7RAR came in from HMAS *Sydney* on a Chinook, followed closely by the gunship that was to be my transport back to Vung Tau.

This time I was the only passenger, comfortably seated and secured. The Huey rose easily above the rubber trees. At 2000 feet it was cool and safe. I looked down at the receding village of Hoa Long and the broken ribbon of road stretching ahead across the mangrove swamps and muddy streams of Vung Tau peninsula. Like a strip map unrolling, the narrow tongue of land slid beneath us. To the east small fishing boats dotted the sea midway to the Long Hai headland. In the setting sun, larger ships waited patiently for their trip up the Saigon River. Below, the map came to life as we descended—villages, the airfield, vehicles, people. We banked low over the flagpoles of 1ALSG headquarters and settled gently on to Vampire Pad. Bending low I trotted to the start of the planked track and turned briefly into the dust-laden wind from the rotors to give a thumbs-up to the pilot. It was twelve minutes since we'd left Nui Dat. The only way to travel.

On Friday night we were invited by the Australian Civilian Surgical Team to a party at the Pink Panther, which I gathered was a Bachelor Officers Quarters for an American Signals Unit. The Australians, from the Prince of Wales Hospital, were assisting the Vietnamese staff of Le Loi Hospital in Vung Tau. They freely admitted they had done very little and they seemed to show no great drive to overcome difficulties.

A stroppy journalist was there, a small man three months in the country and immaturely blowing his own trumpet, calling the Vietnamese lazy bastards, not worth fighting for. Here was I, after five days, noting more deficiencies in the Westerners I'd met! At least I kept my opinions to myself, or I hope I did—there was an amazing amount of booze as well as food.

I was surprised to find the male/female imbalance at the party was only about three to one. There were many US nurses, quite a few civilians and of course the Australian girls from Le Loi. They were keen to talk to recent arrivals from Australia, and I was delighted to chat them up and to be educated. 'The Grand Hotel is a brothel,' said Julie. 'You'd be surprised at what I've been offered.' It was great to be in female company again. I was in happy mode. The CO seized the opportunity to put something to me. Max Sloss would be around for another week and there was little work in the hospital. How would I like to go up to Nui Dat for a few days?

Here was the explanation of my introductory trip to the sharp end. Ralph Meyer was keen to get Mick back to his administrative duties as 2IC at the parent unit. I would temporarily be medical officer of the forward detachment until Jack Blomley arrived from Australia with the 8 Field Ambulance rear party.

'Great,' I said, 'when do I go?'

'In about ten hours' time,' the CO said.

The midnight curfew protected me from a hangover, which was just as well. I discovered at breakfast that my transport would not be a helicopter but a Landrover. The veteran RSM Bandy had given me some parting advice when I left the battalion in Perth. 'If you have to travel, sir,' he'd said 'go on foot or by air. Vehicles get ambushed.' It was a standing order that all travellers on that road wear helmets and flak jackets and that each vehicle carry at least one automatic weapon. In warlike garb with pistol and pouch of reserve ammunition, I joined two Diggers with nonchalantly slung F1s. We climbed into a very dusty and battered Landrover.

There had been no incidents on the road for ten days, said the driver, which was not particularly reassuring if you thought about statistical probabilities.

Our road ran north along the Vung Tau peninsula, the first few miles through apparently peaceful and well-populated regions. Leaving the outer fringes of Vung Tau we skirted the airfield to pass a succession of wayside hamlets as far as the US naval shipyard at Cat Lo and the adjacent village of Nam Binh. Now the country was more open. Small rice paddies and mangrove swamps lay on each side. The two-lane highway had been soundly constructed, sealed and elevated above the low-lying terrain; now its surface was in a bad state of repair, rutted and potholed by continual civilian and military traffic. Our driver only really slowed down when we crossed the few small rivers. Here the Landrover crawled across rickety makeshift structures hastily thrown up alongside the fallen spans of bridges wrecked by VC mines.

We left the peninsula and the swamps and sped on to Ba Ria (which everyone wrongly pronounced B'reea and wrongly spelt Baria), the capital of 'our' province, Phuoc Tuy. Everybody called the province Fook Twee, which was surprisingly close to the Vietnamese pronunciation. Shabby dwellings along the southern approaches to the town suddenly gave way to modern market buildings. Baria is a crossroads, with the main road running westwards to Saigon. We continued north, past a large Catholic orphanage and the Korean-staffed civilian hospital. A gaggle of near-naked children playing in the dusty roadside jumped up to shout unintelligible but clearly friendly greetings. 'Uc dai loi,' said the driver. 'It means Australians.'

Further north, past the outskirts of the town, unsmiling labourers, men and women, ignored us as they tilled dusty fields by hand or using a primitively harnessed buffalo. The scene was biblical and peaceful, the atmosphere distinctly threatening. In the village of Hoa Long, two miles from Nui Dat, a tiny urchin screamed obvious abuse and pointedly urinated in our direction. I felt much happier when we passed through the Task Force perimeter wire and entered the rubber plantation.

Seven

THE GROUND SHOWED there'd been no rain at Nui Dat. The heavily used areas of bare earth were bone dry and fine red dust completely coated everything—the high foliage of the rubber trees, the huts, the tents and the soldiery. I stepped down to greet a Red Indian Mick and my boots at once scuffed up their small contribution to the vast pall created by aircraft, vehicles and a thousand men. No time for idle chit-chat: Mick's chopper was departing in a couple of hours. He took me on another lightning tour, first introductions to the staff at the headquarters and RAPs (Regimental Aid Posts) of the 5th and 6th Battalions, then a visit to the top of the small hill that gave Nui Dat its name.

Some mortars were practising on a target at 3000 metres. I was told that the VC were watching us from another feature about 6 miles (10 kms) away. It was eight months since the major battle of Long Tan. This epic event had seared the minds of Australians fighting in Viet Nam. It took place in August 1966 in a rubber plantation just a few miles east of Nui Dat, where D company of 6RAR held off an attack by a VC force at least ten times stronger. They fought gallantly in the true Anzac tradition. Many earned awards for bravery; many were wounded or killed.

Now, at night, the perimeter fences of Nui Dat were being probed by the enemy with increasing frequency. The sense of alertness at the base was almost palpable, more evident than on my brief visit just a few days before. This was a more interesting place to be than the minimally functioning, changing-over Field Ambulance. The dust, I also decided, was preferable to the wind and sand of Vung Tau.

Over drinks at 6RAR, I met a past acquaintance, Captain George Bindley, who had been adjutant of the CMF artillery unit in Perth and a mate of John Marum, the nurse provider. He was now battery captain of 103 Battery at Nui Dat and he had aged many years. I did not know Lieutenant Colonel Townsend, the commanding officer of 6RAR, but he too looked haggard, with a tiny facial twitch indicating the stresses of the job.

Mick headed back to Vung Tau and I went to the officers' dining hut at Task Force headquarters. An ear-splitting blast rocked the building at the start of the first course. I wiped a spoonful of soup from my left ear and tried to look as unconcerned as those calmly eating about me. It was not a mortar attack, I gathered, but the sound of a 175 millimetre gun from the neighbouring US artillery battalion. There must have been some strange acoustic phenomena around Nui Dat. The noise and blast were of a different magnitude from the din recently experienced when we'd been out in the open.

The Australian gunners now further spoiled my digestion, with reports only slightly less deafening. '105s and 155s,' said the officer across from me, 'probably firing H & I.' I looked puzzled. 'Harassment and interdiction,' he said kindly. In a less public moment I enquired further and learned that this meant just blasting away at an area, rather than a specific target. It did not seem a very sensible or efficient use of high explosive, but who was I to question the conduct of the war?

After 24 hours I became accustomed to the intermittent artillery fire, except for one special effect of the sound and pressure waves. The latrine at Nui Dat was a cunning arrangement of lidded cylinders over a deep pit. A quiet few minutes' read here was seldom possible. The noise of the guns was invariably accompanied by a vertical blast of hot air directed at one's bare posterior.

Apart from the deafening noise, and a ten-foot king cobra being killed less than 100 yards from my tent, things were tranquil at Nui Dat during this brief visit. The 8 Field Ambulance forward detachment was separate from the RAPs of the infantry battalions and the gunners. We ran a small hospital comprising an RAP, minor operating theatre and ten-bed ward. Our responsibility was routine medical care of the smaller units of 1ATF, hospital treatment of minor sick and injured, and liaison with the heli-ambulance crews, particularly in the management decisions on battle casualties.

An American Dustoff Huey helicopter flew in every morning at about 0800 hours and settled down on the pad next to the hospital, its long skids just fitting onto the narrow strip of concrete. Here it remained on standby until every evening before dark, when it would head back to the greater security of 36 Evac or the massive logistics base at Long Binh. The evening run was a very useful means of inter-hospital transport. If the MO at the forward detachment decided any patients from the RAP or in the ward required better facilities for diagnosis or treatment, the Americans would deviate their homeward journey to Vampire Pad.

The main function of the Dustoffs was extraction of wounded from a combat area. This was done by winch or by using a tiny, roughly cleared landing zone (LZ), and it was a hazardous business. The Iroquois helicopters wearing the Red Cross were unarmed but they were frequently subjected to intense ground fire. One crew chief I talked to had been shot down three times and his flak jacket was ripped where a bullet had ricocheted across the region of his left shoulder.

The US crews sent to Nui Dat were very happy to be on a soft assignment, knowing that the Viet Cong were avoiding big confrontations with the Australian patrols. They were babyfaced, crew-cut youngsters, only about 19 or 20, who would lounge through the day lazing under their aircraft, among the trees, or in our small ward, reading magazines and exchanging banter with patients and staff. Those I met were very pro-Australian. They were unfailingly correct and courteous, accepting with puzzled good humour the sly ribbing and the tall stories they were fed. Nobody was too unkind, though—the Diggers being well aware that their lives might one day depend on these quiet young Americans.

An unfair rumour at the time was that the Americans only flew daytime Dustoffs because they were too frightened to fly at night. It was true that they provided nearly all the daytime cover, but that was because the RAAF's 9 Squadron had a very limited number of helicopters and crews, who were required for a whole range of duties. As a policy, neither the Australians nor the Americans flew night Dustoffs except in the gravest emergency, simply because the risks were too great. Skill at night-flying or bravery were not the issue. General Gurner, when he became Director General of the Medical Service, made the comment: 'The code name Dustoff probably came from their speed at pick-up, barely dusting off the improvised LZs, but it now stood for Devoted Untiring Service To Our Fighting Forces.' Few would argue with that.

The Sunday morning sick parade consisted of one case of gonorrhoea and one of diarrhoea. My only remaining work for the day was repair of a split scalp, the result of an engineer's fall. Monday was different. Besides the sick parade, I had to get through the medical examination of 65 troops returning to Australia. This checking and documentation of RTA medicals had to be thorough—no unmissed damage due to war service, no skin infections, no tropical disease and no VD lurking to cause havoc at home. With the heat and humidity inside the bare metal hospital hut it was a demanding session.

The afternoon brought two pleasant surprises. It rained, which made conditions marginally cooler, and Jack Blomley unexpectedly turned up a day early, grinning cheerfully under a pancake makeup of sweat and red dust. On the introductory tour his good spirits were only subdued at the final stop—the saggy MO's tent and the narrow entrance to the sandbagged dugout alongside. I bet him that his ample girth would negotiate this easily if the mortars started to arrive.

That night at about 2200 hours there were mortars, flares everywhere and much noise from the 105s (with my vast experience I could pick them now). Happily the mortars were outgoing, but in the middle of all this activity we got a call from Task Force HQ that a casualty was coming in—a night Dustoff! Jack and I scrambled to the hospital and were all set to deal with a major wounding. When the chopper landed, it proved to be not a Huey but a recce Possum, bringing in one Digger with a temperature of 103°F. He was sick, but he'd been sick for five days and his evacuation could easily have waited till morning! Radio communications badly needed some sorting out.

Tuesday, 25 April, Anzac Day. There was a dawn parade, not compulsory, and to my great surprise none of our veteran Field Ambulance lads were at all interested. After twelve months of heat, discomfort, boredom and occasional danger they just wanted to go home. This was my first clear indication that morale must be going badly wrong in some places.

After sick parade, the forward detachment's sergeant major drove Jack and me first to the PX (he used the American term for the Army store) and then to the Post Office. Nothing worth buying at the store, but the PO produced a letter for me from Australia, a smart piece of catching up on my movements, and very welcome. I read the home news as we continued out to the perimeter for an official inspection of the water point. The filtration, chlorination and testing of the water supply were part of our medical responsibility and we at least needed to know the system, although as usual on hygiene matters the expertise and the work both belonged to Regular Army NCOs. Jack admitted he was shit-scared being this close to the wire. I was happy to discover that I felt invulnerable, or at least I thought I did.

In the afternoon I hitched a lift in a chopper back to Vampire Pad.

At 8 Field Ambulance the rear party had arrived. Morrie was gleefully babbling his news of a son and heir, Tony was in manic mode and Pete was gloomy and withdrawn. Mick almost hugged me; we boozed till midnight.

Eight

OUR OWN UNIT flag was now flying. The changeover was almost complete and 8 Field Ambulance was settling into a routine. On the clinical side Mick was in overall charge, combining the roles of administrator and doctor. Although his first interests were general and tropical medicine, he also chose to establish and run a venereal disease clinic, well aware it would be a huge and disheartening task. Tony took over the RAP, the hospital's outpatients section, Peter was installed in the medical wards and Morrie joined Ron Gregg and myself on the surgical side.

The theatre team was still not complete and the new unit not yet ready to manage battle casualties. I had several days to plan our systems for dealing with elective and emergency surgery, to sort out all the anaesthetic and resuscitation equipment, old and new, and to tutor Morrie and the operating theatre technicians in its use. We went in detail through the functioning of the large Boyle machines, the Midget nitrous oxide and oxygen apparatus (like a mini Boyle) in the minor theatre, the EMO ether vaporiser, the bag, mask and valves for emergency breathing assistance. The Bennett ventilator we discovered to be U/S (unserviceable) and not repairable by the Field Workshops engineers. It would have to go back on HMAS *Sydney*. We concentrated on care in the use of the Bird, our only device now if a patient needed ventilation in intensive care.

It was thanks to this quiet period that I had the great good fortune to join Mick on two visits to Saigon. The reasoning was this. Firstly there would be much value in two senior medical officers of 8 Field Ambulance making early liaison visits to both the Australian Staff and the Headquarters of the US Army Medical Corps in Saigon. Secondly, Mick also had to see Harry Dangerfield at the Walter Reed Army Institute of Research (WRAIR) in Saigon about a task he and I had been given. Fevers of unknown origin were a significant problem among our fighting troops and the Americans had been asked to help.

At the beginning of 6RAR's tour, blood samples had been taken from the whole battalion. Now, after a year in a confined area of operation, they were to be bled again. The WRAIR scientists could then compare the samples to identify what diseases the Australian troops were being exposed to. Mick was to arrange with the Americans that he and I would collect the samples at Nui Dat the following Saturday and deliver them personally to Saigon. This date coincided with the third and most important element, the arrival of the first Australian nursing sisters in Viet Nam. The CO, for reasons that escape me, felt that Majors Boyle and Barr would be the most suitable unit representatives to meet the nurses and escort them to Vung Tau.

On Friday 28 April at 0730 hours Mick and I were back at Vung Tau airfield. The twin-engined Caribou aircraft of No. 35 Squadron RAAF had two regular flight schedules out of Vung Tau, the 'Mission' and the 'Wallaby' runs. Ours was the direct Mission flight to Saigon. The Canadian De Havilland Caribou was designed with an upswept rear fuselage which allowed a steep takeoff angle (in flying jargon it was STOL, for short takeoff and landing). Departure from the safety of Vung Tau was normal enough and the 25-minute flight surprisingly comfortable. But there were VC guns on the approach to Saigon Airport and the Caribou waited till the last moment before diving with alarming steepness to the runway. Minutes later we were deposited outside the RAAF Movements Hut on the blistering tarmac of Tan Son Nhut. This RAAF area was called, for no comprehensible reason, Rebel Ramp.

It was a mild surprise to see on a noticeboard the correct Vietnamese spelling for the airport; the Americans, and therefore all foreigners, called it Ton (rhymes with don) San Noot. The major shock was the scale of activity on the airfield. Tan Son Nhut was a vast brown plain slashed by two shimmering parallel runways and flanked by miles of cement and tarmac. Around this perimeter was a jumble of densely packed buildings—offices, hangars and cargo sheds, with freight, machinery and portable huts overflowing onto the acres of hard-standing. This was all mere background. What was so staggering, almost defying belief, was the multitude of aircraft.

Everywhere there were warplanes, hundreds of them, a mind-blowing parade of aviation from the 1930s to the 1960s. Some were protected in concrete revetments, many more stood exposed in long, orderly rows, others were scattered like toys on a giant's playground. Close by there were planes in pieces outside hangars, planes being towed by tractors, planes taxiing on the apron. On one runway a plane would be landing at least every minute, on the other they were queued to take off. There were old DC3s and Skyraiders, tiny Cessnas, communication craft, modern fighter-bombers and a range of multi-engined transports from the last three decades. The din of aero engines and the smell of exhaust fumes were overwhelming.

The old terminal of Saigon Airport was going about its business, although scarcely 'as usual'. In the middle of this awesome display of military air power, jets carrying the logos of Air France, Pan Am, Air Vietnam and Qantas flew in and out, their crews and passengers having the bizarre experience of being briefly in a war. In front of the civilian terminal an Air Viet Nam Caravelle taxied past a Boeing 707 of Air France. I snapped a quick shot with my new Kowa to show the old adversaries nose to nose and apparently kissing. A nice symbol of international reconciliation and friendliness, I thought. The Vietnamese security guard didn't grasp the symbolism, and threatened to confiscate the camera.

An Australian Army bus drove us to MACV, the headquarters of Free World Military Assistance Command Viet Nam. The journey of just a few miles took a very long time. Along the teeming streets the driver had to constantly halt, weave, halt and weave again, threading his patient way through the stream of cyclists, tricyclists, motorcyclists and pedestrians. The locals simply ignored our bus and all other vehicles, small or large. They made way only for the horn-tooting, battered blue and yellow Renault taxis, whose drivers clearly pursued a policy of yielding to nobody.

The headquarters of the Free World Forces, despite its grandiose name and rooftop display of brightly coloured national flags, was a cheerless warren of long corridors, narrow stairs and cluttered offices. The Australian Staff occupied a three-dimensional maze towards the rear of the building. Mick and I did our formality stuff, up and down the stairs, meeting senior officers and conferring with the Medical Corps staff. I felt a sense of one-upmanship. Vung Tau might not be very exciting, but we were likely to see more of the war than these 'Saigon Warriors'. It was a delusion that would be shattered by the Tet offensive in a few months' time.

We politely rejected the offer of lunch and accommodation in some dreary officers' billet and took our temporary leave. Outside the MACV compound one of the many taxis noisily polluting the streets slammed on his brakes. Squeezing into the rear seat of the little Renault felt like climbing aboard a missile. In English, then pidgin French, Mick announced our destination, 179 Cong Ly (pronounced Cong Lee). The driver looked doubtful. Mick produced an envelope with the typewritten address. A big grin, a stamp on the accelerator, a dense cloud of oil-filled exhaust smoke, and we were launched.

Cong Ly turned out to be not far away and Number 179 a classy address, a large well-kept building in a wealthy inner suburb. This was the Saigon headquarters of the Walter Reed Army Institute of Research, the home and workplace of Harry Dangerfield and his fellow scientists. Harry, Mick and I had found ourselves very much on the same wavelength from our first encounter in Vung Tau. Harry was the most open and direct of men. He spoke in a soft, pleasant voice, with little trace of his Oklahoma origins and none of the polite verbosity common among his countrymen. Not: 'At this point in time our accommodation facilities are necessarily limited, but it would be a real pleasure to have you visit.' What Harry had said was: 'We're crowded, but there's a bunk whenever you're in Saigon.'

Now here we were. Harry appeared, crew-cut and lean, whooping in genuine delight. He almost ran us upstairs, recruiting Don Hunter and some others from offices along the way. In a small, comfortable bar, introductions came with cold Budweisers. The WRAIR (pronounced rare) staff were a rare mixture of ranks, ages and specialties. It was clearly a first-names-only establishment and their friendliness to two strangers was quite remarkable. Don promised to give us a sample of his own brew of chilli sauce, Colonel Phil Russell from SEATO in Bangkok convinced me that the Thai capital was the place to spend R&R. The amiable Major Jack del Favero was presented as a veterinary officer! Where were the horses and mules, I wondered? The answer was nowhere: Jack's speciality was bacteriology.

The hastily assembled welcoming party reluctantly returned to their duties while Harry took us for a 25 cent tour—no skimping ten cents' worth for the Aussies. It was typical of the man that I only now learned that he was the chief of staff here. His unconventional unit had rented the front half of an obstetrics hospital to house its offices, laboratories and living quarters. The rear section still flourished as a maternity home for well-to-do Vietnamese.

Harry led us at last to the 'dormitory'. This had previously been an operating theatre. The white-tiled room was now crammed with double-decker bunks, each one covered or surrounded by luggage, kitbags, radios, books, clothing and personal gear. A couple of the residents were on their bunks, stripped to their underwear and cooling off from the midday heat; though it might be cramped, the ex-theatre was still air-conditioned. The two men hospitably cleared places for us. 'They're out on field work,' they said airily, shoving absentees' belongings off the bunks and into a pile against the wall. We dumped our bags onto two adjacent berths. Our half-naked room-mates switched on the huge pendant operating light and trained it in our direction. 'Some reading lamp, hey?' This was bordering on the surreal!

We grabbed a shower, put our uniforms back on and gladly accepted Harry's offer of a lift in his Renault into town. When we reached Le Loi and the city centre Mick and I were probably goggling like country bumpkins. Apart from Mick's New Guinea service, neither of us had ever been outside Australia—and here we were in this exotic Asian city.

Saigon was rightly called the Paris of the Orient. Graceful colonial buildings and modern apartment blocks, fashionable stores and street stalls, tree-lined avenues and intriguing alleyways, limousines, tricycle rickshaws and Lambrettas, glamorous shoppers and giggling schoolgirls—where were the unhappy war-torn Vietnamese? This was a city pulsing with life and prosperity. Except for the military uniforms, the garish hoardings advertising cigarettes, aspirin and toothpaste, and a couple of hideous political statues, Saigon was a visual delight, a perfect blending of two cultures. I was entranced.

We sampled a *bière pression* at La Pagode in Tu-Do before Harry made for Hai Ba Trung, the next street along. Here was the multi-storey Bachelor Officers Quarters called Brinks and here we ate a very good American lunch. Having thus fortified his guests, Harry dropped us back at the Free World in time for our second round of meetings. We talked staffing problems, logistics and treatment protocols until at last we got to our key briefing—the arrangements for the new nurses. We would definitely meet them next Saturday. Who were they? No-one was prepared to give us the names.

Harry called WRAIR the Cong Ly Hilton. He insisted that our heavy day demanded we watch the sunset from the Hilton rooftop and have a few beers to wind down. Then another shower (no water shortage here), a switch to civilian clothes and we were headed downtown yet again with our energetic host.

The eighth floor bar in the ultramodern Hotel Caravelle was becoming famous. It was very smart and very expensive. Here, like many of the international correspondents, we paid through the nose to watch in some luxury a small bit of the war, the drifting lights of flares from helicopters probing the dark outskirts of the capital. We were joined by the mysterious George Warfe, the jungle expert who kept turning up and who now suggested dinner at the Restaurant La Cave. It was a good choice—the French menu was superb. The acrid Algerian *vin ordinaire* was less than ordinary, but we drank it by the litre.

We headed for home in boisterous mood before the 2300 hours curfew. George, Mick and I, ambassadors at large, were loudly singing a marching song. Harry soon joined in.

> We're a pack of bastards, bastards are we,
> We're from Australia, the arsehole of the world and
> all the universe.
> We're a pack of bastards, bastards are we,
> We'd rather f . . k than fight for lib-er-tee.

In the cool of a night breeze, the quieter Americans were parked in comfortable deckchairs on their roof terrace. The flare ships were still active and from the north came occasional sounds of gunfire. We settled down for some more beers; George Warfe, now in full flow, recounted strange adventures and bloodthirsty jungle exploits. Mick and I basked in the reflected glory.

During dinner, George had quoted a line which took Harry's fancy. Now he wanted a full recitation and George was happy to oblige.

> It was Christmas Day in the Workhouse,
> The happiest day of the year.
> Hearts were full of gladness
> And bellies full of beer.
> In strode the Workhouse Master, to inspect the grimy walls,
> 'A Merry Christmas to you', and the paupers shouted 'Balls'.
> His brow grew dark with anger as he faced the sullen mob,
> 'You'll get no Christmas pudding, you dirty bunch of sods'.
> Then up spoke Jimmy Watkins, with his face as bold as brass,
> 'We don't want your Christmas pudding, you can shove it up
> your arse'.

Harry Dangerfield had three pet hates, which had surfaced during the evening—General de Gaulle, the United States Air Force and USAID. It was the massive aid organisation that had really got him worked up—'tactless blundering in countries they know nothing about'. Now there was a perfect response to smug offers from some self-important authority. When I staggered off to bed Harry was still chortling about it. And 'We don't want your Christmas pudding' became the motto of the WRAIR team.

On Saturday, thankfully not until 0930, we had an appointment at USARV Headquarters to meet some of the American medical top brass. Colonels Raymond W. Blohm, Edmond R. Kielman and Al Gomez impressed us greatly. They conveyed a most useful understanding of the complex medical situation in III Corps, the military zone which stretched east–west across the middle of the country from Phuoc Tuy to the Cambodian border. How big their task was, how small ours. I had no idea of the hugeness of the installations at places like Long Binh, Bien Hoa and Tay Ninh. My cockiness was dampened for all of two hours. 8 Field Ambulance was a tiny part of this Corps, and the colonels had barely touched on IV Corps down in the Delta, let alone II Corps and I (Eye) Corps to our north.

The Americans at that time had about half a million servicemen in Viet Nam. Australia and New Zealand's contribution was about four thousand. Astoundingly, our hosts had considerable knowledge and understanding of our medical problems. It seemed amazing that senior administrators of this calibre were willing to give so much time to a couple of visiting majors. In retrospect, it was a demonstration of American regard for Australia's involvement in an increasingly unpopular war.

Official duty done for the weekend, Mick and I retreated thoughtfully to WRAIR and grabbed a few hours much needed rest. The inexhaustible Harry roused us mid-afternoon. Time for sightseeing again. The culture shock was now diminishing and I could absorb a bit more detail. The dignified complacency of the Continental Palace Hotel (shades of colonialism and Graham Greene); the lawns and tall trees extending majestically down the central reservation of Le Loi; the Hotel de Ville; the ornate white Opera House fronted by a tiny rotunda for the white-uniformed Vietnamese on point duty. These local policemen were called White Mice. This Mouse wore a big pistol and his raised hand stopped even the aggressive little blue and yellow taxis.

We were more interested in the scores of beautiful girls, black-haired, slim and graceful in the traditional *ao dai* (pronounced ow-zigh). The silk tunics were slit to the waist, the thin silk trousers clinging. 'VPL,' commented Harry approvingly. My education was continuing; this meant 'visible panty line', something we thereafter looked for on every occasion.

Towards evening, families were gathering in the side streets. They sat on tiny stools around pavement stoves, chopsticks diving into communal bowls of fish and rice. Food! So far today Mick and I had survived on coffee. Harry urged us along, down to the Saigon River and the My Canh floating restaurant, for great Chinese cuisine and dubious wine in vast quantities yet again . . .

Harry Dangerfield's concept of the ideal start to a Sunday was a trip around the early morning markets. Phil Russell and Jack del Favero were persuaded to join us. We jostled among the chattering crowds, very foreign and touristy in Koratron trousers, open-necked shirts and shoulder-slung cameras. There was plenty to see, including a great range of goods that had been liberated from American PXs. We inched our way through sweaty shoppers along alleyways packed with baskets of reeking vegetables, meat and fish. A small boy offered us 'feelthy pictures'. And this was at 7 a.m.!

The WRAIR idea of Sunday brunch was ham and eggs served with pancakes and maple syrup, American fare normal enough for today's world travellers, mind-boggling then to us innocents abroad. It was surprising how well the combination went down, settling the stomach sufficiently to try a cautious beer. A quiet couple of hours on the Cong Ly sun terrace, plans finalised for the next weekend, and it was time to head for 'Ton San Noot'.

The 1600 hours 'Wallaby' flight called at Nui Dat on the return run to Vung Tau. The Nui Dat airstrip (Luscombe) was unsealed, undulating and short. To minimise the hazard from ground fire outside the small perimeter, the Caribou approached at high altitude, then corkscrewed earthward in a tight spiral, suddenly straightening to touch down. The propellers screamed in reverse pitch and we juddered almost at once to a standstill. The rear loading door opened, the load-master shoved out some crates of fruit and shouted at a group of infantrymen to follow them into the swirling cloud of Nui Dat's red dust. Before the door had whined shut, we were moving, gathering speed for a stomach-grabbing climb to safe altitude.

John Frewen met us at Vung Tau airfield with the news that 8 Field Ambulance had not fallen apart in our absence. The Landrover struggled up the short incline to the Mess. A sudden gust blew sand all over us. We were home.

There was of course much disappointment that we didn't bring back any information on who the nurses were. Presumably the CO knew but he was saying nothing. Although I don't remember, it is likely that Mick and I let it be understood that our lips too were sealed. The unknown ladies were already generating a deal of sympathy. Their quarters, strategically sited in the hollow equidistant between the male officers' tents and the chapel, were nearly completed. The good news for them was they would not be living in tents. The bad news was that their new home consisted of two low wooden boxes partitioned into tiny rooms, each with a tiny window. At the base of the dunes this looked to be a veritable heat trap. To ensure maximum discomfort for the occupants, the area was then surrounded by a wall of plasticised hessian, helpful for privacy but certain to block any breeze.

At 0630 the next Saturday, 6 May, we started our roundabout journey to meet the nurses. The driver, his 'shotgun', Mick and I were in a Landrover armed with two F1s, two SLRs, two pistols and 1000 disposable syringes and needles. Under the rubber trees at Nui Dat, 6RAR was fully set up for our blood-letting. A dozen soldiers were already waiting in the RAP. Vic Bampton, the regimental medical officer, took a hundred syringes and an ice box and flew off in a chopper to the Horseshoe. One company of the battalion were still camped on this feature a few dangerous miles to the east. Talk about research in the field!

Mick and I started work at 0800, the system functioning like clockwork. The sergeant major ticked each man off from the company rolls; the RAP medics had divided up their tasks to keep us supplied with skin wipes, needles and syringes and to get the test tubes labelled and packed. The artillery blasted away all day, the aluminium Kingstrand rattled and the Diggers talked twitchily of a VC battalion in the area. The rumour was that the VC would launch an offensive to mark the thirteenth anniversary of Dien Bien Phu. The fall of this base near the border of northern Laos, on 7 May 1954, was the final blow to the French colonials. The resulting negotiations saw the Viet Minh gain control of North Viet Nam and the South become a separate state. Anniversary or not, the thought of a major action wasn't a pleasant one right now. The short-timers providing their end-of-tour blood samples wanted no part of any big battle. There were a few nervous jokes—'You've got the last blood I'm gunna spill'—but nobody much was laughing.

The 'patients' kept on coming. None were overweight after a year at Nui Dat, so the veins were easy. Thank God too for disposables. Sterilising and sharpening for this lot would have been a nightmare. At about 1600 hours Vic returned, rightly proud that he had a sample from every member of his scattered company. An hour later Mick and I were finished, massaging our hands and wrists, by now painfully stiff from the repetitive movements.

The RAAF chopper which had brought in Vic was waiting impatiently. We clambered aboard, secured the precious ice boxes and were off at once, flying almost due west, where dark storm clouds partly concealed the setting sun. We crossed the rugged ranges the troops called 'Warburton Mountains' and Mick was stirred into song: 'They say don't go, on Wolverton Mountain.' I began to laugh. In the jungled slopes below, Viet Cong would be listening to the helicopter, trying to guess its route and destination. Their intelligence sources probably knew anyway, but they were unlikely to care about our blood cargo, even less about the second phase of our mission. A thousand Australians, on the other hand, were eagerly awaiting news on when the nurses would be coming. Mick and I were getting a 36-hour start on all of them. It was a funny kind of war.

Again we came in high to Tan Son Nhut, but in our helicopter the steep descent was relaxed and gentle down to the heliport, at least a mile from where the Caribou had landed us the previous weekend. Then I had been too fascinated by all the planes to even think about where the helicopters were. Now I knew. As we angled in, rotor blades slashing noisily in the heavy, humid air, we passed over row upon row of them. It was like looking down on some huge car park. The lines were straight, their spacing mathematically neat to allow room for manoeuvring. Some Hueys sidled delicately a few inches above the water-covered tarmac, others rose gingerly to clear their neighbours, then lifted quickly over the perimeter buildings and disappeared in the gloom. Our pilot, perhaps impressed by the Priority Medical label on the ice boxes, ignored the broad parking area and set us down immediately outside the Movements Office.

For the first time the day's organisation developed a hiccup. We had been promised military transport and none was in sight. I sat outside the doorway guarding the specimens while Mick tried to phone WRAIR. The telephone system in Saigon was a relic of French colonialism, outdated and inadequate. The Americans had many lines of their own but this connection must have gone through the French system. During the twenty minutes it took Mick to get through I watched the helicopters rising and setting down against the background of lowering cloud and retreating downpour. Mostly Huey gunships with M60s bristling, they looked like angry wasps disturbed by the rain. I wish I had thought to count them.

The obliging Harry collected us in his ancient Renault. We checked in to the Cong Ly Hilton's 'operating theatre', showered, shaved and put on our best white shirts and slacks. Harry's many kindnesses were now repaid by our departing alone for nurse-minding duties. He and his men would doubtless be very busy with the blood samples. Besides, we reasoned, too many strangers would confuse the new arrivals. It was also a reasonable assumption that with half a million Western servicemen in-country this was a once and only opportunity to squire four round-eyed girls on a night out in Saigon. We would not require any assistance.

The nurses were already installed at the Embassy Hotel on Nguyen Trung Truc, around the corner from Le Loi. We found them just finishing dinner, the only non-Asiatic females in the restaurant, and mighty good they looked in their sleeveless dresses. All four seemed very calm and self-possessed considering the strangeness of their situation, but they were gratifyingly pleased to see us. 'It's so good to hear your Australian voices!' We ordered drinks, sorted out the introductions and then the questions came tumbling out. What were their quarters like? Was Vung Tau dangerous? Where could they buy makeup? How busy was the hospital? What were the Americans like? Was there much malaria? Could they wear civilian clothes off-duty?

The excited inquisition continued as we took our charges on a tour through central Saigon. Heads turned wherever we went—the locals curious, the US servicemen envious. Mick and I demonstrated our great knowledge of the city, showing off like a pair of teenagers. How good was this? Four girls keeping close and hanging on our every word.

While enjoying the attention, I was obviously also trying to make some cold-blooded assessments. These women were going to have a huge influence on our medical work, on the administration of the hospital, on unit morale and on the social life of the Mess; quite possibly on us personally too. Doubtless Mick was making his own first judgements, and notes would be compared.

Captain Amy Pittendreigh, senior by a few years and with the higher rank, was petite, quiet-spoken and serious (as well she might be!). She was from Western Australia and had obviously been primed up on my background. 'I know quite a bit about you!' Sharing the same isolated State gave a surprising feeling of kinship. More importantly, her rather grave eyes were capable of a definite twinkle. Of the three lieutenants, Maggie Ahern was manifestly a live-wire, radiating restless energy. She was demure and peaceable now, but the name and her flaming red hair gave warning of a mercurial temperament. Colleen Mealy was a quiet-voiced brunette, wide-eyed with excitement. Terrie Roche was blonde, with a slow country drawl and unhurried manner.

The most significant thing was that they seemed to get along well. They all came across as having a sense of humour and there was no doubt they were desperately keen to prove their nursing worth. All four were pleasantly good-looking and normal—no stick insects, no voluptuous curves, no Hollywood-style glamour or blatant sex appeal—four attractive women, friendly in a quietly reserved way. It was all most reassuring, everyone relaxed a little and the evening steadily became more enjoyable.

The mature and wise Amy very politely established an early curfew. A good decision; tomorrow they would be coping with the roller-coaster Caribou ride and the first shock of Vung Tau. After a nightcap in the bar at the Caravelle we reluctantly escorted the quartet back to their hotel. It was no surprise to find they were two to a room. Naturally, neither Mick nor I had entertained any thought of dalliance with them. Mick nonetheless had a cautionary word for me against getting too closely involved. It was not the most elegant phrase, but it was very much to the point. 'Be careful, mate. Don't shit in your own nest,' he said.

Full of self-righteousness and the afterglow of agreeable female company we squeezed into a taxi. 'Cong Ly. How much?' Harry had told us the reasonable fare and stressed the importance of settling it first. 'One-twenty P,' said the driver confidently (100 piastres were then the equivalent of about one US dollar). 'Sixty P,' Mick and I roared in unison. The man grunted disappointed assent and was still muttering and shaking his head when we drew up at No. 179. The GI on guard saluted, ignored our proffered identity papers and opened the door for us. It was nice to be recognised as friends.

The Americans, it seemed, were not complete barbarians about Sunday mornings. At a civilised hour Harry, Don Hunter and Ace Adams took us to the Continental Palace. The splendid hotel, gracing the corner of Tu Do and Le Loi, was the very essence of French colonial architecture. Its solid stone structure gleamed white in the bright morning sunlight, the tall windows haughty, the green awnings matching the trees and lawns outside.

The famous Terrace Bar, all white pillars, Mediterranean arches and cool shade, seemed exactly right; the cane chairs were peopled by characters plucked from a dozen novels. The correct drink appeared to be coffee and cognac. Not for us: Harry led our party through to the enclosed rear garden, away from the traffic and the crowds.

Here we sat under a pergola surrounded by beautifully tended tropical plants. Butterflies flitted brightly in the sunshine. Two peacocks wandered among the palms and frangipani. The white-uniformed waiter brought hot croissants, bacon and eggs and a richly aromatic coffee, the best I had ever tasted. It was impossible to believe we were in a war.

A leisurely stroll around Saigon, working our way down towards the Saigon River, continued the exploration of this war-stricken capital. The largest vessel in view was the German hospital ship *Heligoland.* Moored in haughty isolation, her disciplined Teutonic lines contrasted with the untidy, ill-maintained little craft keeping their respectful distance. To us she seemed a bit remote and withdrawn from the people she was trying to help. But what would we know about it? We were embarrassingly ignorant of their activities, or of the many civilian aid

A civilised Sunday breakfast at the Continental Palace, Saigon—Mick Boyle on the left with three quiet Americans, Harry Dangerfield wearing glasses, Don Hunter and Ace Adams.

projects being run by other countries. Anyway, right now we were not interested in hospitals or medicine. We had walked off the late breakfast and there was a delicious smell of Chinese cooking.

We met the girls plus Major Brian Joyce of Medical HQ for lunch at the My Canh. They had found shops displaying up to the minute Western fashions in shoes and clothing, and were expressing amazement at the astronomic prices. Not a very warlike conversation. To give them a frisson of excitement we told them about the restaurant's blasting by Claymore mines a few months before. Not a very effective frightener—the My Canh today was peacefully crowded with Sunday lunchers.

We found a railside table on the top deck. A team of polite waiters served dishes of uniform excellence. We ate slowly, washing down each course with Carlsberg lager, and watched the continuous movement of traffic on the river. A speedboat bounced jauntily across the muddy water, its wake violently rocking the narrow wooden skiff directly below us. A little Vietnamese girl squatted in the stern, alone in the fragile craft. She was quite unperturbed, expertly manipulating a pair of long oars with her bare feet. She held her position alongside, manoeuvring backwards and forwards to catch coins tossed by onlookers from the restaurant. Racing downstream came a Westerner, a single sculler in pristine white singlet, flashily showing off his style. The two examples of skilled oarsmanship were a salutary reminder of Viet Nam's painful contrasts. Whatever any of us had expected Saigon to be like, the realities were most certainly very different.

It would have been nice to spend hours chatting in that exotic setting, but our own reality was now closing in. Mick and I and the girls left the My Canh to get back into uniform, collect our belongings and catch the afternoon Wallaby to Vung Tau.

To avoid any overexuberant demonstrations of welcome, the date of the big arrival had not been widely broadcast. The Caribou ride, apart from the usual impressive demonstrations of short takeoff and landing, was notable for the gaping disbelief of our fellow passengers when they saw uniformed Australian nurses on board. We slipped Amy's team quietly into 8 Field Ambulance and with some misgivings conducted them to their new home.

Mick and I had painted them a deliberately gloomy picture, hoping the jail-like actuality might be less of a shock. They seemed to take it in their stride. We breathed a silent sigh of relief and left them to it. Our retreat was not rapid enough to miss the sounds of a lively discussion. Words like 'floor coverings', 'decorating', 'decent furniture' followed us up the hill. It was time for a gin and tonic.

That night, as president of the Mess Committee, I officially welcomed the nurses to 8 Field Ambulance Officers Mess. We had wine with dinner and many celebratory noggins afterwards. In a quiet moment outside, my shoulder served when a few tears needed to be shed. Towards midnight, when the women began to wilt, several gallants eagerly volunteered to form an escort party to see them to their quarters. Our protection was not really necessary; in the moonlight an armed guard stood stolidly outside the hessian barrier. The Army was determined that its latest reinforcements would sleep undisturbed.

Nine

CAPTAIN PITTENDREIGH AND her lieutenants transformed both their quarters and the hospital in a matter of days. Bright curtains, bamboo screens, wallpaper, ornaments and flowers all appeared with magical swiftness. Their living area was now indubitably feminine, and it was also relatively comfortable. The much-sneered-at hessian screen actually shielded their buildings from the heat reflected by the white sand; they were often cooler than the wise men exposed on the hill.

At work, to be successful in taking over from experienced male NCO medical assistants, they had to both look the part, which they did in starched uniform and veil, and be the part. Their formal training (in those times happily concentrated on real nursing rather than academic theory) meant that better ward routines were soon in place. Femininity plus nursing skills ensured instant affection from the sick and wounded; the displaced NCOs and the orderlies now under more rigid management took longer to be won over. Even they eventually accepted that improvements were being made. For the officers it was an embarrassing experience to see through the nurses' eyes how scruffy our hospital had been.

Manners and language too were distinctly improved. After the weeks of rumour, alarm and doubtless lustful fantasy about the nurses' arrival, the degree of respect they were shown was remarkable. Among the convalescents in particular there was a tendency towards greater interest in personal appearance and an occasional flirtatious remark, but the nurses were treated always as nurses. I did not see or hear of any incidents of what today would be called sexual harassment. It was a tribute to their own impeccable behaviour. All four were always perfectly turned out and coolly professional in the hospital environs, despite the heat, humidity and long hours of work. Even in jungle greens, when they visited Nui Dat, the nurses maintained a ladylike deportment which effectively held the sex-starved soldiery at bay.

Red-headed Maggie was allocated to the surgical team. Now we were complete and on Monday 8 May the new team accepted its first casualty.

The primary function of the surgical staff was the best possible management of battle casualties. By now it was old hat for Ron; he was happy for me to rehearse the new team for all the duties ahead, other than the actual operating procedures, offering an occasional pertinent suggestion on changes we made to the previous routines.

Our team of operating theatre technicians were absolutely essential in the effective treatment of the casualties. The OTTs looked after the operating theatre with its surgical and anaesthetic equipment; they sterilised the instruments and dressings; they formed litter teams to meet the Dustoffs; they checked and made ready the resuscitation equipment and drugs; they assisted in cutting off clothing and positioning the patients for examination and X-raying; they recorded the key information of pulse and blood pressure, drug doses, tourniquet times and other events as dictated by the MO; they helped with giving oxygen, maintaining the airway, taking blood samples and setting up intravenous drips. In the theatre one OTT was always scrubbed, gowned and gloved to assist the surgeon, another acted as the anaesthetist's assistant and at least one other was the theatre 'runner', unscrubbed and free to fetch and carry.

These OTTs were led by Sergeant Bruce Turnbull, a man slow of speech, taciturn, quietly competent and with many worries. Much of the leftover equipment was in a bad way, needing testing and repair; his staff were inexperienced and there were too few of them for the workload. Worst of all, from his viewpoint, was the arrival of female nurses, and officers at that—his authority and status were immediately undermined, perhaps even his job. Corporals Brian Connelly and Paul Crowe and Privates Ken Youngson, Geoff Harris and Cisco Colbran all shared his concern about the nurses. It was a great stimulus to training; they were not going to be told how to do their job by some overbearing female.

Maggie was an experienced theatre sister who had very definite ideas on how things should be done. Bruce Turnbull and the OTTs were indeed treated early in the piece to some flashes of the anticipated fiery temper. These subsided, once she had her way, to a bantering camaraderie, and she brought us an extra charge of enthusiasm which would be greatly useful in the months ahead.

The OTTs were divided into teams as first and second on-call. Maggie and Bruce Turnbull concentrated on the theatre activities of sterilising, preparing instruments and assisting the surgeon. Morrie and I lectured and rehearsed the teams in resuscitation and anaesthesia duties. The ideal was for the OTTs to be interchangeable, each one capable of any task, which was never completely achievable. Some did have specialised tasks, such as Bob Burgess, Peter de Worboies and Bruno Davis who shared the X-ray duties. Some had favourite jobs. Private Colbran's was the most unusual; the petrol-fired autoclave for sterilising was a constant source of trouble and Cisco enjoyed the challenge of keeping it going. He would sit cross-legged in the sweltering heat of a tiny alcove, twiddling knobs, adjusting valves and tapping steaming pipes. It was like watching an industrious goblin in a corner of Hades.

These OTTs were very young soldiers. Many were National Servicemen, many had had very limited hospital experience and their standard of education varied widely. It is a tribute to their team spirit that I never completely sorted out who were National Servicemen and who were regulars. I rarely heard any of them complain about their lot or criticise their workmates. Many years later I discovered that this was a somewhat rose-coloured view, but it was how I perceived things at the time. Undoubtedly they were all desperately keen to put their training into wartime practice. I developed the utmost respect for each one of them.

The boys had much to learn, particularly about anaesthesia. It was most fortunate that the red-headed National Serviceman Ken Youngson became my first anaesthetics technician. The role is not easy. Many anaesthetists, and I was one, adopt the carefree, jokey attitude exemplified by Grimsdyke in *Doctor in the House*. (Richard Gordon the author was previously Gordon Ostlere the anaesthetist.) This might in some cases be a genuine personality trait, but on the job it is a pure facade. Anaesthesia is the one specialty where the patient's life is truly in the doctor's hands.

Death on the operating table was rare by the 1960s, but a mistake at any stage of general anaesthesia can cause disastrous complications and death may well follow later. However breezy and confident you might appear, underneath there is always the worry of something going wrong. The stress is much less when you can rely on your assistant, when you know the right drugs will all be ready, the equipment properly checked, the intravenous drip constantly watched. When your own hands are otherwise occupied your technician must be able to maintain the airway by supporting the jaw and keeping the facemask in position, a combination which takes much training and practice. Intubation bypasses the airway problem, but for this a muscle relaxant is usually given, which then means the patient can no longer breathe for himself. Since we had no mechanical ventilator in our theatre, another vital task which my assistants had to learn was 'squeezing the bag'. It's not as simple as it sounds: the relief valve needs continual adjustment and the hand must be educated to squeeze with the right pattern of pressure and rhythm.

It is essential too that your assistant can see through the jokey facade. He has to recognise when the situation is changing from routine to possibly life-threatening and to anticipate your needs. If a real emergency does arise he must respond calmly and resourcefully: the right syringe, the sucker in your hand, the table tilted, the reserve laryngoscope ready. Ken Youngson was a very intelligent young man. He soon became highly skilled, a trusted assistant and an ideal model for others who followed.

Despite his fiery red hair, Ken appeared to accept his enforced military service with minimal grumbling. The National Servicemen I got to talk to were certainly unenthusiastic about Army life and discipline but most seemed resigned to their lot. Some were quite happy to have a taste of adventure, to see a bit of Asia and to gain some financial benefit from their call-up. Again, I later heard very different opinions. Maybe they decided to tell the officer what he wanted to hear; maybe they changed their attitude. In any event, although on Diggers' ridge the atmosphere might sometimes have been near-mutinous, in casualty and the operating theatre all the OTTs worked with willingness and pride, and with ever increasing skill.

Our 'patch' began on Vampire Pad, the litter teams waiting when a Dustoff landed. They gave the spare litter to the chopper crew chief in exchange for the one being used, then hand-carried the casualty along the causeway path (on which there never were any accidents) to enter triage. This first half of the surgical Kingstrand hut was known variously as Triage, Casualty, Resus or Pre-Op, all the names being appropriate. Here the wounded were resuscitated, given a priority for treatment (the French *triage* means sorting), and made ready for the operating theatre.

Triage was a strictly functional room. The ceiling and walls were of corrugated aluminium, a box of bare metal relieved only by a row of

A Dustoff chopper circles Vampire Pad, crossing above our 'movie theatre'. (Photo: P. Davis)

A litter party leaves Vampire Pad en route to the hospital. (Photo: P. Davis)

tall louvred windows. There were half a dozen simple lightweight trolleys, head ends nearest the windows which offered good daytime lighting. Opposite the trolleys were large white equipment cupboards festooned with the personal weapons of the surgical team. Overhead, the bare aluminium beams sprouted electric lights and a couple of ceiling fans whirring ineffectively in the heavy, humid air.

Each resus trolley had its own double drip stand, a couple of hanging stethoscopes and a wall chart behind. Nearby were suction apparatus, oxygen cylinders, bag and mask emergency breathing gear and drape-covered trays carrying emergency drugs, intravenous equipment and intubating gear.

The next part of the Kingstrand housed a small portable X-ray plant and a minor operation room. The remainder, the eastern section of the building, was sealed off as the main operating theatre. This really looked like an operating theatre—a major and a minor operating table with operating lights, two anaesthetic machines, stainless steel equipment trolleys, glass-fronted instrument cabinets, white-painted finish to walls and ceiling, and the supreme luxury of air-conditioning.

Following surgery the patients were kept in the Resus area until they had recovered from their anaesthetic. The more seriously ill went straight to the small Intensive Care Unit in the adjacent Kingstrand; here they continued to benefit from air-conditioning and here we were still involved, looking after specialised drips and airway problems, and frequently bringing them back for further emergency surgery. The less severe cases were transferred from Resus to the surgical ward, where they were no longer a direct responsibility of the theatre team.

Within this area of operation, from Vampire Pad to the Intensive Care Unit, Morrie and I modified and refined the plan of action for severely wounded casualties. It was a plan based on very simple principles, which appealed to our no-nonsense surgeon.

The injured soldier would usually arrive within an hour of being wounded. It was rare for an IV drip to already be in place and this was not necessary, because of the speed of delivery of the soldier to hospital facilities. In modern ambulance terms it was ‘scoop and run’ rather than ‘hold and stabilise’. Notified of an approaching Dustoff, we would assemble the first on-call team and check the availability of second on-call staff. Before the helicopter landed we had the resuscitation equipment and inflatable tourniquets set up and tested, intravenous drips assembled and syringes of pethidine, penicillin and tetanus toxoid drawn up. The mobile X-ray machine would be in place by the resus trolley. Staff Sergeant Vonk's laboratory staff would be set up for blood crossmatching, one technician in the lab, one ready to collect the samples. In the operating theatre, Maggie, Bruce and their assistants would prepare for major surgery.

The first principle we taught was reassurance. From the moment the litter team picked up the wounded soldier the OTTs gave constant words of encouragement: 'You're OK now, sport. This is the Australian hospital. You'll be right.' On the resus trolley all but the most minimally injured were given oxygen and told it was doing them good. Inflatable tourniquets were used to control bleeding from the limbs. Two wide-bore cannulae were placed in different veins; blood was taken from one for immediate cross-matching, then intravenous fluid was run in through both lines. Pethidine was given intravenously in repeated small doses until pain was completely relieved. Massive doses of intravenous penicillin were started at once.

While this was going on, all clothing was cut away and the patient turned so that every part of his anatomy could be inspected for entry and exit wounds, small shrapnel fragments, burns and other damage. X-rays were taken on the trolley, looking for metallic foreign bodies, suspected fractures and internal injury to lungs or belly. Sites for

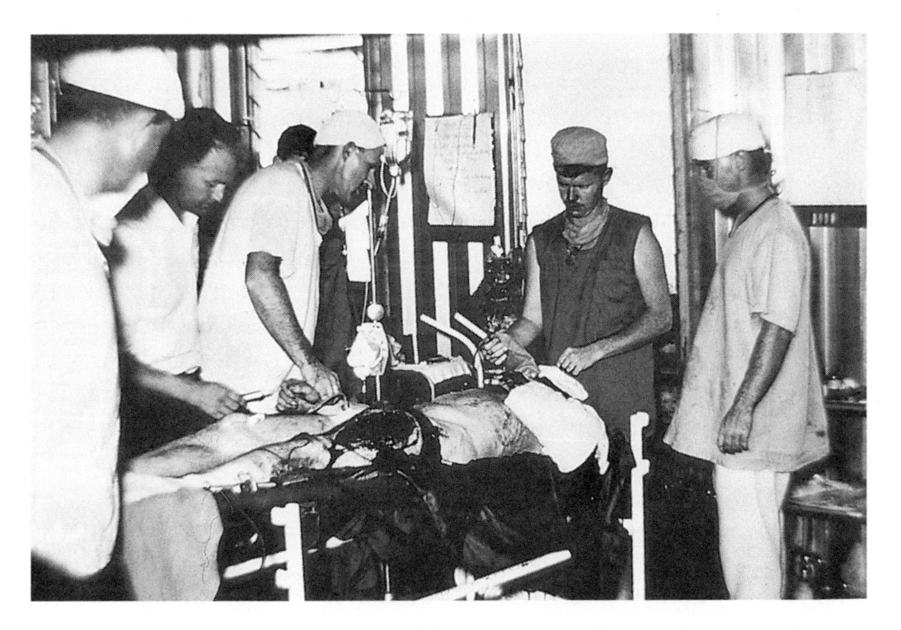

Resus in action: Paul Crowe is behind the mask; Ken Youngson looks after the head and airway. (Photo: M. Peacock)

operation were cleaned and shaved. As soon as Ron had completed his triage assessment of the casualties, the first patient was moved to theatre where the rest of the operating team were already scrubbed and waiting. No system is perfect, but thanks to the OTTs this one worked well. Our severely wounded and shocked patients were treated with a speed and efficiency impossible in the best civilian hospitals of the time.

While the medical and nursing care of casualties always gets the publicity and the limelight, a huge contribution to the care of the wounded came from the supporting staff. One such was the medical liaison officer, another role for the overworked bearer officer, John Purser. The important task of getting the Casualty Personal Particulars Form completed was a priority among his many administrative duties.

This documentation was vital in keeping accurate records on all injured soldiers, but the surgeons battling to save life or limb were not always sympathetic to form-filling. John showed maturity and sensitivity beyond his years in picking the moment and the method to get the required information. Ron and Morrie might be drooping with fatigue after hours of operating; John, just as pressed with his own work, would be waiting outside theatre, signal pad in hand, for a brief statement. Injuries treated and patient's condition: the signals had to be sent.

The bearer officer was assisted by an admission and discharge clerk, who transferred details on to further forms, for fuller documentation and accurate statistics. The duty pack storemen from John Kelly's department had the task of collecting and documenting all equipment that came with the patient. Hand grenades, rifle, ammunition and other lethal items were grabbed before the litter reached the triage door. The Kelly gang had to wait then for the remaining equipment and clothing, until the drama of resuscitation was over and the stripped patient safely in theatre. Private Garcia, the unit barber, assisted with shaving the sites for operation; the photographer was there to record particular injuries or operations and to assist the OTTs when not filming.

The chaplains were called to every Dustoff. They waited quietly in the background until given the OK, sometimes to offer words of comfort or prayer and sometimes, when we were hard-pressed, to become assistant OTTs—blood-moppers, light-holders, messengers—any task we might spring upon them. The often maligned cooks played their part during long operating sessions, delivering coffee, hot soup, chicken pieces or steak sandwiches which we would wolf down between cases. Civilian hospital disaster planners underestimate the importance of hot food and drink in maintaining morale.

It is probably true that every member of the unit was keen to help in some way when major casualties came in. This was 8 Field Ambulance providing the most dramatic justification for its presence in Viet Nam. For those taunted by visiting Nui Dat warriors about their safe and comfortable war, personally taking some part was a considerable tonic. Spectators were never allowed but we sometimes had difficulty keeping resus clear of an excess of willing workers.

Ron's surgical management of war wounds closely followed the routine used by the American Army surgeons and proven successful in thousands of casualties. After full resuscitation, when pain and shock had been dealt with and blood volume had been restored and the circulation was stable, the wounded man was anaesthetised and his wounds widely debrided. This meant the removal of all damaged tissue to minimise the risk of infection. High velocity injuries from land mine blast or rifle bullet cause extraordinarily extensive damage, with traumatised muscle often concealed beneath apparently normal skin. Major Gregg was expert at seeking, identifying and removing all such dangerous tissue. Many soldiers owe their well-being or their life to Ron's skill and experience.

Full debridement left a wide open wound. All bleeding was controlled, then the bare area was packed and the whole swathed in heavy sterile bandages. After the operation, massive doses of penicillin were continued via the IV drip. The patient returned to theatre after five days. Another anaesthetic, and the dressings were removed. Any further suspect tissue was excised. If all was well, with no sign of infection, the clean, healthy wound edges were brought together by sutures—so-called 'delayed primary closure'. The importance of 'debridement and DPC' in treating war wounds, so different from most civilian injuries, is a lesson surgeons have to relearn in every conflict.

This system of resuscitation and surgical management was all relatively straightforward while casualties remained infrequent. Our first dozen or so emergency cases were in fact not caused by enemy action but by a depressing run of land mine and grenade accidents, drop-short shells from friendly fire, and burns and other accidental injuries. None of us had anticipated this scenario in our trauma management. There was little satisfaction in repairing damage so unnecessarily caused. There was, however, one advantage: not being faced immediately by multiple combat casualties gave us time to modify and perfect our new routines.

Each morning Ron and Morrie (who proved to be an excellent assistant surgeon and is now a senior thoracic surgeon in Adelaide) would do two or three cases from a waiting list for elective surgery. I used the opportunity to teach different anaesthetic techniques to the OTTs, and to give Morrie, Mick (when he was available) and Maggie (as a backup) experience with the equipment. The operations varied. Never anything too long; our minds were always on a sudden influx of casualties. There might be removal of plantar warts, say, relief of an ingrowing toenail, even a haemorrhoidectomy. But the most common procedure was circumcision.

This most ancient of operations probably originated among desert tribes as a hygienic measure to eliminate balanitis—inflammation of the foreskin. Whatever the arguments nowadays against routine circumcision of infants, if the baby boy is going to be a soldier he will undoubtedly benefit from it. Constant heavy physical activity in tropical conditions with inadequate facilities for washing led to a remarkably high incidence of balanitis among the jungle fighting troops. The OTTs soon dubbed the surgeon 'Rabbi'.

For a few days after their circumcision, the victims were acutely uncomfortable. We gave them a refrigerant spray to quell the painful involuntary erections which commonly occur in the early post-operative period. Among the other convalescents wandering about the hospital area, these patients were easily recognisable from their crouched gait, with pyjama pants held well clear. One night the movie show newsreel included a parade of Miss World finalists in their swimsuits. A distressed figure soon hobbled out, moaning as he went past: 'I gotta get me spray!'

Ten

THE NURSES HAD arrived at just the right time; we were about to experience a big increase in the casualty workload. During the first surgical list with Maggie in charge of theatre we got a call: 'Dustoff with four seriously wounded.' If true, this was more than we could reasonably cope with. We would take two, and send the chopper on to 'Cotton Gauze'. Maggie led the scramble to finish the routine case, cancel the others and clear and prepare the theatre. We had just finished setting up the resuscitation equipment when we learned they had all been taken to 36 Evac. The Dustoff crew had made the right decision. Pity we didn't know earlier.

Ron, Morrie and I jumped into a Landrover to see if we could lend a hand. In 36 Evac's tunnel-like triage we found Bob Watson and his team dealing with four Australian sappers who had been blown up by a mine. The most severely head-injured man already had a tracheotomy tube in place to keep his airway clear. Two medics were putting in intravenous lines. The other three victims each had a resuscitation team battling to get their lines in. All obviously were in urgent need of fluid and blood. Bob waved an arm inviting us to help.

The US system of casualty management was very rigid. The number of doctors needed to staff their huge medical commitment meant that most had been conscripted (drafted), and the level of experience varied greatly: many were very junior. For severe injuries their routine was always to do at least one 'cut-down'. This means cutting the skin overlying the vein, using forceps to dissect away the tissues to isolate about an inch of the vessel, running a loop of thread around the freed segment, then nicking it and pushing a cannula (a plastic tube) into the vein. The cannula is secured in place by tightening and tying the loop; finally the skin incision is closed with one or two stitches. This is a very certain means of getting in a large intravenous cannula and ensuring that it does not become displaced—but it does take time, especially if the operator is not surgically experienced.

It is far quicker to slide a large needle directly into the vein, as when a blood sample is taken. The needle itself would soon cut through the vein, but it can be provided with a plastic sheath which becomes an IV cannula. An alternative method is to have a longer plastic tube passed through the needle and along the vein as an IV catheter. In either case the needle is withdrawn and the plastic tube fixed in place with just one suture. Since our replacement supplies came from the US Medical Depot we used the same types of IV equipment, the most common being Angiocaths (sheath over needle) and Intracaths (catheter through needle).

This longwinded account is intended to help explain the fact that, while the Americans were struggling to get a cut-down in the arm, I asked for a 14 gauge Intracath and positioned the line in the external jugular vein at the first attempt. Bob looked up from the adjacent table and nodded: 'Good shot, Marshall'. It was a nice moment making a useful contribution on the first occasion I worked with the Americans, but any small triumph belonged to my Perth training. The technique I used had been taught to me years before by Archie Simpson and Peter Gibson, who were then Perth's only thoracic surgeons. They had shown the advantages of cannulating the external jugular in the neck to get quick, simple and safe access to a large vein before heart or lung surgery. By tilting the patient's head down you can find the external jugular vein even when other veins are collapsed by blood loss and shock. I had used the technique routinely, had taught it to junior anaesthetists and had made it a key element in our system of resuscitation at 8 Field Ambulance.

I hope you will accept—well, try to—that the purpose of these technical digressions is not to blow my own trumpet. I am trying to give a picture of some of the ways in which major casualties were dealt with and to highlight the big difference between the American medical set-up and our own. Their vast organisation could not function if each doctor was allowed to do his own thing; any deviation from the protocols was regarded as a serious offence. But with just one specialist surgeon and one anaesthetist, Ron Gregg and I literally wrote our own rule book and could vary it at will. Bob Watson's appreciative comment was also a nod of envy for our freedom of action.

There were several important ways in which our practice differed from the Americans'. We would not do cut-downs as a routine, but only when I could not even get into the external jugular. This neck vein had two extra advantages besides simplicity and convenience. By connecting a simple manometer tube, the jugular line could be used to measure the central venous pressure. A rising pressure in the veins returning blood to the heart gave a good indication if the heart was failing to pump adequately or if too much fluid was being pushed into the circulation. Secondly, when the patients were convalescent, the line in the neck usually meant that no IV drip was needed in the arm—and therefore no splints, bandages or plasters to interfere with movements of the arm, wrist or hand. The men quickly got used to the small dressing on the side of the neck, and were both more active and more comfortable.

The next question was the choice of fluids to be poured into the veins. The Americans used huge quantities of crystalloids (salt solutions) in the early stage of resuscitation. This was the modish therapy at the time, based on research in the United States which many of us frankly disbelieved. The fluid was likely to rapidly leak out of the bloodstream and cause waterlogging of the tissues, particularly the lungs. For blood transfusion they had large stocks of low titre O Positive blood. 'Low titre' meant it was unlikely to cause transfusion reactions and the Americans gave this blood immediately, uncrossmatched.

My policy was to give the salt solution but to restrict the volume to two litres during the initial resuscitation period. Before transfusing blood I preferred to wait for crossmatching, which our laboratory could normally achieve within twenty minutes. If there was a delay in getting a crossmatch, we followed the commonly accepted principle of giving a synthetic solution of colloid until the blood arrived; the large molecules of the colloid acted like proteins in blood plasma, supporting the circulation and allowing the fluid to leak only slowly into body tissues.

For major casualties, the fluids and blood were pumped in under pressure (another important task for the OTTs) until the central venous pressure began to rise. After every ten units of stored blood, we routinely gave a pint (about half a litre) of crossmatched fresh blood, drawn from volunteers in 1ALSG. The purpose was to overcome the hazards of using large volumes of stored blood, notably the risk of bleeding due to lack of clotting factors.

With four resuscitation teams working flat out this was no time for discussions about our different approaches to casualty management. The 36 Evac staff, commendably efficient, soon had the two patients with head injuries sufficiently stable to be transferred. Morrie went as medical escort on the helicopter taking them to Long Binh and the neurosurgeons at 24 Evac. This left only the two patients for theatre, so Ron and I were now surplus to requirements. But we stayed to observe, and to bring back a first-hand report on the Australians' wounds. The injuries from the explosion were shocking. One lad's leg was so shattered that a hindquarter amputation was needed, and both his hands were mutilated. The other had multiple wounds to body and limbs from blast and flying shrapnel. The anaesthesia was of high quality, the surgery good but slow. Speed of operating is another major difference between American and British traditions of medical practice.

Late in the day, with their patients safely in post-op, the Americans invited us to join them for coffee and doughnuts. Ron reckoned that if all went well the sappers would be back with us before very long. Our hosts agreed. Despite the good medical care, the air-conditioning and the bevy of female attendants, the Australian wounded were always urging to be transferred. They did not like the claustrophobic Quonset wards and they wanted to be with their mates. But they did like the ice cream!

We swapped a few stories as the theatre staff wound down, then got more serious about what improvements could be made. Better communication with the Dustoffs was a priority. The helicopter crews

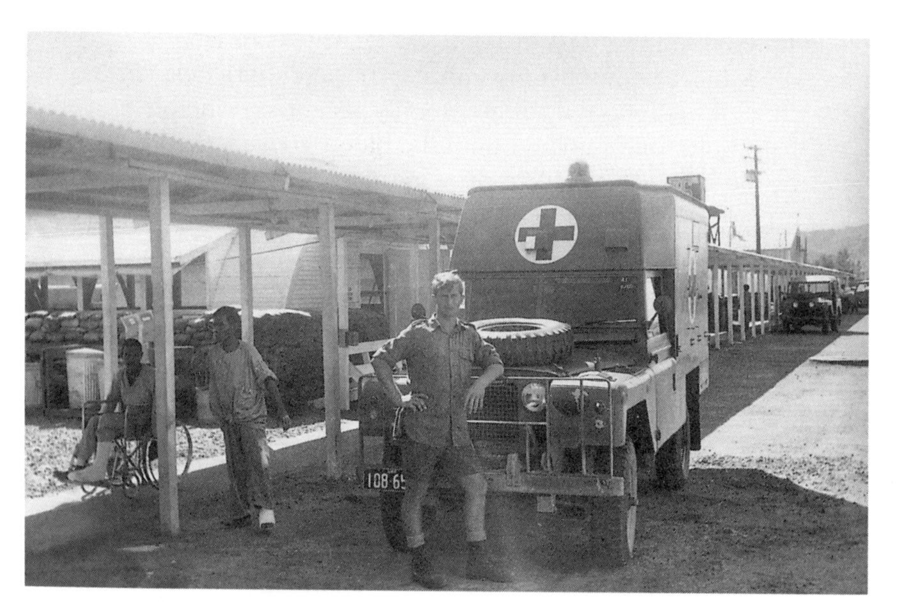

'They also serve . . .' An 8 Field Ambulance duty driver waits at 36 Evac to take our surgical team back to the Australian lines. (Photo: P. Davis)

needed more help in making a decision as to where to take casualties, depending on the numbers, the type of injury and the urgency. At 8 Field Ambulance we could comfortably deal with one major case and a few lesser injuries at a time. If all the staff were available, if Ron and I each had experienced assistance, it might be possible to handle simultaneously two major cases in the main theatre and a less severe injury in the minor operating room. We needed accurate, up to the minute information on what was coming; we should have the means to advise on what we could cope with; if multiple casualties were going to 36 Evac we needed to know early what help they could use. 36 Evac had radio contact with the helicopters. We would push for an effective three-way radio link between Vampire Pad, Cotton Gauze and the Dustoff.

The day spent at 36 Evac made me considerably more knowledgeable about some of the systems and nomenclature in US military medicine. I had rapidly learned not to call the nurses 'Sister'—it was a term of disrespect, except for nuns. Our theatre sisters were their operating room nurses. The US staffing system for anaesthesia was very different from ours in both civilian and military hospitals. Australia follows the British tradition that anaesthetics should only be given by qualified doctors. In America, as in many European countries, specially trained nurses give the majority of routine anaesthetics. An American doctor qualified in anaesthesia is called an anesthesiologist, as against an anesthetist, who is a nurse. To confuse matters further, it was quite common in Viet Nam for a long-serving career Army nurse anesthetist to carry the rank of major, while working alongside a much more highly trained anesthesiologist recently conscripted as a captain. This was the situation at 36 Evac, which I found bewildering, but it seemed to work. There may have been friction between the Medical Corps and the Nursing Corps where rank did not match technical capability, but I never saw it.

The commanding officer of 36 Evac, according to the unit noticeboard, was LTC Paul E Siebert MC. It took a little while to work out that this didn't mean the CO had been decorated for bravery but that he was a lieutenant colonel in the Medical Corps. His executive officer, equivalent to our adjutant, carried the postscript MSC for Medical Service Corps, while the nurses were identified by ANC. This was all eminently sensible, as were the cloth name badges sewn to each officer's shirtfront, a policy we very soon copied. These gave the surname in large black lettering, very helpful to those of us who seemed never able to catch names, or to remember them.

It was a pity the name tags did not include rank, because the US insignia could also be a bit confusing. For example, on a second lieutenant's lapel the single metal bar would change from gold to silver when he was promoted to first lieutenant. This peculiar, very unOlympic ranking of the metals also applied to a major's oak leaf when he became lieutenant colonel. The really important promotion in Viet Nam was to 'chicken' colonel—a full colonel got an eagle with outstretched wings. But we didn't meet any of those exalted beings working in triage or theatre.

Eleven

THE DEPARTURE OF 2 Field Ambulance had meant a reorganisation of the Officers Mess. The commanding officer had made me PMC or President of the Mess Committee. This was a prestigious and important appointment; the PMC was responsible for the conduct, discipline, social life and etiquette of the Mess, the bar trading and all financial transactions, and in the current circumstances also for the general living conditions of the officers. It was a disturbing prospect for one so militarily inexperienced.

The post should have gone to Mick, as second in command, in the normal course of events. The frostiness between Ralph Meyer and his 2IC was by now well developed, but it was probably not the only reason for my appointment. With several CMF doctors already members of the Mess, and the likelihood of many more to come, making one of their number PMC might help to avoid misunderstandings and potential conflicts. My natural modesty is again sacrificed in the interests of truthfulness when I admit to some degree of skill in smoothing ruffled feathers and massaging bruised egos. Fortunately, at the time of the appointment I had little idea of just how much diplomacy would be needed as the months wore on.

Whatever the CO's reasons, Mick was hurt and angry. It was a severe test, a decision which might have destroyed our friendship, but we dared not risk dissent. No way was Mick going to beg, and if I tried to step down God knows who might get appointed! On many subsequent nights, full of gin and tonic, Mick would curse and rant. But it was always for my ears only and it was to me, not at me. His support never failed. I badly needed guidance on military etiquette and ritual, and on the PMC's role as host to senior officers and VIP guests. Mick saved my bacon time and again with advice on how to do the job that was rightfully his.

Jack Blomley, although currently absent in Nui Dat, became Mess secretary and Morrie Peacock treasurer. The ordinary members of the

Mess Committee were John Kelly and Tony Mooy. Only one Regular Army officer in the lot! Perhaps Ralph Meyer was protecting his stretched administrative staff. Time, money and effort outlayed in trying to improve conditions would be pretty much wasted since a new Mess was in the construction schedule. Indeed, despite our dilapidated circumstances, within 1ALSG we were regarded as fortunate. No other unit had its own Officers Mess.

Besides the doctors, administrative and technical officers of 8 Field Ambulance, members of the Mess included my tent-mate Ron Benyon, officer commanding 33 Dental Unit, and the three padres of 1ALSG. We also had three very welcome associate members, the Australian Red Cross girls, who actually lived in the large downtown villa housing officers of the American Medical Corps but preferred to spend most evenings with Australians, at 1ALSG Officers Mess or with us. And of course soon after our Committee was established we got our four nurses as full Mess members.

The task of the Mess Committee was to keep this disparate group happy in their off-duty hours, in a battered tent tormented by wind and sand and offering minimal facilities. It was established immediately that keeping the bar refrigerator fully stocked was the number one priority. At our first Committee meeting, in the CO's air-conditioned pad, there were no demands for temperance (the treasurer was a tolerant teetotaller) and no serious disagreements. The weekly Mess fee was reduced from $1.00 to 50 cents—cheap enough, but then so were our surroundings.

I was given the job of persuading Mama-san and Baby-san, the mother and daughter servants employed to look after the officers' lines, that they had to improve the speed and effectiveness of their cleaning. This was my first real contact with any of the local population and it was spectacularly unsuccessful. They spoke no English and I had no Vietnamese. My pidgin English, mimed threats and gesticulations were met by giggles, which moved me to a blustering anger. Later I learned that such giggling was not amusement but a sign of embarrassment. Any improvement in the cleaning and sweeping following my outburst was infinitesimal.

We fared only slightly better with Private Pettifer, the sole batman assigned to the officers' lines. He was never convinced of any great need for punctuality or tidiness. I had tried to shame him into activity with the information that four nursing sisters were soon to arrive, which news moved him not at all. I cannot recall his ever showing any interest, amusement or excitement. As he wandered expressionlessly about the lines, Pettifer seemed to be in a dream world of his own.

So the Mess remained a depressing place for us, let alone the nurses. Work parties were called for and many officers volunteered to make conditions in and around the Mess tent more pleasant for the newcomers. We got things a bit tidier, but the only long-term benefit from our efforts was the earlier mentioned Tamworth Triangular Toilet.

Another early decision of the Mess Committee was to prepare a shopping list for the CO who was shortly off to Singapore. Specialised shopping was something of a problem. The ASCO store stocked a standard range of goods at duty-free prices—cigarettes, beer and spirits, of course, but also things like transistors, tape recorders and clothing. Trading in these, however, tended to be in short, hectic bursts which rapidly disposed of each new shipment from Australia. The American PX was a much larger concern, jammed into the airfield complex just a few hundred yards from 36 Evac. But its good stuff also seemed to be sold out by the time we got there. I was able to nab for my own use a single lens reflex Kowa camera for $49.00, a bargain which, having escaped confiscation at Ton Son Nhut, served me well for years. Goodies for the Mess were not so easily found.

Adjacent to the PX was a 'concession arcade' of gift shops flogging Vietnamese and other Asiatic goods, mostly pictures, lacquerware and pottery. Again the Americans always seemed to clean out the quality goods, which were impossibly overpriced anyway. None of us were interested in sending home tatty souvenirs and the last thing the Mess needed was cheap and nasty decorations. We had no guidance on where to find genuine local handcrafts at reasonable prices. Singapore was definitely a better option.

Despite making this use of the commanding officer's Malayan trip and despite having myself already been twice to Saigon, I was not above dropping snide remarks about 'junkets' or 'swans', as such excursions of dubious military value were termed. Soon, though, I would be keeping my trap shut: I became a dedicated swanner, worthy of my Swan River heritage.

For the majority of Australian servicemen, their tour of Viet Nam was restricted to the small piece of Phuoc Tuy Province around Nui Dat and the Vung Tau peninsula, and often to just a small part of that narrow strip. It was perfectly possible, indeed likely, for the soldier to know less about the country he was fighting for than anyone at home who read the right books and magazines and watched TV news and documentaries. Major Barr intended to do much better than that. Really serious swanning, or boondoggling as I discovered the Americans called it, takes a combination of ruthless wangling and the seizure of every piece of good fortune. I would do my PMC best for the 8 Field Ambulance Officers Mess; when work permitted, I would also make every effort to escape.

Our parent Mess was 1ALSG Officers Mess, to which we were invited every Friday night for Happy Hour. The joyful hour of drinks at half price was followed by a usually magnificent curry-based buffet. The place was always crowded, but never more so than when we first brought along the nurses.

That Friday at the end of the nurses' first hectic week brought a surgical crisis. One of the post-op cases, still being transfused, had a further massive haemorrhage. His blood had stopped clotting and he was rapidly going into shock. We called urgently for B Positive blood. Several donors appeared at once from our own unit. I pumped in the ultra fresh Field Ambulance blood while his wounds were repacked and re-dressed. The extra clotting factors did their stuff, the bleeding stopped, his circulation picked up. By late afternoon he was safely back in intensive care and we were more than ready for Happy Hour.

Until that night the only female guests seen at the 1ALSG Officers Mess had been the Red Cross girls and occasional nurse from the Civilian Team. Amy, Maggie, Colleen and Terrie were brought in under a close escort of male officers from 8 Field Ambulance. There was a chorus of enthusiastic cheering. We greeted the Support Group commander and his PMC and formally presented our ladies. They were engulfed at once by an eager throng and we pushed our own way to the bar.

This Mess was a solid structure, and by our standards equipped to the height of luxury. The walls had floor to ceiling louvres offering the possibility of ventilation without sand, there were numerous glass-topped tables and comfortable chairs, a radiogram with amplification system, and a piano. The only flaw was that the bar, staffed by Vietnamese girls more decorative than efficient, struggled to cope with the Happy Hour rush. The panelling above the bar displayed a row of plaques representing every unit in the Logistic Support Group, and a thirsty bunch they were.

Most were also good friends of 8 Field Ambulance. The headquarters of 1ALSG, always under pressure and not always appreciated, did their administrative best for us. Ken Rawnsley and his officers of

102 Field Workshops looked after our dicey generator like a delicate baby. Jim Walton, our fearless leader on the battle efficiency course, was now in charge of ASCO and prepared to reserve items for any of his former infanteers too busy in the hospital to join the post-shipment buying spree. The engineers took care of the 8 Field Ambulance buildings, and RAASC our transport. As with our own non-medical staff, everybody wanted to make some contribution to the care of the wounded. There was also the point that we were their own medical service. During a twelve-month tour with 1ALSG many would be seeing us professionally. It was good to have such friendly and reliable support. Doctoring, too, has its benefits.

My responsibilities as PMC were minuscule compared to those of Major Ken Peterson, who presided over the 1ALSG Officers Mess. Ken was CO of the Provost (Military Police) Unit, a big man not to be taken lightly. He ran Happy Hour night as a beaming dictator. He knew the names of every member and every guest. He and his Mess Committee worked hard at making every Friday night a boisterous success. It was a most important commitment. The food, drink and entertainment they provided offered the safest form of escape from the combination of hard work and tedium that was the lot of the Support Group officers at Vung Tau.

There was one boring but important element to these evenings, which was to farewell all officers returning to Australia. The PMC's speech was of necessity pretty routine since there could be two or three departures every week. Their speeches of reply were usually slurred, rambling and studded with clichés: 'A year's tough but interesting work' . . . 'Fellowship of brother officers' . . . 'Comradeship of the Mess' . . . Tiresome and bland stuff. On the nurses' first Friday night one refreshingly honest lieutenant spoke more pertinently. Irrespective of lady guests the rules of the Mess strictly forbade swearing, but he had no need of profanity to make his feelings crystal clear: 'Colonel Chambers, Mr PMC, ladies and gentlemen: When I reach home, I will recall three highlights of my tour in Viet Nam. Two have passed, the third is yet to come. The first was receiving the orders posting me home; the second was the day my replacement arrived; and the third will be when I step on the plane for Australia. Thank you.'

After the formalities on these occasions Mick came into his own as entertainer. He would drink huge quantities of gin and tonic, then gravitate to the piano. Solo and in combination with musicians like Dave Abernathy and Mike Smith he would pour out blues and improvised jazz. When a crowd gathered, if they were in the mood he would switch to saucy ditties. Meanwhile Morrie, bless his teetotal convictions, came into his own as my saviour. Keen, young, willing and competent to provide cover, he let me forget the week's worries by keeping up with Mick on the G&T.

There was a general reshuffle in the officers' accommodation at 8 Field Ambulance in early June and the tent closest to our Mess became free. It was claimed by Barr and Boyle although, as a residence for relaxed and gracious living, it left something to be desired. The tent was nylon, a standard eleven feet by twenty-two (3.3 by 6.6 metres) structure erected on wooden floorboards and surrounded by a low wall of sandbags. Facing east–west, it offered some possibility of protection from the monsoonal rain soon to beat against the southern wall. However, like the Mess itself, the tent was worn out and it welcomed us with a midnight soaking when the wet season proper suddenly arrived.

We woke cursing as the water cascaded in and saturated our bedding. We started emergency repairs to the splitting nylon; the pelting rain then stopped as if a tap had been turned off. We stopped swearing, opened the entrance flaps and sat quietly smoking, the coolest and freshest we had felt since arriving in Vung Tau. That tent, our home for the next six months, has achieved a sort of immortality since it features, together with the Mess, in a painting by Bruce Fletcher that is now at the National War Memorial in Canberra.

In many ways I was sorry, on moving to the new tent, to leave Ron Benyon, the quiet dentist, although he was in any case about to go home. He had been more affable than most of the 'short-timers' and had welcomed my appointment as PMC with genuine warmth. Ron had a slow, statesmanlike way of speaking, with emphasis on every syllable. 'Do not underestimate the might of the United States Airforce,' he would gravely intone, as we listened to the distant thunder of a B-52 raid. And his advice on swimming was wisdom itself: 'No-one,' he pronounced in the Mess one Sunday afternoon, 'has been bitten by a sea-snake while sitting at this bar drinking gin and tonic.'

I must have taken some of his manner with me when I moved out. It would explain in part the strange style of communication that Mick and I gradually developed, including solemn pronouncement, over-gentility, joke words and coarse slang leavened by New Guinea pidgin.

'Would you consider the time has come for further liquid refreshment?' . . . 'My deee-ar chap' . . . 'G&T?' . . . 'The Great Provider!'

. . . 'Ron-baby yonder would appear depressed!' . . . 'On account of the fact he needs a bit of the old one-two' . . . 'That ALSG shithead, 'im bigfella bastard anyway' . . .

Soon a sprinkling of Vietnamese would make the verbal mishmash even more extraordinary. We used the style of talk without any deliberate intent. Some expressions came quite naturally in conversation with others, causing the occasional raised eyebrow, but mainly the odd language was between ourselves. It became a comforting code, a verbal reinforcement of our unique and special friendship. Over three decades later a strange phrase or peculiar cadence still occasionally surfaces, and brings with it a stabbing sense of loss.

Twelve

One of the things I admired about the Americans' chief anesthesiologist, Bob Watson, was his interest in the welfare of the Vietnamese. He didn't spell it out but it was apparent from offhand comments he made. Colleagues at 36 Evac told me he spent much of his spare time organising a children's clinic and that he was trying to establish a dairy to provide free milk for the local infants. This was very different from the attitude of the average US serviceman, to whom the locals were 'gooks' or 'slopeheads'. The equivalent Australian term 'noggie' (or 'nog') seemed somehow less offensive and almost all of us were guilty of its use.

Like the Americans, most Australian servicemen appeared to show little interest in the Vietnamese people, or even to openly dislike them. I don't believe this was simply racism. The soldiers were fighting an increasingly unpopular war. Given the choice, they would not be in 'this lousy country', with its heat and its smells. Unless they were actually being attacked they could not know who was the enemy. Any noggie, man, woman or child, could be VC—and some of your mates were being wounded or killed by vicious homemade boobytraps. The only locals the men got to know were the highly suspect bar girls. So it was best to regard all Vietnamese as potentially treacherous. It was not an unreasonable policy.

But Bob Watson's way seemed preferable, not that I was suddenly converted to any highminded idealism. I had always vaguely intended to learn about the country and the people. The few available books peddled unreliable propaganda for or against the war and I had so far been too busy for anything more practical than this bedtime reading. The first weeks had been taken up with getting the resuscitation and anaesthesia service organised and in sorting out the Mess. The few days at Nui Dat were entirely cut off from the local villages by the perimeter wire; Saigon had been just a mixture of military errands and tourism. As the casualties and workload increased I was spending most nights tiredly boozing.

Bob's example, though, persuaded me the time had come to get out, to at least explore Vung Tau, and not merely its restaurants and bars.

As it happened, this was just the moment at which an obscure organisation called the United States–Vietnamese Cultural Group advertised a beginners class in the Vietnamese language, to be held in the local high school—one night a week for 14 weeks, price 1300 piastres. This had to be a sign, the start of my new program of cultural enrichment. Some support, however, would give me encouragement. Mick was not interested, Wally Williams and John Kelly were halfhearted. Maybe I could persuade the nurses . . .

I picked the right time: the day we accepted and treated our first 'two major casualties'. The new Dustoff radio communication system had worked as planned, the organisation in triage, theatre and the post-op ward all went well, both patients came through in excellent shape and the nurses were feeling rightly pleased with their contribution. All four agreed to start the language course with me.

They went shopping in Vung Tau and found copies of *Speak Vietnamese,* the recommended text, and Private Murdock drove us in for the first session at the high school. He was too polite to express his obvious surprise at our destination. The duty driver was more used to transporting officers to and from the Vung Tau nightspots.

The school building was in very poor condition. The classroom walls were grimy and crumbling, the wooden shutters on the windows were broken; the lighting from two bare bulbs was dim and flickering, the stools and desks battered and rickety. About 30 Westerners trickled in, mostly Americans in small groups like ours, and the room was filled. We squeezed ourselves behind desks made for children of a much smaller race. There was a hubbub of noise from the classroom next door. A horde of grubby urchins clustered outside our window chattering and pointing at the strange spectacle we undoubtedly made.

Our teacher was Ong (Mr) Phat whose day job was teaching history in the school. His command of English was poor and he did not seem to be a good disciplinarian. He was totally ineffective in shooing away the giggling onlookers, nor could he quiet them when they delightedly began to mimic our efforts at Vietnamese pronunciation. But he was a conscientious teacher. He had us repeating the same few words and phrases till mouths and tongues ached from the unaccustomed exercise.

On paper, Vietnamese is simple. The words are short, the grammar sensible and uncomplicated. To speak it is appallingly difficult: single syllables can have four or five totally different meanings, distinguished only by subtle variations in tone. The class were dismayed, Ong Phat philosophical. In his broken English he explained that the lessons would become more rewarding when only the serious students remained. He expected a 75 per cent dropout.

A month later, this forecast had proved a bit optimistic. The class was down to five, including Colleen and me. Our homework, written exercises from *Speak Vietnamese,* was coming along fairly well. In embarrassing contrast we were humiliatingly slow in picking up the words and their different intonations from Mr Phat's singsong chantings. Even worse were our attempts to sound anything like him. 'Chào ong. Hom nay ong manh khong?' (Hello, sir. How are you?) It is meant to sound something like 'Chow omh. Homm nye omh man commh?', with a gradually rising inflection to make it a question. This is one of the easiest phrases and none of us came close to the right pronunciation.

The two-hour lessons included a ten-minute break during which I tried to learn something about Mr Phat. He seemed pleased enough at my interest but was too worried about his English for any deep discussion. I did glean a few snippets of information (or possibly lies, if he happened to be a Viet Cong sympathiser). The most surprising revelation was that he had French nationality and was extremely proud of the fact. He showed me his citizenship card to prove it. He had been educated in a French-run college; he expressed much satisfaction that the colonial regime had ended, but his dearest wish was to visit Paris. This love–hate attitude to France was common among the few educated Vietnamese I met. They wanted their national freedom (we didn't discuss whether this meant North *and* South Viet Nam). The French had been ruthless oppressors, but they were still an elite people: Paris was the cultural centre of the world.

In the French colonial days Vung Tau had been Cap St Jacques, a favourite seaside retreat for the families of businessmen and government officials sweltering in Saigon. The resort lay between the two hills at the tip of the Vung Tau peninsula. The beachfront of the sheltered bay had been developed with a palm-lined promenade and the town had spread more and more untidily inland. Rising above the tiny houses and shacks lining the shabbier streets, splendidly built French villas occupied choice positions near the seafront and on the hillsides. With a touch of Gallic imagination it could be the Cote d'Azure—bright sunlight, orange-tiled white villas dotting green foothills, palms along the foreshore—but closer scrutiny soon showed that the days of wine and elegance at Cap St Jacques were over.

The tiled roofs of the villas were clumsily patched and green paint peeled from the doors and shutters. The once beautiful gardens had degenerated to tangles of jungle behind crumbling high stone walls. By day there was still some semblance of dignity, at night Vung Tau surrendered completely to its new role. Tawdry bars and massage parlours polluted the waterfront promenade and the market streets with their garish lighting, raucous pop music and crudely soliciting prostitutes. It was a soldiers' town, a leave town crammed with drunken servicemen in civilian clothes: Americans, Koreans, Filipinos, Australians, all of them seeking a few hours of pleasure, forgetfulness or total oblivion.

On Saturday night, clinical and administrative duties permitting, a group of us began going to the 'Pacific'. This was the US Vung Tau Open Officers Mess, where Australian officers were welcome if they paid their membership fee. We made one of our number a member and the accompanying 8 Field Ambulance officers went as his guests. We weren't really being cheap Charlies, we reckoned, since we only used their facilities on the one night a week.

The Pacific was a three-storeyed building, previously a hotel, set in large grounds. It was very well guarded and provided the only secure parking in Vung Tau. Elsewhere an unattended vehicle was likely to lose its battery and wheels within minutes or to vanish completely. The Pacific was the one destination where at night we didn't have to rely on a duty driver for transport. Any officer with a G11, the Army driving licence, could take his colleagues in a unit Landrover.

Because 8 Field Ambulance had more vehicles than available duty drivers, we were accustomed to taking a Landrover whenever we wanted it. I didn't have a G11 on arrival, but made sure I soon got one. An RAASC captain put me through a tough test, reversing along narrow tracks, using four wheel drive over the dunes and negotiating the 'wrong way' traffic in Vung Tau. We returned to the Transport Office, the examiner issued my licence and offered to drive me back to the hospital. He took a short cut, snagged a drooping power line with the Landrover's gun mount and cut off a lot of electricity. I thanked the swearing captain and hurried on to urgent clinical duties. Not before checking, of course, that neither of us had a whiplash from the jolt and that my pocket still held the precious G11, my pass to personal transportation.

Not surprisingly, to enter the Pacific was to enter the US—poker machines, jukeboxes, hamburgers, Budweiser, Bourbon and Coke. Local flavour was provided by miniskirted Vietnamese waitresses scurrying between the crowded tables and their sisters, the Vung Tau bar girls, who had been brought along as guests. An invitation to the Pacific was the ultimate status symbol. In *ao dai* or miniskirts the girls would sit demurely watching the ungraceful antics of Western civilisation at play. Only the slimmest and most poised of the round-eyes did not look bovine and clumsy beside the petite natural elegance of these girls. Innate grace is not synonymous with virtue, however. A girl might briefly leave her escort to whisper in your ear: 'Voulez vous couchez avec moi?' Undoubtedly the safest answer was: 'Merci, non.' The attraction for us on Saturday night was live music plus a floorshow.

Three soldiers from 8 Field Ambulance had teamed with two Americans to form a guitar band called The Outer Limits. This twang gang were regular performers at the Pacific, and very slick and professional they were. The soldier who was their lead singer was almost unrecognisable, confident and stylish in satin trousers and frilly shirt, but he was none other than our radiographer, Private Burgess.

The featured floorshows were something else again. The servicemen's clubs in Viet Nam formed a lucrative circuit for adventurous and talented entertainment groups. These shows usually provided first class music or beautiful girls, and frequently both. I most vividly remember The Pretty Kittens, a band of curvaceous Californians in mini-culottes and white boots pounding out go-go numbers while hundreds of sex-starved, homesick men stamped and shouted their approval. For their last number the mood changed to soft and slow: 'Last night I went to sleep in Detroit City . . .' Suddenly the raucous audience went quiet. In some extraordinary way the silence built up a crescendo of expectancy; the whole room waited, then roared out the heartfelt chorus: 'I wanna go home, I wanna go home; Oh, how I wanna go home!'

For the journey back to 8 Field Ambulance, Ron Gregg was our most exciting chauffeur. He would drink prodigiously and not leave the Pacific until well after the 2200 curfew. We would then head erratically towards 1ALSG. Instead of stopping at the sentry points, he would slow down to a sober but purposeful 10 mph, report loudly to the guard, 'Major Benyon and party!', and continue confidently on his way.

That was our Saturday night entertainment. It was on Tuesdays, after the Vietnamese lessons, and particularly once Colleen had given up the linguistic struggle, that I began to make acquaintance with Vung Tau's seedier night life. I would stay in town to rendezvous at about 2100 with Mick, Kelly, Frewen or any others finding themselves in need of a break from the high life of the 8 Field Ambulance Mess. We tried many meeting places and eventually settled on the Thunderbird Bar.

The bar world was a remarkable social phenomenon. In Vung Tau these establishments varied from undisguised brothels to respectably run miniature nightclubs. Although external appearances could occasionally be deceptive, once inside the bar the girls' behaviour soon made clear what delights were on offer. Whether she was a micro-miniskirted stalk-grabber, giggling flirt or quietly attentive hostess, no matter what that particular bar's place in the social spectrum the bar girl was the essential attraction.

The system of a girl's employment never seemed to vary. A Mama-san worked her from 10 a.m. to 10 p.m. seven days a week. The price of female company in the bar was the purchase of Saigon teas. Immediately you came in and sat down you were joined by a bar girl. She either sat wriggling on your lap or demurely beside you. If you were unlucky she was a 'dog', the nasty description we used for those who were plain, over thirty and over-made-up. But if your luck was in, your companion could be a woman of rare grace and beauty.

Irrespective of what drinks you might order, a thimble-sized glass of amber liquid would be brought for the girl. The accompanying chit would blandly read Cognac Coke, 120P. Of this money half went to the bar girl and half to Mama-san. The bar was always so dimly lit it was impossible to see what was happening at other tables. A clever girl could flit between widely separated customers, capturing two or three Saigon teas simultaneously. Newcomers to the bar were soaked for as many Saigon teas as the market would stand. For regular customers the incidence of replenishment dropped sharply. Favoured servicemen might escape at a rate of one Saigon tea per hour, with the girl casting anxious glances towards Mama-san.

If she wanted time off during the ten-to-ten working shift, the bar girl had to pay for the privilege. A customer wishing to take her out of the bar would similarly have to pay Mama-san something between 600 and 1000 P. The commonest purpose was not the invariable reason for such an exit. Occasionally a girl might be taken as a shopping companion or for a Sunday afternoon swim. Many did accept such invitations and many became genuinely attached to a particular soldier. They might become faithful and jealous lovers, but rarely would they give up the lucrative work in the bar.

Almost as universal as the demand for Saigon tea was the life story of the bar girl. She always came from Saigon, which was a real status symbol, and she had to work in the bar to help educate a younger brother or sister. Alternatively she had been tragically widowed by the death of an American serviceman, usually a pilot. In a few instances the sad tale may have had a basis of truth. How could you know? What did it matter? You just enjoyed the feminine attention. Political correctness did not feature prominently in the Vung Tau of 1967.

The Thunderbird Club was a bar in the upper range of respectability. It was on the western outskirts of Vung Tau, close to the RAAF villa but a long way from 1ALSG and therefore rarely visited by Australian soldiers. It was a favourite haunt of a group of American officers who were the first to introduce 8 Field Ambulance to its attractions, I suspect via John Kelly or Wally Williams. The rest of us were easily converted, which is how we became regular patrons. The Uc-dai-loi (Australian) officers became very popular—or at least were given that impression by Mama-san Helene and her bar girls.

Each customer had his 'own' girl, based purely on which one joined you the first time you came to the bar. Trying to switch girls caused much consternation and bad feeling. It was safer to change to another bar. My good fortune was to get Xuan (pronounced Suan) the first time I entered the Thunderbird Club. She was as petite and delicate as a Dresden doll, with shoulder-length black hair soft and shining, flashing almond eyes, beautiful teeth and a flawless complexion. She was quite the loveliest girl I ever saw in Viet Nam and I was instantly smitten.

Xuan understood some English and probably quite a lot of French but she chose to speak in the patois of the bar girl: 'You buku butterfly', if she heard I had been to another bar; 'Never happen', when accused of making eyes at John Purser; 'Same same baby-san', when asked how good my Vietnamese was.

This bar girl language caught on like wildfire among the Australians. They happily admitted 'Uc-dai-loi cheap Charlie'. From *beaucoup* and *petite*, they might be 'buku' or 'titti' drunk. *Troi-oi*, a catch-all exclamation for surprise, dismay or disgust, was the most used and most useful. It was pronounced 'choy-oy!' by the Australians, who outdid the Vietnamese in the variations of inflection used to convey particular shades of meaning. *Xin loi* meant 'sorry about that'. 'Number one' was good, 'number ten' was bad and 'number twelve' was terrible. Smart students of the language such as myself knew another category—*ba mouilam*, number thirty-five, was the living end, the age when all men became randy old goats.

At the Thunderbird I was introduced to the oriental technique of avoiding giving unpleasant or unwanted answers. Xuan could never come out with me tonight, maybe next week. Her occasional absences from the bar were smoothly explained by Helene. Xuan go to Saigon, Xuan at market today. From several sources I gradually got the picture that she had two children in Saigon and a husband working in the Philippines. *Choyyy–oy!!* Much later a jealous girl in a rival bar told me, and spies from 36 Evac confirmed it, that Xuan was shacked up in Vung Tau with an American dental officer. *Xin loi*, old boy!

Thirteen

MY INTRODUCTION TO the Vietnamese medical setup occurred through the Australian Civilian Surgical Team at Le Loi Hospital in Vung Tau. Colin Friendship invited me to see them at work. I watched a hare-lip repair, which was done very well, but my admiration was for the anaesthesia. The patient was an undernourished child, obviously anaemic. There had been no pre-op laboratory tests; there was no guarantee of an empty stomach and no premedication. Because there were so few beds and so few staff, he had come in 'off the street'. They were using the EMO apparatus to give ether/air, plus a trickle of oxygen from one precious cylinder, which would help cope with the anaemia. This was brave and skilful stuff in difficult circumstances. Better them than me!

The other Australian civilian teams, at Bien Hoa and at Long Xuyen down south in the Mekong Delta, all apparently had similar difficulties in the local hospitals. Typical treatment by the French-trained Vietnamese doctors of even minor illness was the blunderbuss combination of streptomycin (for infection), cortisone (for anything else) and camphor as a 'stimulant'. The older doctors were mainly to be found in the most pleasant and least dangerous parts of the country where they indulged in lucrative private practice. The young ones, fresh from medical school in Saigon, were drafted into the Army. Little wonder that the provincial hospitals were so in need of outside assistance. French-built, they had all suffered progressive deterioration. The buildings were simply not being maintained, they were dirty and plumbing was almost non-existent. Two patients to a bed was not uncommon. At least one member of the patient's family came to hospital, usually sleeping on the floor. It was the custom and a necessity for the relatives to supply the feeding, clothing and basic nursing care.

The teams sent in for three-month stints were mainly surgical. Usually the full complement was about six doctors, six trained nurses, a radiographer, a laboratory technician and an administrator. They normally also had at least one physician and one paediatrician whose lonely burdens must have been great indeed.

Adjusting to a different system was quite a problem, as I was to discover. The Vietnamese doctors and nurses seemed more concerned with their social status than with maintaining high standards of patient care. Then again, who was I to make judgements? The local attitude to sickness was essentially fatalistic. Nurtured in this concept, poorly trained and impossibly understaffed, it is not surprising that they accepted conditions deplorable to Western eyes. As a matter of course they worked an eight-hour day and left their seriously ill and post-operative patients for the relatives to look after at night. I was still a bit surprised when the entire Australian team left Le Loi Hospital for lunch and a swim. Maybe a small example of continuity of care would have helped. I admit, this was a pretty highflown sentiment from someone looking for any and every opportunity to swan off from 8 Field Ambulance!

The basic medical commitment of my unit was the care of all Australian and New Zealand servicemen in Viet Nam and of Vietnamese injured by Australasian action. These duties permitting, as part of the policy of winning 'hearts and minds' we were also encouraged to give some medical assistance to the local population. This was a tricky assignment: how to give help without overstretching our limited resources of staff and medical supplies, without treading on the toes of the local practitioners and the Australian Civilian Team, and without compromising security.

One civilian programme we took over from our predecessors, 2 Field Ambulance, was as much for the benefit of our own troops as for the health of the local community. This was the Vung Tau dispensary, housed in a small brick building about a quarter of a mile from the entrance to 1ALSG. The dispensary displayed an emblem of crossed Vietnamese and Australian flags. It was run as an outpatient clinic by a well-trained Vietnamese nurse called Louane. I think she must have been paid by USAID since her medicines and drugs came from USAID stocks, distributed by Wally Williams. Poor old Wally used to tear his hair out trying to cope with the stringent regulations and endless paperwork involved with USAID supplies. *Pace* Harry Dangerfield, these did constitute a worthwhile Christmas pudding, although the metaphor in this instance was not quite appropriate.

The Field Ambulance supplied a medical officer to attend the clinic on Wednesday afternoons and help Louane with her more difficult problems. I went a few times, but Tony Mooy was the regular clinic doctor. In practice, the Wednesday afternoon sessions were mainly VD clinics, dealing with gonorrhoea (and with chlamydia, although we didn't know it) among the local bar girls. This was no simple matter because the girls all tried to treat themselves first, presumably to avoid being barred from work by the military authorities. They would pay exorbitant prices to pharmacists in the town, receive antibiotics of dubious age and purity and take them in inadequate doses. The result was frequently a chronic infection, treacherously free of symptoms and resistant to penicillin.

Having infected many more clients, when the discharge recurred or she got pain from her pelvic inflammation the girl would come to the clinic. A stringently controlled regime of high-dose antibiotics usually resulted in a cure. Within a few weeks our patient would be reinfected. Louane accepted the inevitability of these repetitive attendances; for us it was depressing to make the slides and have gonococci appear under the microscope for the second, third and fourth time.

Fortunately for my mental equilibrium I got involved in a much more encouraging health programme. This was based in the village of Nam Binh, about twelve kilometres on the road to Nui Dat (twelve clicks up the track, in the current jargon), just north of the naval yard at Cat Lo. The Australian Medcap (Medical Civic Affairs Programme) team had established a good liaison there. The villagers were Roman Catholics who had fled from North Viet Nam. They were law-abiding fishermen, very poor, led by a Vietnamese priest who was anxious to provide them with some medical or nursing care.

Ralph Meyer was enthusiastic for an ongoing medical aid project and suggested a weekly clinic at Nam Binh. I jumped at the chance. Here was an opportunity to learn more about the local population, to try out my Vietnamese and hopefully to establish something practical in the way of long-term assistance. We agreed it was no use just turning up intermittently and dishing out a few pills. I would take a small team and aim to set up a proper clinic with some limited facilities. We would keep patient records and offer as much continuity of care as our hospital commitments allowed.

First, though, I needed some linguistic help. My spoken Vietnamese was infinitesimal and on current form likely to remain so. Father Paul, the village priest, spoke French. I had benefited from two years of

French at Wesley College, but irregular verb tables and *la plume de ma tante* were scarcely adequate for comprehending symptoms or giving medical advice. Enter Lorenzo Montesini . . .

One of the most astonishing things about the Army is the range of abilities it can conjure from the ranks. Like a rabbit from a hat, the Orderly Room produced Corporal Montesini to be my interpreter. This unlikely military clerk was reputed to be some sort of Count from southern Europe. He did not volunteer any background except that he had lived in France and gloriously wasted an Arts year at Melbourne University before being called up. His French proved to be excellent, he was smart and he was not put off by sickness, blood or needles. Monty became The Great Interpreter. He also came along for a while to the Vietnamese classes at the high school. Monty and I tried sometimes to socialise with a drink in a bar after class, and John Frewen and I got involved with his 21st birthday celebration at the Chinese restaurant in Vung Tau. It was depressing to me that the divide between officers and other ranks meant that these occasions were never really comfortable. There was much about my interpreter that I didn't discover, but 25 years later I was to learn a bit more about him.

In Australia's high society the big story of 1992 was Prince Lorenzo Montesini walking out on his planned wedding to heiress Primrose Dunlop. It happened in Venice, and Lorenzo went off with his best man, Robert Straub, who had been with us in 33 Dental Unit. Monty subsequently wrote an autobiography in which his civilian aid work in Viet Nam was barely mentioned. A pity—it may have been a minuscule part of his extraordinary life, but his contribution was of the utmost value to our work at the Nam Binh clinic.

For our first visit I borrowed an F1 and rode beside the driver as 'shotgun'. Montesini, two eager medics and several crates of drugs and equipment were packed into the back of the Landrover ambulance. Our arrival had an element of the spectacular. As we drove in, the village Boy Scouts, smartly uniformed, were paraded as a guard of honour in the school yard. The priest, small, bespectacled and wearing a black robe and sandals, stood at their front; at least a hundred villagers hovered expectantly in the background. Some formality was obviously the order of the day. I left the machine-carbine with the driver, dismounted and came to attention. Still with pistol on hip, I gave a Boy Scout salute that David Hill, scoutmaster of the 1st Miles Troop, would have been proud of. The guard returned the salute with huge enthusiasm; Father Paul beamed a welcome and shook my hand. He marched off the Scouts, I introduced Corporal Montesini, pleasantries were exchanged in French and we were invited to accompany the priest to his *maison*.

We crossed the road to the church. It was a surprisingly large building, only a few years old. Already the exterior plaster was badly cracking and the paintwork flaking. (On later visits, I went inside. Despite the obvious poverty of the village and lack of maintenance, the altar pieces and cheap statues were most lovingly cared for, and there were always one or two worshippers.) Behind the church was Father Paul's low wooden bungalow. He pushed aside a couple of yelping, mangy dogs and a ginger cat, settled us at the small kitchen table and extracted two bottles of beer from an ancient kerosene refrigerator. It was *Ba muoi ba*, the local version of Biere 33 and not at all bad. We sipped our drinks while he looked on approvingly.

It was pleasing to discover that I understood much of what Father Paul was saying. He had been trained in a French seminary in Saigon and spoke his French quite slowly and grammatically. When the subject matter was obvious, I could cope and respond appropriately; when I could not, Monty did his stuff. The priest chatted on, politely and unhurriedly. I began to worry. We were here to see patients and ALSG regulations insisted that all vehicles be off the Nui Dat road by 1700 hours. In June 1967, security on that road after dark was non-existent.

At last, after a very long twenty minutes, Father Paul produced an enormous key and led us back across the road to the school. The crowd were still there, now in an untidy queue leading up to the school door. It suddenly dawned on me that they were not just spectators, but prospective patients, all one hundred and something of them.

The giant key unlocked a very tiny room which had been prepared for our clinic. This boasted a barred window, a small wooden table, two chairs and a cupboard bare except for one unused set of midwifery equipment. With the massive lock on the door, the barred window and a padlocked cupboard we had to be in some kind of storeroom. It was like an oven. Outside, babies yelled and their mothers jostled for position to see the new *bac-si* (doctor). Our medics, who had been patiently waiting by the ambulance in the shade of a small tree, brought in the crates and began unpacking. We started work.

The symptoms were presented in Vietnamese to Father Paul, in French to Monty and in English to me. A surprising number of complaints proved to be trivial or imaginary. It was soon apparent that many of the villagers just wanted reassurance from a Western doctor that they and their children were healthy. On the other hand there were a few with signs of genuine disease, who offered only some unrelated symptom. When I tried to ask about the real problem they were silent. My guess was that they were holding back, wanting to assess our competence and our style of treatment before embarking on a serious consultation. We cannot have seemed very professional, unable to speak their language, armed to the teeth, clad in dust-covered jungle greens and sweating profusely in the tiny 'consulting room'.

I asked Father Paul to write each patient's name on a filing card and then jotted down the date, the key findings and treatment. Everyone expected some medication, which we had anticipated with a supply of aspirin, iron and vitamin tablets. A small number with obvious infections such as boils or bronchitis got an injection of penicillin, which they loved, and a few days' course of antibiotic tablets. The medication instructions were transmitted in reverse order—me to Monty, Monty to Father Paul and he to the patient, a classic scenario for confusion and error, but I never learned of anyone coming to harm.

Many hopefuls remained unseen. We packed up only just in time to beat the 1700 hours road curfew, creating great restiveness among the people waiting outside. Father Paul carefully padlocked the box of case cards and remaining drug stocks in the cupboard, then used his giant key to lock the door behind us. I promised the crowd, in fractured Vietnamese, French and sign language, that we would return next week. They looked desperately disappointed and disbelieving. I sincerely hoped that next Thursday there would be no emergencies at Vung Tau.

The driver sped us back in a thundering tropical downpour. We were not very satisfied with our first session. A few simple things, though, could make a vast improvement. And during the next few weeks the Nam Binh clinic was transformed.

Room to work was the first priority. Carpenters from the Army Civil Affairs Team put in a door which gave us access to an adjacent room. Somehow they also produced an examination couch, then shelves, more cupboards and a wash basin. There was no tap, of course. We were more than happy to bring our water in jerrycans from the Army's purified supply in Vung Tau.

Happily, Ralph Meyer agreed that, providing there were no security scares, I could add a Sister to the Nam Binh team. Having a nurse would be a great help. As well as dispensing tablets, ointments and medicines and assisting the medics with injections and dressings, she could provide a female touch that would undoubtedly calm worried mothers and distressed babies. Usually our nurse was Maggie; if I was free to leave triage and the operating theatre she was too.

There were important developments on the Vietnamese side. Father Paul issued the patients with numbered tickets, which solved most of the arguments as to who would be seen next. The big advance was the appearance of a young Vietnamese nun who spoke excellent English. Sister Mary knew all the patients. She was a mine of information about their background, their diet, their daily activities and their past injuries and illnesses. She was also best at filing the case cards which frequently got confused: three words in a name seemed to be used interchangeably. It was puzzling that she only came to the clinic irregularly. ('Today Sister Mary is in Saigon'—the excuses were reminiscent of the Thunderbird Club.) When she did attend the clinic our problems were halved.

The young nun was intimidated at first by the injections and minor surgery, covering her eyes and turning her head away. Very soon,

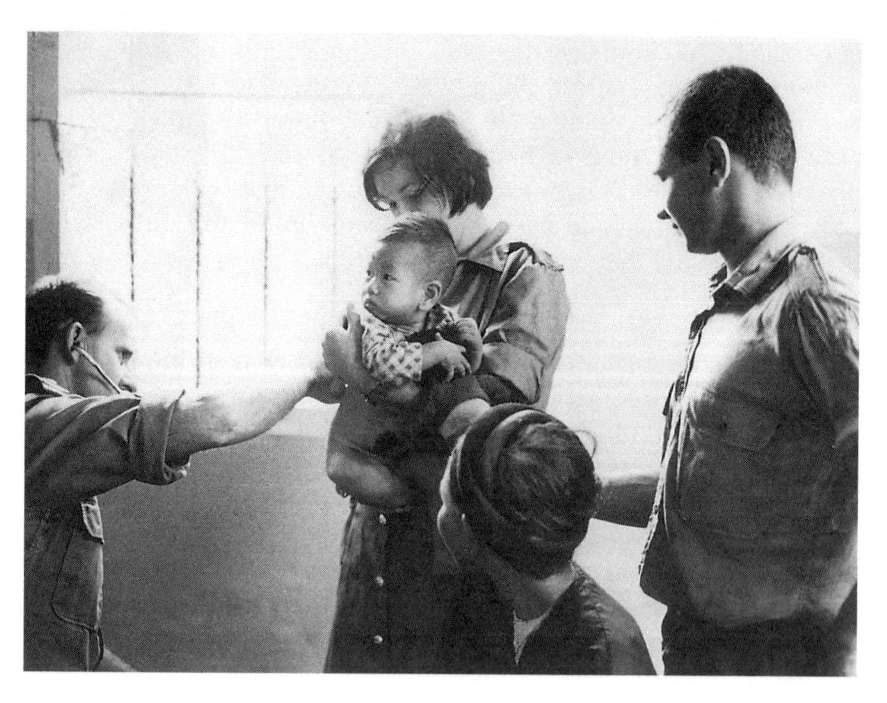

Our clinic at Nam Binh in operation; one of the first four Australian Army nurses in Viet Nam, Colleen Mealy holds a small patient, assisted by Corporal (later Prince) Lorenzo Montesini, our interpreter. (Photo: P. Davis)

though, she became a clinical enthusiast, peering with interest as I sutured a cut or released the pus from a carbuncle. She also developed some talent as a diagnostician. 'Hot and cough,' she would say, translating the commonest set of symptoms in a little chant, and have a bottle of cough syrup ready before I had put aside the stethoscope. She recognised the pallor of anaemia and would start labelling a box of iron tablets in confident anticipation of the treatment. She even tried to treat the doctor when she thought I was wilting. At the end of particularly heavy clinics she would produce a glass of water and urge on me a couple of multi-vitamin pills.

Aside from the language difficulty and primitive conditions, after the early confusions were resolved the Nam Binh clinic sessions were much like general practice in Australia. Coughs and colds in the children, lacerations and abrasions among the adolescents, muscular aches and pains in the adults—most patients didn't need skilled attention and many just wanted reassurance. Sometimes, though, we were able to provide life-saving treatment. Severe gastroenteritis and pneumonia in young children responded most gratifyingly to antibiotics and advice on fluids and diet. A floppy, dehydrated, feverish toddler seen on one Thursday would be brought back the following week bright-eyed and active. When this happened all of us would get a real buzz—priest, doctor, nurse, interpreter, medics, and especially Sister Mary—beaming faces and satisfied murmurs all round. It was the same as the feeling in a delivery room when a healthy baby is born. For a while I would feel a bit less world-weary.

A few clinical problems were very different from a Perth suburban practice. Many patients had huge abscesses of the buttocks. These were caused by unsterile injections given by a quack practitioner (not in the village, Sister Mary would hasten to declare). Others bore evidence of treatment by Chinese-influenced doctors: paper patches on the forehead for headache, pinch marks and scratches on the neck for sore throat, red circular weals and burns from cupping and moxibustion.

Another common practice was for grandmothers to pierce the earlobes of small girls. We saw several cherished granddaughters with face and neck swollen from a spreading infection, and a bead of pus oozing from the tell-tale needle hole. Penicillin in this isolated, highly moral society (no bars or bar girls in Nam Binh!) was the wonder drug it had been in the Western world twenty years before. One shot and the sepsis melted away.

Malnutrition in the sense of starvation was not a problem. The village was amply supplied with rice, fish and tropical fruits. The children, however, loved sugar cane and sweets and many of their parents chewed betel nut. As a result most mouths were in a terrible state. There was no evidence of any form of dental treatment. *Dau rang* (sore tooth) was as frequent a complaint as 'hot and cough', and bush dentistry became our commonest operative procedure. Again I had cause to thank my training. The small group who returned from Adelaide to Perth as final year medical students had been taught to do simple extractions in the Dental School of Western Australia. When I went back to the Dental School as an anaesthetist, the staff had kindly let me keep my hand in.

That was quite a few years before, but for the villagers it was me or no one. I took a set of dental forceps as a priority item on our second visit. The children would stoically accept the quick removal of a very loose tooth. The less simple cases all got a local anaesthetic. Father Paul and Sister Mary were deeply impressed to see the patient remaining cheerfully unconcerned while I struggled, with little skill and much force and wrenching, to extract a difficult molar.

Many of the dental problems were of course far beyond me. These we referred to 33 Dental Unit. By this time Ron Benyon, unmolested by any sea-snake, was safely home. His replacement was Major Peter Kentwell, who most nobly agreed to spend each Tuesday afternoon treating patients from Tony's local clinic and from Nam Binh.

The Dental Unit's CO had his revenge for my frequent referrals of dental disasters. Just occasionally he was served up a totally uncooperative little patient, for whom treatment was only possible under general anaesthesia. No excuses—I had to devise some paediatric apparatus from bits of tubing, and get on with it. Ken Youngson would prepare the minor theatre and happily set up the makeshift apparatus. The theatre technicians welcomed a diversion from the daily succession of adult males. I was not so cheerful. Anaesthesia for dentistry is difficult at the best of times. With unprepared, frightened, bronchitic children it is close to a nightmare. The kids were in pain from their rotten teeth, but they would not die from caries. It would be appalling if I sent a child to the dentist and had him die as a result of my anaesthetic.

Peter and I assessed each case most carefully. I used the minimal amount of halothane, he worked with lightning speed and fortunately there was never any drama. One grubby urchin did express his appreciation with an enormous post-anaesthetic vomit. This sprayed over me a combination of undigested fish and rice, brightly coloured by the bleeding from his sockets. It was the one occasion when Ken Youngson temporarily lost his enthusiasm for paediatric anaesthesia.

Apart from the dental cases, I had another avenue of referral from Nam Binh. This was to the Australian Civilian Team at Le Loi Hospital. If a patient needed surgery or a specialist medical opinion, we would take him back with us in the ambulance. The difficulty was that by the time we got to Vung Tau, it would be past 5 p.m. and the Vietnamese doctors and the Australians would often be gone. Our patients never worried. They were quite happy to settle down in a corner, clutching my referral note, and wait to be seen in the morning.

My most stupid referral was a 75-year-old with probable leprosy. (More useful training: I had seen leprosy among the Aboriginals of Palm Island in north Queensland and in the leprosarium at Derby in northwest Australia.) I took this old man to Le Loi because, having made the diagnosis, I didn't know what to do about him. He went reluctantly; in retrospect, at his age and with mild disease, I should have done nothing. Despite its reputation leprosy is not very infectious and I still had much to learn about Vietnamese attitudes to illness.

From Sister Mary and from the Australians at Le Loi I gradually did come to understand a bit more. The Vietnamese were hypochondriac people when young, seeking attention for the most minor complaint. In old age they became philosophical and much more resigned to ill-health. The families were supportive and reverential to their elders and preferred to have them at home, well or ill. Very few patients died in hospital. The relatives knew the signs. At night they would take their kinsman home to die peacefully in accustomed surroundings, comforted by the family. It was more than a little thought-provoking to compare this policy with our society's attitude to its older members.

For the majority of the sick patients, those who stayed at home, the lack of any nursing supervision in Nam Binh was a constant worry. We had, for instance, children with burns which I could clean up and bandage using IV pethidine, but which needed attention before our next visit. I tried very hard to persuade Father Paul that a responsible person should attend every clinic. It did not have to be a nun or teacher. A mature, sensible villager could be trained in basic first aid and the management of common ailments. Whenever I raised the subject, the conversation always swung to another topic. Catholic-reared Corporal Montesini attributed this to a fear of competition.

Such a person would carry a great deal of prestige and might pose a threat to the priest's leadership. Monty was probably right. I suspected that Sister Mary's attendance was kept intermittent for a similar reason.

The Thursday pre-clinic ritual of a drink and a chat never varied. Occasionally it was a Coke instead of beer, and I never knew whether this was in observance of a religious day or just a question of availability. I would still have preferred to get on with the work. Time was important. The 1700 curfew remained rigid. Each clinic averaged 35 to 40 patients—a considerable strain with no laboratory investigations, no X-rays and no colleagues to give advice. It would have been nice to have more thinking time.

Nevertheless, my education was broadened. The schoolboy French came back well since the priest spoke slowly, with few colloquialisms, and Monty helped by restricting his translating to the less familiar words. And I gained some insight into life in this small part of South Viet Nam.

Father Paul's story was a fascinating one. His village had been given the opportunity to leave North Viet Nam in 1961. He had shepherded the flock of 1300 souls to the South and they were now permanently settled on the Vung Tau peninsula. He had named their new village after two province chiefs near Hanoi. The villagers' economy was

Colleen and our driver amuse the kids at Nam Binh. (Photo: P. Davis)

almost entirely based on fishing, indeed the church was only 100 yards from the sea. Although not wealthy, they were contented. Even if communism were to disappear from their home district very few would consider returning to the North.

The village school was run by Father Paul and a staff of nuns and lay assistants. They educated the children up to the age of seven or eight, the tuition fee being 60 piastres (less than one US dollar) per month. Further education was then available at the state school in Vung Tau. There the monthly fee was 250 piastres, but the cost of travel from Nam Binh was another 300 piastres a month. Only one in ten of the village children progressed to the Vung Tau school; the remaining eight-year-olds went to work on the fishing boats.

They did indeed seem a contented community and our unit established quite a rapport with the village, particularly through the Catholic padre. When I was safely in England, reading in the *Daily Telegraph* about the incursions of the communists and eventual fall of South Viet Nam, I felt a huge sense of guilt. In our small way we had started something in Nam Binh that we could not continue. Our political leaders had started a war in Viet Nam that proved to be unwinnable, and safe refuge for Father Paul's flock had been a cruel illusion. The huge bloodbath I feared in the South did not happen—but what became of that small community, of the smiling priest, of Sister Mary and the other nuns and assistants? My conscience is troubled still.

Fourteen

ONE BENEFIT FROM the Vietnamese language classes was that I began to get through to Mama-san and Baby-san, if only in a small way. They still waved ineffectual brooms at the sand-coated floors of the Mess but, trotting about our lines in their conical straw hats, long-sleeved blouses, black silk pyjamas and sandals, they at least seemed pleased to see me.

'Chao ong. Hom nay ong manh khong?'

'Chao bà. Chao co.'

The dreadful accents of my reply always gave them a fit of the giggles, now undoubtedly of amusement. My triumph as a linguist was to point at some particularly dirty corner; this time they would nod and actually do something about it.

'Winning hearts and minds'—Mama-san in the officers' lines.

What fascinated, and most delayed, Mama-san and her daughter were the family photographs on display in the officers' tents. They would pick up the photos every day and dust them ostentatiously, chattering all the while about the hairstyles and clothing (and probably much else besides) of the Australian women and children. If the owner happened to be about, they would ask very direct questions in the oriental fashion: 'She wife you?' . . . 'How many baby-san?' . . . 'Why not more?'

Their second great pleasure was listening to the portable radios we all bought duty-free from ASCO or the PX. The servants had no qualms about switching on and twiddling the knobs, no matter who was in the officers' lines, and were not too particular about turning the sets off. As they moved from tent to tent they would tune in the next radio, always skipping the Vietnamese stations. What they liked was American pop music.

Unfortunately for our servants, Armed Forces Radio Viet Nam mixed three things in with the music. The best was worldwide (i.e. Viet Nam and US) news coverage, updated hourly. Next, instead of commercials we got repetitive, often ungrammatical homilies: 'Buy US Savings Bonds; see your unit pay clerk today.' 'Keep your personal weapon clean. Practise preventive maintenance.' 'Rabies is fatal.' 'Turn in bogus bills.' 'Help preserve the local economy, keep those piastres in your pocket.' Last and by far the worst was the inane patter so well captured by Robin Williams in *Good Morning Vietnam*. The DJs' nonsense was itself interspersed with personal messages: 'For the guy in hooch 17 Pleiku, love from Susie.' Although it was infuriating, in order to hear The Supremes, The Mammas and the Papas, Gladys Knight and the Pips, even Petula Clark, we soon learned to tolerate the drivel. Mama-san and Baby-san obviously agreed.

Our Logistic Support Group employed several hundred such civilians as kitchen hands, labourers, clerks and interpreters. All were earning more money than ever before in their lives. Many, like our two, probably exercised fine judgement in working just sufficiently hard to keep their jobs. They were called for and returned home in military vehicles; presumably their background and papers were scrupulously checked, but it was a cast-iron certainty that some of our workers were agents of the Viet Cong.

The outdoor and manual workers all took the sensible midday siesta. At noon Mama-san and Baby-san would down tools and curl up together on a table in the laundry. They were asleep within minutes, undisturbed by any of us foraging for a clean shirt or towel. It surprised me that the Australians, like mad dogs and Englishmen, never tried varying their own working hours to allow a rest period during the heat of the early afternoon. Mama-san and Baby-san were also worried about our stupidity. They became very solicitous if any of us seemed ill or exhausted: 'Better you sleep.'

Only two months in the country and already there were plenty of signs that the servants were right to be concerned. Our early enthusiasm was waning, and being replaced by a creeping lethargy. The heat and humidity, the wind and sand, got you down very quickly. Now that the wet season had started it was just more humid, with lightning and thunderstorms thrown in.

Sometimes the wind switched suddenly from the south and blew the rain horizontally from west to east, which put it right through our tent. Sod's law meant this usually happened in the middle of the night. Mick and I would stagger out of bed swearing, close the flaps to the western entrance and use our nylon 'capes half-shelter' to partly block the gaps. We would dig an irrigation channel through the sandbags on the eastern side, to drain away the inches-deep flood above the floorboards, but by then everything was soaked.

Mick, the great digger, makes refinements to the drainage from our tent—another night's sleep lost.

Sleeping was never easy, even on non-rainy nights. Beneath the mosquito net, wearing only underpants or naked, you would lie in a pool of sweat, kept awake by the noises of distant shelling, planes taking off, choppers practising night landings, and by the mind churning over and over. There were plenty of problems . . .

A two-year-old child had been knocked down in a traffic accident. She was brought to us on a Sunday morning because there were no doctors at Le Loi! I spent an anxious hour trying to improvise some even tinier paediatric anaesthetic equipment before a Le Loi vehicle arrived and took her to the civilian hospital. We had never given a thought to specialised children's equipment when Wally and I went through the anaesthetic gear at Puckapunyal. (God, that seemed a long time ago!) There were obviously going to be times when we would have to make do.

Then there was brachial plexus block, an excellent local anaesthetic for operations on the arm and hand. The more cases we could do under local, the more I would be available for emergencies. I had shown Mick the technique: positioning a needle behind the collarbone and on to the first rib, injecting lignocaine into the nerves going down the arm. The block worked perfectly, but I had nicked the top of the lung and produced a pneumothorax. This was a recognised complication and fortunately it was only a small leak of air around the lung. But instead of making things easier I had created a new problem. The nerve block could be done in the upper arm with no risk to the lung but with less certainty of success. Should I avoid any local techniques with known hazards?

The dicey generator had broken down just as Ron started a leg amputation. The surgeon had the battery-operated theatre light. I was left in near darkness just as the patient's breathing became obstructed and his blood pressure was falling. Things got sorted out using hand torches and a laryngoscope, but it was not an episode readily forgotten. I should have organised better emergency lighting. Should every patient be intubated to protect the airway?

If I was feeling this buggered after every mishap, how would I cope with another ten months?

I could always switch to different worries, particularly in the Mess. A variation of $140 between chits and the stocktake had to be reconciled (would you believe, the adding machine was adding wrongly). Ron was getting more aggressive at night with the booze and I was forced to tell him publicly to pipe down. Pete Grainger, the Great

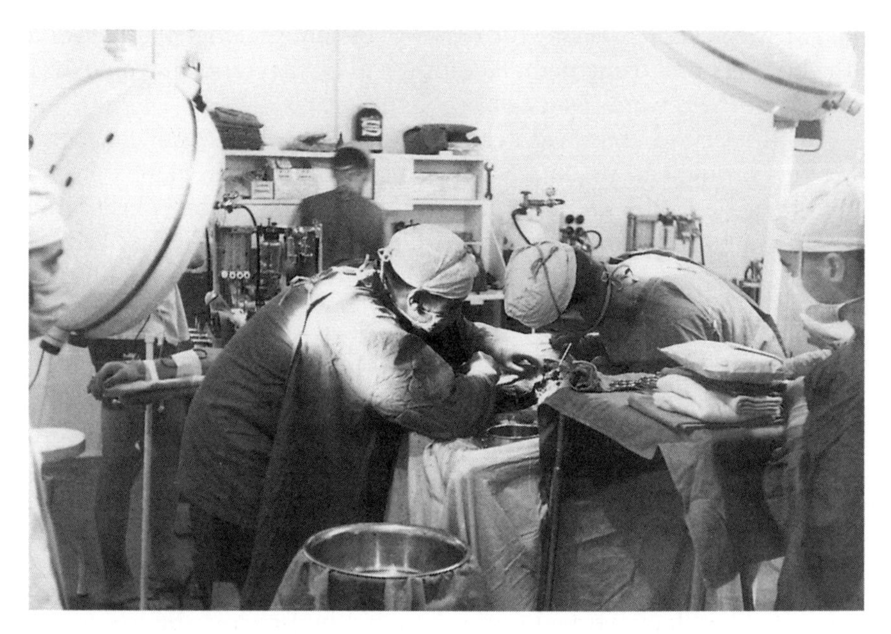

Our team at work—Ron Gregg operating. (Photo: P. Davis)

Wines Adviser, had missed the ASCO shipment, so we had no white wine for our first guest event—Sunday elevenses followed by a buffet. With the nurses and Red Cross girls on display, this would be a big do. Morrie demanded a reduced contribution for teetotaller members.

The elevenses was a great success. Everybody came and most stayed on. The ALSG commander appeared with a Vietnamese dollybird. It was late afternoon before we farewelled them and the COs of our neighbouring units. We were recuperating in the Mess when, at 2000 hours, a Dustoff arrived unannounced.

There were two Australian wounded, shot in the chest and the belly. Ron Gregg was in town. Mick and I agreed we were fit enough to check them before sending the chopper off to 36 Evac. We put a dressing on the chest wound and an IV drip in each patient. I went with them and stayed in theatre while the Americans got on with the operating. It was 3.30 a.m. when I got back to 8 Field Ambulance.

A garbled version of this episode, giving Mick's name, appeared later in some Australian publication. Obviously a member of our unit had sent home the story. The gist of it was that the wounded soldiers had received inadequate treatment because the Australian doctors were drunk. The facts were: firstly, the Americans were the official backup facility when our surgeon, anaesthetist or theatre was not available. It was accepted that we could not provide a 24 hour, seven day a week surgical service. The Dustoff should have gone straight to 36 Evac, but it was almost on Vampire Pad before we were informed. Secondly, although Mick and I had been drinking, we both had a very high tolerance of alcohol and were quite capable of making an assessment and giving emergency treatment. We wanted to ensure that neither patient, having been brought to the Australian hospital, suffered any deterioration while making the trip onwards to 36 Evac. The treatment we gave was correct, and might have been lifesaving.

Mick was understandably incensed at being named and blamed. He was all for writing a rebuttal and contacting a lawyer. My advice was to do nothing. With no follow-up material the story disappeared. Our dislike of journalists did not. Nor did we ever discover who tried to put the knife into the 2IC.

Another problem was our own health. I was getting intermittent episodes of colic and diarrhoea. Nothing very nasty, but wearing and uncomfortable. As all doctors do, I treated myself, by nicking a supply of codeine tablets from the RAP. Mick, not too surprisingly, got gastritis. It also came in bursts, and was sufficiently severe to put him off the grog—for a few days each time, not permanently.

There is no doubt that our physical symptoms were made worse by mental and emotional stress. The noise problem was more than just sleep deprivation. Twenty-four hours a day there was a ceaseless roaring from trucks, graders, generators and machinery, while the flightpath out of Vung Tau airfield ensured a continual stream of low-flying aircraft just over our heads. The naval guns and the rumbling tremors from B-52 bomb strikes were additions to the nerve-grating local cacophony. Mick and I had already had two respites from this incessant noise and the uncomfortable living conditions, and we were still depressed. My admiration was great for those who were stuck in Vung Tau and who stayed on an even keel.

Mick had his worries, not least with the CO and the adjutant. He reckoned one was ineffective, the other was lazy, and the unit was not under proper control. Getting matters improved was like 'trying to push shit uphill'. I could understand enough to at least sympathise. My technical anaesthetics worries were mine alone. Already I was twitchy from the shattering bursts of activity with the Dustoffs and the anxious waiting in between. My early sense of invincibility had gone too. It was unpleasant to feel that whenever you were outside the perimeter a grenade might come your way.

Home, family and friends seemed far away. Letter writing was a chore. I had bought a tape recorder to make communication better, but had to will myself to tape messages home. Kind, loving letters still came most weeks. Family and friends were thoughtfully protective, but it was becoming steadily more apparent just how unpopular this war was at home.

Many of the letters were a reminder of something else. Mick and I actually liked women, which was unusual for Australian males of the 1960s. We really enjoyed female company, and not simply in bed. Besides the way they looked and smelt, we got a kick out of feminine conversation and behaviour and relished the 'oddness' of their emotions. The arrival of the nurses helped, in a two-edged sort of way. We flirted on the brink of romance, Mick with Maggie, me with Colleen. We took them out for a while: enjoyable meals at the Soai Kin Lam Chinese restaurant, go-going at the Pacific. When things got a bit heavy we reminded each other that this was our own nest!

Mick the VD doctor was not going to risk going with a bar girl; nor I except, perhaps, if she could be persuaded, the delectable Xuan. The odd kiss and cuddle under the stars were a comfort but no cure for frustration. Two perfumed letters from Australia arrived on the same day. Would that my love were in my arms and I in my bed again. Too true, sport, and make it an air-conditioned room.

Alcohol was still the great comforter. In a state of maudlin self-pity I told Mick: 'I'm going to piss off.' The rain pelted down, thundering on the drooping nylon. Sleep was impossible. Our tent was a stifling hothouse, cluttered with sodden jungle greens, filthy boots and sand-covered books and journals. 'You already have, mate,' he said, 'this is the end of the pissing line.'

Fifteen

HOW ABOUT ANOTHER break from the stress and frustrations of Vung Tau, an almost legitimate boondoggle? Thank you, Lieutenant Colonel Paul E Siebert. What with the increasing surgical activity and frequent exchange of visits between us and 36 Evac, their commanding officer was by now a helpful friend. The consultant anesthesiologist to the American Army in Viet Nam, he said, was working in the 45th Surgical Hospital at Tay Ninh. This unit was a MUST (Medical Unit Self-contained Transportable). Colonel Siebert reckoned that as I was the senior anesthesiologist to the Australian Army in Viet Nam, it was appropriate that I should visit my opposite number. I could liaise with Major Bivens on our anaesthetic problems and I would see their brilliant new air-inflated hospital in action. Tay Ninh lay northwest of Saigon, near the Cambodian border but still in III Corps. The good colonel was easily able to tee up arrangements for a two-day trip. As usual, his surgical teams at 36 Evac would cover my absence from 8 Field Ambulance.

On 6 June at 0600 the duty driver drove me through the rain to the airfield office of the 54th Aviation Company. I presented myself to the clerk. He was expecting me and knew where I wanted to go, which was reassuring. The 54th was a US Army unit which flew Otters out of Vung Tau. This information was not so heartening. The Otter was a cumbersome, old-fashioned single-engined plane made by de Havilland Canada, which liked to name its aircraft after Canadian animals—Chipmunk, Beaver, Otter, Caribou. Why not types of birds? I had never seen an Otter, but I knew it was slow and noisy, and called by some 'the flying housebrick'.

A major appeared, carrying a briefcase, and hurried into the back room. 'Is that our pilot?' I asked the sleepy-eyed clerk. 'No, sir. He is the instructor. Colonel de Fore will be your pilot.' Thus cheered, I was ushered out into the rain, across the wet tarmac and into the squat and ugly Otter. I got the forward seat, in front of a young American soldier

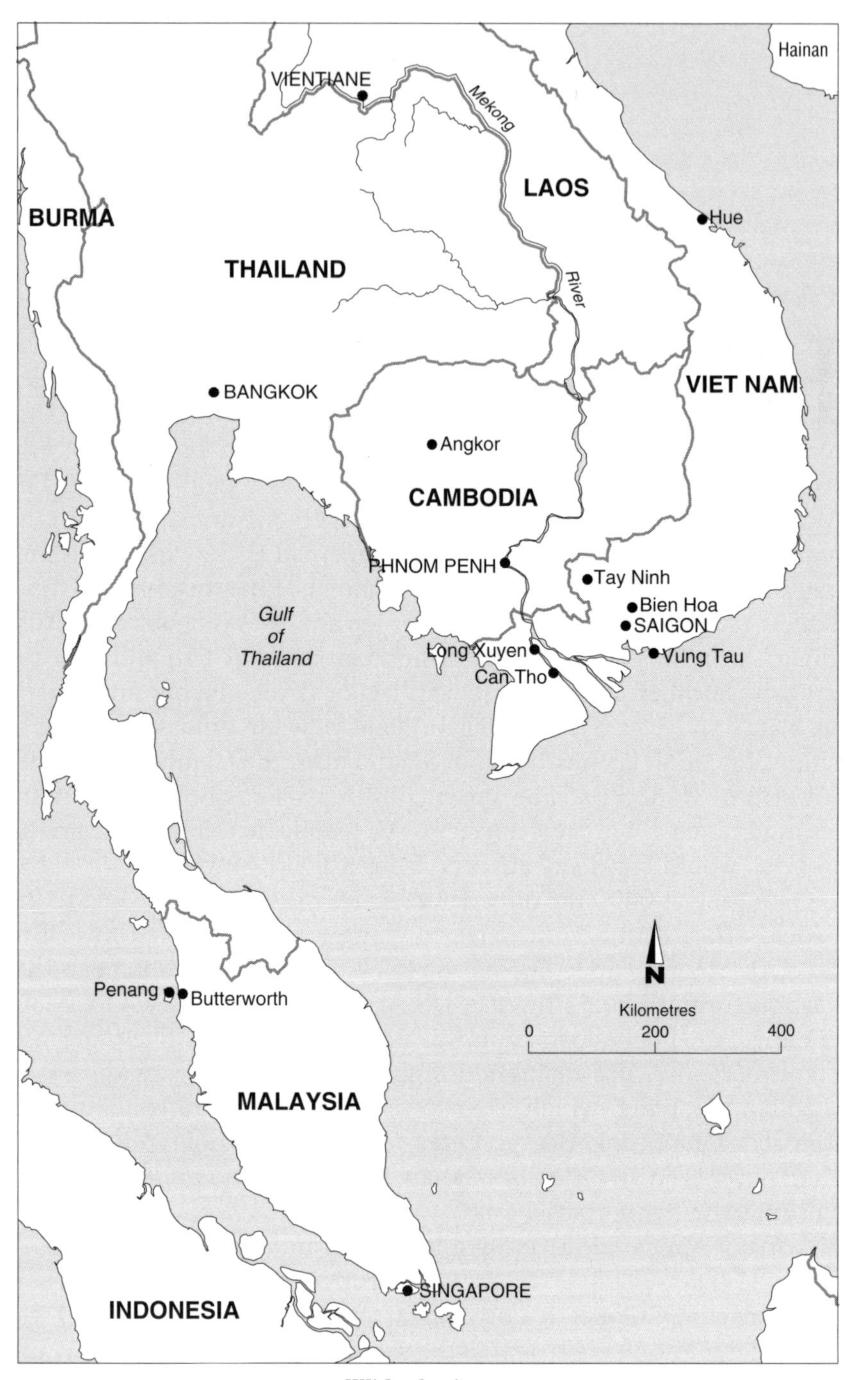

Wider horizons.

and a Vietnamese girl dressed like a New York secretary. We were the only passengers. A squall of rain beat a tattoo on the roof. No-one was very chatty.

I fastened my seatbelt, rubbed a hand across the fogged-up window and peered at the sheeting rain. An anxious-faced colonel settled into the pilot's seat and the major climbed in beside him. It was immediately clear that our pilot was not on familiar terms with this type of aircraft. I was right behind them so I could watch and listen, gripped equally by fascination and fear. The major launched into a detailed tutorial on the instruments, the engine performance and the controls. The latter included, just inches in front of me, an ancient-looking handcrank for raising and lowering the flaps. The teaching session went on for twenty minutes while I rehearsed possible excuses for a sudden cancellation of my trip. It was too late. The engine sprang to life and we were taxiing splashily towards the runway.

The takeoff was terrifying. The Otter wobbled slowly down the runway in a stiff crosswind. Just as the wheels reluctantly left the ground a gust tilted the port wing viciously downward. A belated surge of power and we leapt obliquely upward, almost pole-vaulting on the tip of the left wing. The colonel showed no concern—at least, the back of his head didn't. He put us into a wide climbing turn, heading towards Saigon and a black tropical storm. The Otter bucketed along through teeming rain, wind gusts and air pockets while I meditated on the chances of surviving the landing.

Over Tan Son Nhut we descended out of the storm. The colonel made a perfect touchdown and steered us safely in through the usual melee of aircraft. The GI and the girl departed and the pilots invited me to join them for a coffee. 'Sorry 'bout the sloppy takeoff,' said Colonel de Fore, explaining that he had just been transferred as Exec of the 54th. It was many years since he had flown an Otter. Half an hour ago I could have believed he had never flown a plane in his life.

The major had some snippets of information, not all good. 'Nobody shoots at the Otters,' he remarked, as we watched half a dozen Vietnamese civilians board the plane. 'We provide too good a taxi service for the Viet Cong.' Only last week a VC leader had written personally to the battalion commander thanking him for a pleasant journey. Our flight was to be a routine circuit of six military outposts. Tay Ninh was last, not on the regular schedule. The major was astonished that anyone should choose to go there. 'Everybody at Tay Ninh wants to get out,' he said.

We left Saigon at 0900. The storm had gone but it was still cloudy and surprisingly cool. Our first stop was Don Xoay, not much of a place from the air. All I saw were a few huts and fortified gun emplacements, the flags indicating it was occupied by a unit of ARVN (Army of the Republic of Viet Nam). The 'strip' was a widened section of Highway 14, which runs to the north from Tay Ninh. My faith in the colonel's flying was further boosted when we rolled to a safe, dusty stop. Some ARVN soldiers appeared and eagerly accepted two large packages. The Otter's engine roared, we continued along the highway and were rapidly airborne, the receding Don Xoay obscured by our brown dust.

Song Be was a proper village. Again with a good view from the air, I could see a large central building, a marketplace or civic hall, surrounded by many tin-roofed huts. It must also have been a more significant military post because there was an all-weather airstrip, overlooked by a jungle-clad hill whose peak was lost in the lowering cloud. A smartly liveried white Pilatus Porter, one of the civilian planes of CIA's mysterious Air America, stood on the strip, keeping its distance from a US Army Beaver. Nobody was about until a vehicle came to collect four of our civilian passengers and present us with an equivalent load, a huge US Army sergeant.

The fat sergeant wanted to talk. Above the roar of the engine I gathered that Song Be had a US Military Advisory Team which included members of MILPHAP (Military Provincial Hospital Augmentation Program). He worked as an operating room technician in the Song Be civilian hospital. Much of his day's routine concerned minor surgery under local anaesthesia. It sounded as though he was on his own. I hoped he knew what he was doing.

This country, to the north and west of Saigon, was much more fertile than the sand and swamps of the Vung Tau peninsula. We were flying now over lush green vegetation and water-filled rice paddies interspersed with the geometrical patterns formed by neatly ordered rubber plantations. At Bu Dop we landed on a muddy strip, brown against the green fields and rubber trees. Here the separation of civilian and military elements was complete. On one side of the airstrip lay the village of thatched huts; on the other was an ARVN fortified base. This was a large square—a ditch outside, then thick walls made of timber and sandbags covered with corrugated iron. The enclosed compound of flat bare earth had huts, vehicles, gun emplacements and a central inner defensive square. From our eagle's-eye view it all looked highly susceptible to mortar attack. I remembered the major's comment about his passengers and wondered through what eyes Bu Dop was being scanned by the Vietnamese sitting behind me.

Hon Quan was much larger, a town rather than a village, with tiled roofs, well laid out streets and a bustling central market. The sun broke through as we approached and banked over the marketplace for another squelchy landing. It was now midday. With the sun shining, the Otter on the ground had become a hothouse. Up again at a few thousand feet it was still very warm. The sergeant and I both fell asleep.

We were woken by the pilots to watch four jets making a rocket strike on a target about two miles (three kilometres) away. From this distance it was a beautiful sight. The planes wheeled and dived in the bright sunlight. Golden flashes danced on the hillside, lazy puffs of white smoke rose dreamily from the treetops.

The illusion that there may be beauty in aerial bombardment was soon dispelled as we neared Prek Loc and met miles of defoliated forest. Mud-filled craters gaped between the blasted skeletons of the trees. The tattered remains of parachute flares, thousands of them, hung among the gaunt branches, tiny flutters of white against an unremitting greyness. It was a spectacle of the utmost awfulness. The extent and the completeness of the destruction made my thoughts whirl. The parachutes were waving like flags of surrender, no, no . . . like white shrouds . . . the forest had died long before.

Prek Loc's landing strip was a flat, muddy clearing surrounded by a scene of devastation. A few hundred yards of pierced steel planking grated and shook under the Otter's weight. The only person we saw was a young American lieutenant who came sprinting out of nowhere. He grabbed a bag of mail, turned and ran back across the mud, shouting over his shoulder: 'Get the hell out.' For me, Prek Loc was a vision of Hell. After more than 30 years, that appalling scene is still imprinted on my memory. I often wonder if the lieutenant got out.

Tay Ninh, in complete contrast, seemed a pleasant, peaceful town, greenly tranquil, nestled into the bend of a river. The airfield was a grassy enclosure. There was a windsock and a small hut; in a few places the grass was flattened by faint wheel tracks; there were no other planes, no hangars, no activity. I said goodbye to the fat sergeant, thanked the pilots, grabbed my bag and jumped down awkwardly, my legs stiffened by the hours in the cramped seat. The Otter trundled bumpily away, turned into the wind and roared back a few feet overhead. Its wings dipped, presumably this time in salute, and my aerial taxi disappeared southwards, heading back to Saigon.

The facilities at Tay Ninh aerodrome consisted only of the hut. It contained a white-shirted Vietnamese policeman, two ARVN soldiers, a male civilian and a baby sleeping in a hammock slung from the rafters. My arrival and hesitant greeting evinced no interest whatever. The soldiers continued to play a kind of draughts, the White Mouse yawned and the baby kept on sleeping. I could have been stepping into a scene from Alice in Wonderland.

At least there was a phone on the wall, a decrepit looking military telephone. My instructions via Paul E Siebert were to ring from the airfield and someone would collect me. I lifted the ancient receiver and turned a rusty handle. A non-English-speaking Vietnamese came on the line. In schoolboy French I asked for someone who could *parler Anglais*. There was some jabbering, a pause, a buzzing noise and then an American voice from the deep south. 'This he-aah is Sergeant Xxxxx (I never caught his name), Special Services, Tay Ninh. Sa-ay, who is this?' I began explaining. The puzzled drawl changed rapidly, through polite to incredulous, then alarmed: 'Sir! You're where? *Where*? Do-an't move, Ah'll be raaht there.' He appeared five minutes later in a jeep, a carbine across his knees, beckoning me urgently. The airfield staff, if that is what they were, watched impassively as I jumped aboard and the jeep accelerated away.

The sergeant drove fast and concentrated on that alone until we drew up inside a heavily guarded compound. Then he put me in the picture. I had arrived at the wrong place. All military aircraft used the airfield at Tay Ninh West. The 45th Surgical's MUST was there too, inside the perimeter. The Otter pilots, following my request precisely, had deposited me on the civilian field of Tay Ninh itself, right alongside the town and highly susceptible to VC attack.

Apparently the outward serenity of this pretty town was misleading. It was full of active VC, my saviour said. He invited another driver to take me the few miles I still had to travel. This soldier was even more anxious and tense, and was not at all keen on sightseeing. We crossed the river close by a floating market and flashed past several Cao Dai temples. I had read up on this extraordinary religion, based on Confucianism, Taoism, Buddhism and Catholicism. The temples were architectural monstrosities in ghastly colour combinations of pinks, blues and yellow, but that was all I could see as they passed in a blur. My driver was not prepared to slow down, let alone stop for me to take photographs. 'Too easy for snipers,' he grunted.

Outside the town, the countryside changed completely. We left behind the trees, winding river and green fields to start across a grey, desolate plain. This terrain was ideal for the vast military enclave at Tay Ninh West with its huge airfield, the one at which I had been expected. But it was a godforsaken landscape. Only one natural feature rose from the plain, a solitary mountain just to the west. This was Nui Ba Den, the Mountain of the Black Virgin. It was regarded as a holy place according to my book. From the moment I first saw it, shrouded in cloud and misty rain, the Black Virgin gave me the creeps.

The 45th Surgical, set against this ancient plain and mountain steeped in superstition, was a triumph of modern technology, although it didn't look it. Rather, the hospital seemed to be a blow-up version of 36 Evac. The same open walkways linked the wards, but instead of solid Quonset huts, the familiar half cylinders were created by inflation of some tent-like material. An airlock door led you in from the walkway through a few yards of flaccid tunnel, whose surface drooped a bit between hoop-like supports. The giant curve of the ward, however, was smooth: it was constructed of multiple sections, like a lilo mattress, each segment kept individually inflated to maintain the geometric outline. Huge tubes spread out from a central powerplant to each of these inflated 'buildings'. The whole effect was ugly in the extreme.

I did not confide this opinion to Major Gerald A Lyons MSC, the commanding officer, nor to Major Hollis Bivens MC, the anesthesiologist I had come to visit. It was apparent that these two had been heavily involved in developing this MUST project; to them it was a thing of beauty. I immediately got the full 'ten dollar tour'.

The guided tour was a characteristic feature of life in most military institutions in Viet Nam. All units, especially medical ones, suffered a constant stream of visitors wanting to see the setup—officers from other branches, local dignitaries, journalists, top brass, politicians—their appearance was frequent enough to threaten smooth and efficient functioning. The Americans were much better at coping with this problem than we were. They had a few set patterns, adjusting the extent of the tour and the quality of the spiel according to their rating of the visitors. Tiresome nonentities got the five or ten cent tour (36 Evac and WRAIR had given me much better than that on my first visits; their cheap classifications had been in jest). Here, as the senior Australian Army anesthesiologist and a visitor prepared to stay overnight to really learn how the MUST functioned, I got very special treatment and a fully detailed briefing.

The design of the hospital was ingenious. The central power unit (UPAC), duplicated to guarantee constant service, could run on any form of fuel. It supplied the compressed air, lighting, hot water and air-conditioning. The inflatable wards were spacious and comfortable, if a bit noisy. A laboratory and three operating theatres were cunningly contrived out of giant-sized metal boxes capable of folding into each other for ease of transport. Each operating room could be sluiced out with antiseptic and wet-vacuumed at the end of a surgery session. I was given a demonstration, and very impressive it was. A lot of clever thinking had gone into this hospital. The staff accommodation, however, was pretty basic, in wooden huts or tents. Presumably they had only tents when the unit was transported.

My two enthusiasts were dedicated men, almost messianic in their praise for the 45th Surgical. Nevertheless, as we progressed around the unit, I found myself more often puzzled than impressed. Despite the million dollar gadgetry, it was like walking among a herd of prehistoric elephants; the droopy entrance tunnels somehow animated the huge curves of the wards. The curling tubes to the UPAC were elongated trunks stretching out for food. Although mine is not a fertile imagination, those bulky grey monsters seemed to belong on Tay Ninh's primal plain, watched by the brooding mountain.

There was a sinister air about this whole place which seemed to communicate itself to the staff. The many we met on the tour were polite, but very quiet. There were no jokes, no laughing. The two majors exuded seriousness. Hollis Bivens was not a young man; I could not guess his age but his face was careworn and lined. It was clear from his conversation that he was a deeply religious man. My usual jokey style was severely curbed. The CO, though younger, was equally stern. Why, I wondered, was someone so young, and a Medical Service Corps member rather than a medical officer, running a hospital as important as this?

There was another peculiar thing. The bare walkways and a few sections of the barren grey ground were decorated by delicate small white fences, curved wooden bridges over ditches, oriental gardens and shinto-like arches. These restful features should have helped to soften the functional buildings and high-tech plant. Instead they looked out of place, serving to emphasise how ugly the MUST really was.

I was politely trying to gather how and why these local elements were decorating a US Army unit when our tour arrived at a memorial in front of the hospital. This was a red wooden arch framing a polished brass bell and a marble tablet inscribed:

Major Gary P. Wratten M.C. United States Army
First commander 45th (MUST) Surgical Hospital
Killed in action, November 1966
Tay Ninh, Vietnam

Members of the Cao Dai faith had built a beautiful oriental garden around the memorial, and they were maintaining it with the utmost diligence.

The first CO must have been a remarkable man. Presumably he had established strong links with the local community. It had been a mortar attack, said my hosts, within weeks of the MUST being set up. Had there been others? Oh, yes, a few. I began to appreciate a bit more how special their treatment of me was. These were two very worried and preoccupied men.

I was photographing the memorial (and silently wondering about the politics of those who tended the garden; what a sick thought), when a Dustoff came in with three seriously wounded.

Major Bivens took me to triage where he had a full staff working. Instead of diving in himself he carefully supervised the resuscitation, moving from table to table to check on progress. Where one team were having difficulty he expertly slipped in an Angiocath and continued his rounds. He saw his job mainly as keeping himself free to advise and to cope with crises. In a much lesser way, this is what I was trying to do. In the event of multiple casualties at 8 Field Ambulance, Morrie would nearly always be caught up with the operating, Mick might sometimes be available to give anaesthetics. I needed to train Ken Youngson and hopefully another OTT so they too could take over an anaesthetic and free me to deal with other problems as they cropped up.

In the operating room I admired the neatness of the box design, small but adequate, and the modern surgical and anaesthetic gear. Again, Major Bivens just kept a watchful eye on his staff and we had time for useful discussions. As usual the surgery was slow; as usual it finished in the small hours. The chief anesthesiologist said goodnight, leaving me in the hands of Major Helen Fugowski, the senior OR nurse. She produced fresh doughnuts (straight from the oven, but not as satisfying as our chicken and steak) and I tried to pump the theatre staff.

It was impossible to obtain anything close to a complete picture of what it was like to work in the 45th Surgical, but I got some idea. They were all pleasant and friendly, yet an air of gloom and bereavement pervaded the place. Someone told me of the shock when they were first mortared. Their CO was killed and the hospital design failed. The multiple inflated tubes were meant to cope with mortar attack: undamaged segments would support those decompressed by shrapnel. But several fragments had passed lengthwise through an entire wall, deflating every section and causing a major collapse.

For months they had been confined inside the perimeter; they had been mortared several times and every night American and Filipino artillery hurled a thousand shells into the menacing darkness outside. Interestingly, without prompting, Helen and a couple of others said how much they disliked the Mountain of the Black Virgin, not just as a VC hideout. 'She is never the same. The sun touches different features but part of her is always dark. The cloud and mist move about but never leave her. She's an eerie, eerie Mountain.'

There was no talk of parties or drinking. The air among doctors and nurses alike was a tired, subdued melancholy. Most of them wanted out and were not ashamed to say so, but they were sticking together and obviously helping each other to keep going and do their job.

'Still a few hours of sack time,' said Helen. 'Just ignore the artillery.' I took directions to the guest's hut and left that group feeling pretty small indeed. It was embarrassing to recall my whingeing in the relative security of Vung Tau. I slept fitfully. The wooden hut was not air-conditioned: the UPAC's output was only for the wards and theatres. The surrounding wall of sandbags made for heat and stuffiness, but no complaints about that. Overhead there was no significant protection. Which way had those mortars come in? How close was Nui Ba Den, that creepy mountain?

Paul Siebert had not organised my transport back, in case I wanted to stay a bit longer. Not bloody likely, but it had been a worthwhile visit. Major Bivens and I had established a degree of rapport. The blow-up hospital was not as good as it sounded, although it offered some nice equipment. I had been humbled by the dedication of the staff and I had been scared from the moment I arrived. Time to retreat.

The US system of in-country air transport was strangely haphazard. The schedules were vague and irregular. (Although the RAAF Caribous came under American control the Australians seemed to run a much tighter organisation.) Non-American passengers frequently missed their flight by not arriving well before the scheduled time. If a plane arrived early there was no hanging about at the airfield. Conversely an aircraft might be hours late or never appear at all. This did not represent inefficiency; planes were rarely idle. The tremendous, uneven demands for air transport often resulted in delays or diversions. Stranded passengers would be accepted for later flights on an 'as available' basis. The results I had seen: tired soldiers cluttering the apron at air terminals, sitting or sleeping on heaps of equipment; officers, impatient or optimistic, harassing the movements clerk by flourishing useless documents and demanding priority travel. The Otter was due in, 'probably early afternoon'. Someone on the admin staff of the 45th had a better idea.

An R&R flight was due that morning, which could take me as far as Saigon. Accidents excepted, these flights were never cancelled. Just a farewell cup of coffee and I was whisked to the airfield. Here I joined a group of Americans and about twenty Filipino soldiers, all clutching cameras and bulging airline bags. They were continually scanning the sky—only five days' leave and the plane was late.

As I had discovered, Tay Ninh, in hostile country near the Cambodian border, was not a popular stopping place. The airfield had a huge surfaced runway and acres of tarmac but no aircraft. The sun rose; we sat around in the blazing heat. The clerk announced that our plane would arrive in another two hours. An enterprising private first class (in both senses) hitched a lift back to his unit and returned with ice-cold cartons of chocolate milk. One was for me. Thank you, mate. I was saved from dehydration and starvation.

When the plane arrived it was an aircraft I didn't know. It looked like a small version of the Hercules, with two engines instead of four. The loadmaster stood on a crate by the rear door and addressed us thus: 'Your plane is a C-123, your pilot is Major Xxxx, your destination Ton-san-noot. The flight will take about 30 minutes. The weather will be extremely rough. Those of you in a seat must keep your belt fastened at all times. Those sitting on the floor must hang on to the strap provided. In the event of a crash landing, the alarm will sound six times, and again one long ring prior to impact. The emergency exits are there, there and there. If you become airsick try to move, using any support you can, to the trash can, and avoid soiling our aircraft any further.'

Three officers and I were shown in first and we got the seats. The troops sat on the bare metal floor with a canvas strap across their laps. Several large crates were loaded in behind them and lashed down. The rear door creakily closed.

This C-123 was a grimly functional aircraft. Inside it had the barnlike quality of the Herc, but it was less spacious and bare to the point of nakedness. The noise and vibration were appalling. On the plus side the bad weather did not appear, nor did the alarms sound. At Tan Son Nhut I had a mid-afternoon lunch of chicken and fried potatoes from a Vietnamese snack bar next to the C-123 terminal, then lugged my overnight bag the half mile to RAAF Movements' tiny office. There was plenty of room on the Caribou to Vung Tau.

The promised rough weather made its appearance on the Mission flight. We lurched and tossed through a leaden sky. My greasy lunch churned precariously. The Caribou wallowed sideways like a drunken crab on to the windswept runway at Vung Tau. The last two days had seriously diminished my enthusiasm for aviation. The American and Australian flyers could keep their Christmas pudding. For the time being, I would stay on the ground.

Sixteen

IT WAS NO SURPRISE that our workload from battle casualties was so spasmodic. A characteristic of war is that only a small percentage of the soldier's time is occupied in active combat. What surprised me, although it shouldn't have, was the constant stream of medical and surgical work quite unrelated to military activity. This influx was totally to be expected because our hospital was the primary referral centre for several thousand young men. As well as the problems caused by the climate, the rough living and the war itself they were going to have all the illnesses and complaints of their counterparts in a civilian population.

Appendicitis was a very good example: we operated on our first case within a couple of weeks of arrival and it was rapidly followed by another. It was a remarkable coincidence that these first two appendectomies came from our own unit, although the total number we would eventually deal with could have been forecast from statistics.

Morrie was perfectly competent to operate on straightforward appendixes and I sometimes acted as surgeon's assistant while Mick gave the anaesthetic. These arrangements offered some relief for Ron Gregg, who was more than happy to take a break from routine operating. By now the solo surgeon was a very tired and jaded man. It was also useful to change the combinations of medical officers and theatre staff working with each other on routine procedures. It meant that when multiple casualties threw different members of the operating team together, our efficiency under pressure was that much higher.

Later in the year the statistics came even closer to home when Corporal Brian Connelly of the theatre staff was admitted with a classical acute appendicitis. Sod's law applied: it was a Sunday night and I was enjoying an evening out in the pleasant company of the Red Cross commandant. Brian's operation would be done by the specialist surgeon and both of them agreed that no deputy would be giving the anaesthetic. Driver Andy Bubb was dispatched to find and retrieve me, a task he performed most efficiently, if perhaps with unnecessary relish. In fact I would have been furious not to be called; after several months of intensive work our theatre team were very closeknit. This was looking after a member of the family.

For the smaller non-emergency cases I sometimes used the EMO apparatus with ether. Our supply of oxygen and nitrous oxide from the Americans seemed secure, but we had to have an alternative and we all had to be familiar with it. I did not ask awake patients to breathe ether, still remembering the horrible feeling of sinking into a whirlpool when they gave it to me for tonsillectomy at the age of seven. So it was thiopentone first, then, as soon as the patient was asleep, a gradual increasing of the concentration of ether from the EMO to deepen the anaesthesia. Ether is still a very good anaesthetic, widely used in the third world, although too flammable for cases where the surgeon wants diathermy. In 1967 the younger members of our team had not had any experience of its use and we had no means of scavenging the ether-laden air that was breathed out. A resulting difficulty was that the staff as well as the patient tended to fall asleep.

As well as varying the personnel of the operating and anaesthetising teams and giving everyone some experience with ether, I also used the routine cases to give Maggie and the anaesthetic assistants practice with endotracheal tubes and intravenous lines. If we became swamped with casualties, all of these things might become vital.

The non-military surgery itself provided excellent experience in a variety of procedures. We had tonsillectomies, hernias, abscesses, cysts, injuries from machinery, burns and scalds. We removed a stone which had passed from the kidney and jammed in the ureter. Further down the waterworks we dealt with a leech which had insinuated itself up the penis of a very unlucky Digger. Ron even did an operation for an undescended testicle. In the background the OTTs sang enthusiastically: 'Tie me testicle down, sport, tie me testicle down.' Against all regulations presumably (I was not making any enquiries), we sneaked in an American pilot and I gave his anaesthetic for a vasectomy. It was an odd request. The patient did not want it done at 36 Evac. The US surgeon, a captain, was prepared to stick his neck out, and we owed the Americans many favours. Some difficult questions would have been asked, though, had there been any complications.

From the start, whenever the theatre was quiet I had volunteered to help with the morning RAPs. Perhaps I should have heeded the old hands' advice to stick to my speciality and avoid general duties. The major complaint was urethral discharge. Some had obvious gonorrhoea, the diagnosis easily confirmed under the microscope. Fortunately for them, penicillin was a near certain cure. Many more had an NSU or non-specific urethritis. We did not know then about chlamydia, our laboratory facilities were very limited and antibiotics only sometimes worked. The problem cases were all referred to Mick's special clinic. It was always going to be very busy.

How on earth were these blokes getting infected so quickly, sometimes before they had any leave? Pretty easily, as one young man explained. On the day he arrived in Viet Nam, he and his mates were trucked to 1ALSG, dumped their gear in a sweltering hut on Diggers' Ridge, and headed straight for the beach. In the dunes he was met by a sweet young thing offering another sort of quick dip. Now he had the burning pain on peeing and the telltale yellow drip. In a sense, you could argue his condition was war-caused.

In vain Mick visited and lectured all the units, showing grisly pictures which magnified most horribly on the slide screen. In vain he ranted at the patients in the clinic, while doubling their dose of penicillin. The most resistant cases were admitted to the ward, where Black Pete would glower and forecast the direst consequences for any future infection. It was all to no avail: the soldiers were randy; the bar girls were beautiful and practised in enticement, yet too ignorant, frightened or too small to readily accept a contraceptive sheath. The VD problem was never solved.

By volunteering to do nights as duty MO as well as running the occasional RAP, I also met many of the medical problems other than VD. There were plenty of respiratory infections, with much bronchitis made worse by two packets of cigarettes a day; and of course gastrointestinal problems, which mainly resulted from sampling the local cuisine. The risks were known—the tasty 'noggie rolls' available from street traders were also known as hepatitis rolls. Whatever its cause, the diarrhoea was no respecter of persons. Every medical officer must have suffered at some stage; I seemed to cop it more than most, although I only ate in establishments approved by our hygiene inspectors. Jack Gardiner had to close one of his Sunday morning services when visited by a sudden attack of gut-rot. This was something of a redressing of balance by the Almighty. The padre had cleaned up on the Saturday night by drawing three cards and taking the biggest pot of the game with four sevens.

PUO (pyrexia of unknown origin) was a common and worrying problem. At one morning RAP, I saw six patients with a temperature over 100°F. There were plenty of nasty possibilities including dengue, leptospirosis and tick-borne typhus and we did not have the laboratory facilities on site to sort these out. Again we relied on our well-equipped American colleagues. Malaria we could usually diagnose, the parasites being only too obvious in blood smears put under the microscope.

Malaria was a major concern, and the official medical line was that it was due to lack of discipline. With adequate precautions, soldiers should not be bitten by the mosquito; if they took their anti-malarial tablets they should never get malaria. But the cases appeared and some were very ill indeed. We had a huge fright when Corporal Grace in the quartermaster's office was admitted with a raging fever. For an NCO from the administrative section of the medical unit to go down with malaria would have been a disgrace. To everybody's relief his smears were negative and the temperature soon settled. Later in the year there was a mini-outbreak of malaria involving soldiers on search and destroy operations. It raised a great hoo-hah, although my bet would be that the cases were due to drug resistance.

Mental illness was surprisingly rare and the excellent psychiatry lectures from our course at Healesville were not really needed. I saw one 19-year-old who froze on his first contact with the enemy, and one schizophrenic who charged through the cinema screen because there were Japs behind it; otherwise the mental cases were all due to alcohol. A cook was brought in by the provosts, having been missing for four days. He had been on a bender and had no memory of the second 48 hours. An American captain brought in one Digger who needed four others to hold him down. He was down from Nui Dat at the R&C (Rest and Convalescence) Centre having a rest from operations and he was literally mad with the booze. We only got him under control when I managed to sneak an intravenous needle into a thrashing arm and keep it in place long enough to lay him out with 300mg of Amytal.

None of the officers, despite our constant patterns of heavy boozing, got into trouble with alcohol except for hangovers and episodes of gastritis. We did all have our share of other health problems as well as the recurrent colic and diarrhoea. I developed toothache and had three teeth filled by Peter Kentwell, The Great Dentist—mightily impressed and grateful for his skill with the local anaesthetic nerve block.

More seriously and more painfully, I got a middle ear infection, which I asked Mick to treat. A big mistake: friends should never doctor each other. Clinical objectivity was lost and he agreed to my plea for no injections. After two days of antibiotic tablets Ron became concerned that his anaesthetist was obviously unwell. He took my temperature, peered at the inflamed eardrum and prescribed high dose intramuscular penicillin. Maggie Ahern was instructed to administer the course of injections.

Maggie took me to the minor theatre to have my cowardly backside punctured, which she did with professional skill but most unethical glee. This undignified and painful procedure happened twice daily for a week and the OTTs loved it. Many of their buddies had had similar treatment. They grinned knowingly and brushed aside my protestations of innocence. Ken Youngson more charitably suggested this was the right time for a big night in Vung Tau: it would be therapeutic for my bad temper, and safe since my bloodstream was loaded with penicillin. I felt so lousy that there was no possibility of putting the suggestion to the test.

Jack the Quack came down from Nui Dat with a really bad case of prickly heat. This is a joke condition except for the sufferer; his entire body was covered with the itchy rash. No expert dermatologist was required. We had dealt with several similar cases. The only treatment needed was 48 hours respite in the air-conditioned intensive care ward: the rash always vanished like magic. Padre Pres Sullivan's problem was less simply sorted out: he got chest pain and was speedily shipped off to Saigon as victim of a probable heart attack. The diagnosis was confirmed by the cardiologists; happily just a small area of heart muscle was affected.

All these, even the padre's mild coronary, were mere inconveniences compared with the injuries and mutilations that came to us from the bursts of military operations in and around Nui Dat. And if we moaned about our discomforts it was rarely for long; the wounded soldiers taught us many lessons about uncomplaining courage and dignity in distress. It was astonishing how often their concern was for their mates rather than themselves. The value of their training was proven again and again. Loyalty to the unit was everything. Your battalion, your company, your platoon and your section were always the best: your mates must never be let down.

By no means did all the wounded go back to Australia, nor did they want to. The holding policy of the Field Ambulance was 30 days. If a soldier could be got fit to fight in that length of time, we kept him in-country. For many, getting back to their mates was more important than the chance of home and safety. The bravado must sometimes have been pretended, when it was obvious to a soldier he would be going back to his unit, but I have little doubt that most times it was genuine.

One soldier with the Special Air Services walked angrily from the Dustoff, furious that he had been brought to hospital. His patrol had been inserted by helicopter; he was forward scout and had been hit almost immediately. He marched in, face blackened, camouflaged greens dirty and bloodstained, and his first question was: 'When will I be right to go back, Doc?' It was his twentieth birthday and his present was a chunk of grenade in the left shoulder. The Kiwis were similarly gung-ho. A massive Maori was brought in at the end of a two-day patrol. He had fallen and fractured a rib just as they set out but had kept quiet and stayed with his section rather than leave them one short.

A Scottish sergeant, riddled in an ambush, was brought in close to death's door. After hours in the theatre and some twenty bottles of blood he woke minus a leg and an eye. Yet his concern was not for

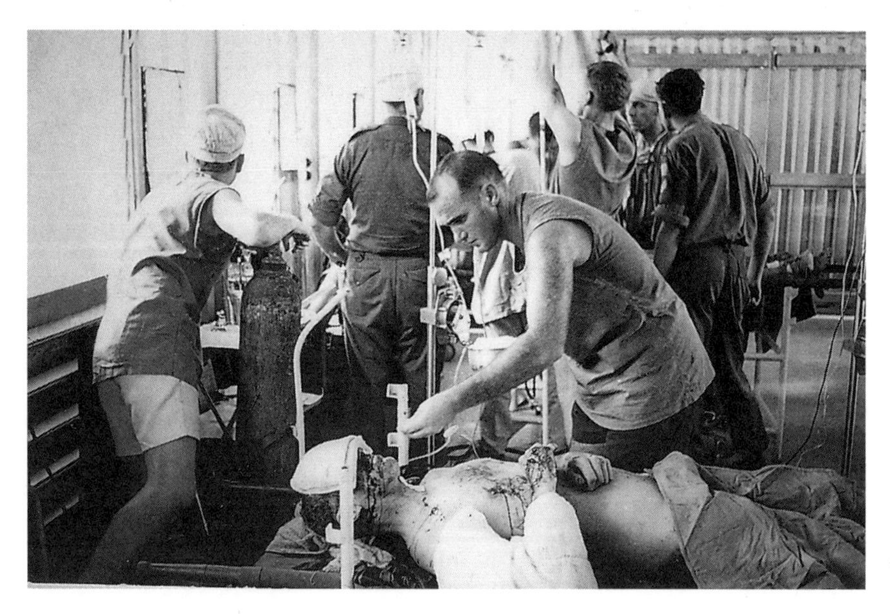

With forward planning, even management of multiple casualties usually went smoothly; Sgt Bruce Turnbull in the foreground. (Photo: P. Davis)

himself. Jock's first question was: 'How are the rest of the boys?'

Another infantry company got into a nightmare of booby traps around a VC camp. Six of them came to us; two were very badly wounded, the remainder had shrapnel injuries, superficial but serious enough, to face, trunk and limbs. Their section corporal had missed that patrol because he was about to go on R&R. He came to the hospital next morning in an agony of guilt, not wanting to see them because he had 'let the boys down': he just wanted to know how they were doing. Morrie, the great psychologist, calmed him down. They were doing fine, he said; furthermore he would cough up a hundred bucks if 'the boys' spat at him. With that, he pushed the corporal into the post-op ward. 'Strewth, it's the bloody corp! Where were you, you bludging old bastard?' Morrie's money was safe, although a foreigner might not have recognised that the barrage of oaths and abuse was an expression of affection.

In treating those six casualties we had experienced our most satisfying day in Viet Nam, a day when everything went right. Partly this was thanks to my swanning off to Tay Ninh. Immediately I got back I had applied the lesson learned from Major Bivens. By then our doctors and OTTs were experienced enough. Unless the work was overwhelming, I would stand back and observe as they went through the process of resuscitation we had devised. I did this for the next couple of Dustoffs, finding it very difficult to keep back and keep my hands off. But they were not needed; there were no mishaps, no difficulties and no serious delays. There were some areas for improvement, though, particularly in making clear who did what, and in what order of priority. I wrote a revised screed and this went into the medical section of the unit's Standing Operational Procedures (SOPs) for Battle Casualty Management.

As well as revising the logistics in managing the severely injured, and the duties of individual members of staff, I took the opportunity to review our policies on the details of clinical treatment. The sudden arrival of six casualties at one time was an exacting test of the system as developed and revised. Thanks to the radio linkup between our A&D and the Dustoff chopper we had good warning of the problems we would be facing. Thus before they arrived we had an outline plan for dealing with the different injuries. The triage assessment, pain relief, clerking, crossmatching, intravenous fluid replacement, X-raying and the use of two operating teams all went like clockwork. We started at 0800 hours and took the last patient to recovery at 1900. These rules had been tried, tested and found very satisfactory. Nothing I had seen at 36 Evac or at Tay Ninh gave me reason to alter them. We stayed with the external jugular line, measurement of CVP, using colloid solutions and waiting for crossmatched blood. After that day, apart from the blow of losing our radio link, the system was never seriously changed.

Our results by any standards were very good. No patient died who could have been saved. There were no uncontrollable bleeding problems due to lack of clotting factors, thanks to routine use of ultra-fresh blood. We had no cases of pulmonary oedema or fluid in the lungs, which was so common among the US hospitals it was called Da Nang Lung. Not one of our patients needed to be put on a ventilator after operation. It was a proud record, and I am proud to have made a major contribution to the system.

But we were not as brilliant as might first appear. Our patients were all young men, in superlative physical condition, brought to us usually within three-quarters of an hour of wounding. Most significantly, we were not getting those with severe head or chest injuries: they normally went to 36 Evac and to Long Binh. It was damage to brain, chest wall, lungs and heart which most commonly created the need for ventilation and the risk of pulmonary oedema. Da Nang Lung was by no means due only to overenthusiastic infusion with salt solutions. Our American counterparts had to cope with the most difficult cases.

All the same, we did well and there was much pleasure to be had in seeing the speed of our patients' recovery. Within a few days most would be up and about; they would hold their intravenous bottles high and wander around the hospital swapping 'warries' with their mates. The communal lavatory was a popular meeting place. After breakfast, a row of bandaged heroes would be seated on the latrine, smoking and chatting, while their penicillin bottles dangled in a line from the rafter overhead. It was a sight at once ludicrous and satisfying.

Seventeen

THE SATISFACTION OF doing their job well and seeing the Diggers make a good recovery was what kept our team of OTTs going. Like all of us the theatre technicians had episodes of tiredness and irritability, yet only occasionally did I see evidence of real stress. Once was when the victim of a mine blast was brought in, dead on arrival from horrific injuries. One of the team was cleaning up and decently covering the mangled remains. He had spread out the bloodsoaked jungle greens and was sorting the contents from the pockets—a crumpled pack of cigarettes, a lighter, a broken pen, two sweat-stained letters now spattered with blood. His eyes were moist and he was trembling. And all I did was give him a sympathetic pat on the shoulder—the Great Supporter!

We were probably better prepared to deal with psychological problems among our patients, but they rarely surfaced while the wounded soldiers were in our care. A severe wound was a 'homer'. Once the decision was documented 'For Medevac' the toughest, most dedicated soldier had no need to feel further responsibility to his platoon. If he was going home, then the sooner the better. The first objective was to be fit enough to make the next medevac flight. There were very few problems among this group in getting medication taken and dressings kept clean and dry. This anxiety to 'catch the silver bird' was of course perfectly natural, as were the other worries that mounted as medevac day approached. Had the family been contacted? Did they know a limb was missing? How would the wounded men be looked after on the journey? Could they take gifts with them? How would they collect their pay? These concerns did not require exploration of deepseated emotional problems; what the Diggers needed was reassurance and friendly, practical help. Enter the Australian Red Cross.

The Red Cross girls did all sorts of good works in Viet Nam, of which I only saw a part. From my limited viewpoint their most valuable contribution was in dealing with our post-operative patients and especially with those returning home. The Red Cross complement was three, but changes in staff during the year meant I had the privilege of working with five terrific women, and of course as PMC it was I who officially offered them the hospitality of the Mess. Janice Webb, Marie Hunter, Robin Harris, Margaret Young and Barbara Buchanan graced our hospital and our Mess. All were unfailingly cheerful; each had her distinctive personality. They brought feminine comfort and companionship to the sick and injured. They read letters from home and helped to write the replies. They sent urgent personal messages to next-of-kin. In their Red Cross Landrover and station wagon they took the fittest patients for shopping runs and trips to the beach. And they brightened many a tedious evening in the Officers Mess.

Because they were not Army officers, their relationship with the Diggers was quite different from that of the nurses. The Red Cross girls were recipients of the most personal of confidences, and sometimes, regrettably, of unsubtle innuendo or more direct harassment. It was a revelation to see their individual ways of handling these difficult situations while remaining good-humoured and uncomplaining. Deviating the returning energy of our post-op patients was the real trick. Convalescent sex-starved rogues usually found themselves unpacking crates and sorting books and gifts.

The maximum support from the Red Cross came in the hectic last few days before a medevac flight. From May 1967 every alternate Monday was medevac day, when the RAAF flew in a Hercules to evacuate our seriously ill and wounded to Australia via Butterworth, Malaysia. Anyone going on this flight had to come through our care because 8 Field Ambulance was the clearing station for all Australian and New Zealand servicemen returning home on medical grounds. Those originally treated at 36 Evac, Saigon or Long Binh were all transferred to us a few days before, for final assessment before evacuation. If the hospital became overcrowded, we would request and receive an extra flight to keep beds free for incoming new casualties. Before any medevac flight the hospital would be pushed to the limit. The hospital staff, as well as the patients, had many reasons to be grateful to the Australian Red Cross.

Twenty-four hours before the flight, the RAAF medical officer at Vung Tau would do a round of the wards with the surgeon. This was a morning of dreadful suspense for the post-operative patients. There were plenty of problems associated with air travel. Even with pressurisation the oxygen level would be down, a bad thing if you were seriously anaemic; the fall in pressure could cause expansion of gases in a post-operative belly or increase the volume of air trapped in the chest with a pneumothorax; irrespective of wounds and dressings, effective restraint was essential against turbulence. The Hercules, despite its size, was very short of space when central upper and lower bunks were fitted. There was no room for major medical equipment, nor for the RAAF staff to perform any procedures beyond first aid, the noise level even prevented use of a stethoscope—basically nothing serious must go wrong once the patient was on the aircraft.

Each man's fitness for air travel therefore had to be assessed with clinical detachment, a task much easier for the RAAF doctor than for those who had been caring for the patient since his arrival on the Dustoff. Doubtful starters were given a last chance, a transfusion overnight, even an early morning trip to theatre for surgical review and redressing of wounds to reduce the risk of infection or a sudden bleed.

On medevac mornings, while the surgical team was busy with last-minute procedures, the quadrangle in front of the wards seethed with activity. The ambulant homegoers milled about in a happy state of confusion, collecting their gear, saying goodbyes, sometimes losing their vital International Health Certificates. John Purser and his A&D clerks scurried around checking and searching for missing documents; our four sisters fussily adjusted bandages, cleaned faces and combed untidy locks, determined that the RAAF nurses would receive immaculate patients. The Red Cross girls coped with a last-minute stream of errands, changing money, packing gifts, sending telegrams, collecting messages, organising follow-ups with the Red Cross staff at Butterworth. Between operations Ron and I would pop out of the theatre to check the condition of our star patients.

The Hercules usually arrived over Vung Tau at about 1030 hours. As it swept in low and majestically over the hospital, the fittest medevac patients would whoop and dance a jig of excitement. Until this moment there had been a tinge of disbelief. Seeing the 'silver bird' was beautiful confirmation that their 'homer' was for real.

Each flight brought an RAAF medical officer and two nursing sisters who would be caring for the patients on their journey. They came to us fresh from civilisation, smart, relaxed, well groomed. Each fortnight it came as a shock to see them and compare myself—scruffy, tense, rough as bags in speech and in manner. Twice the medevac's flight surgeons were friends from hospital days in Perth. Neil Fatin

From May 1967, every second Monday was medevac day: Mick Boyle and RAAF Flight Officer Jean Liddicott aboard a medevac Hercules. (Photo: Marie Boyle)

and Stew Brash looked the same, and why not? It was not that long ago. I felt older and not necessarily the better for their coming. They would arrive suddenly, like aliens from a different world, but that world was home and their presence brought stabbing memories—family, friends, the fellowship of hospital doctors, parties, Cottesloe Beach, the Swan River sparkling in spring sunshine . . .

The first part of the patients' journey home was to Vung Tau airfield. Depending on their condition they went by helicopter, Landrover ambulance or bus. The second part was the easy two-hour trip to Butterworth. There they spent the night in the supreme comfort of 4 RAAF Hospital. Any who were unfortunate enough to deteriorate overnight would be held there; the remainder went on next evening on a night flight to Richmond in New South Wales.

These medevac arrangements had had a somewhat chequered history, which was embarrassing to the Australian Government but providential for dedicated swanners. Again I seized an opportunity, and got myself and a very nice American into deep trouble. That story can now be related, but to keep events in some sort of chronological order, the Dining-In Night and one or two other things must come first.

Eighteen

IT MUST HAVE been the Regular Army officers who decided we should have a Dining-In Night. The idea was madness. Dining-In is the most significant social event in the life of an Officers Mess. It is military history brought to life: the traditions of centuries, the silverware proudly displayed, white-jacketed stewards rigidly correct. Formality is the essence: to be a success, even merely to pass muster, everyone must be dressed up; the food and wine have to be at least of reasonable standard. The atmosphere of a Dining-In is one of dignified elegance.

And we were to provide this beneath sagging canvas on the shifting sands at Vung Tau?

Our normal foodstuffs, supplied from US rations, provided menus which often sounded promising; the depressing actuality of the roast chicken, grilled ham or braised steak was usually a singular level of tastelessness. The day's anti-malaria pill might well be the most memorable feature of a meal, and the bowl of paludrine tablets kept at the centre of the table would certainly be its only decoration. A Dining-In was laughably implausible. The Mess Committee, considerably strengthened in purpose by the addition of Lieutenant Ahern as Female Member, agreed to make it happen.

The generally acknowledged truth was that we needed some happening to brighten the social scene. It had not taken long for nights in the Mess to become drearily monotonous. During the day there were opportunities to while away off-duty periods: shopping and sightseeing excursions if a vehicle was available, a couple of hours on the beach if not.

The 'Back Beach' was a pleasant stretch of gently sloping sand which extended from our frontage for about a mile to the rocky headland of Cap St Jacques—'Back Beach' as opposed to the 'Front Beach' of Vung Tau township. It was divided into three sections, Australian, American and civilian. Our area was seldom crowded; a swim followed by lazing on the beach could be quiet and relaxing. High-spirited chopper pilots would buzz the beach at an alarmingly low altitude if any of the nurses were sunbathing; the air-gunners liked to test-fire their M60s a few hundred yards out to sea; the high winds and crosscurrents tended to create a dangerous undertow; ugly corpses of sea-snakes appeared on the shore; underfoot in the shallows lurked a small fish with viciously spiked fins: the pain of its sting was only relieved by injecting local anaesthetic; but all in all the beach was a restful place.

Since the Americans had lost several servicemen by drowning, a lifeguard had been permanently posted on their beach and he was often busy. To the surf-loving Australians it came as a surprise to see how many GIs were totally unfamiliar with the sea. Obviously few Californian beach bums had ended up in Vung Tau. We seldom negotiated the broken-down barbed wire fence between the sectors. There was not much appeal in being mixed up among locals hawking cheap souvenirs, gaudy cardboard hats, doctored watermelons and pineapples—nor with the pallid, dog-paddling Americans interested in buying the stuff. The more distant beach used by the Vietnamese boasted a row of dirty cafes and sleazy shanties. Any visits there had nothing to do with swimming.

Sun and surf on our own beach, shopping trips to ASCO, the PX or the market in Vung Tau—these were safe and acceptable daytime diversions. It was filling the long evenings that posed the problem. Not everyone found Saturday night at the Pacific to their taste. Once a week was usually enough for buying Saigon teas in the Vung Tau bars. Basically, the officers of 8 Field Ambulance spent their evenings in the Officers Mess. Except for those on duty, we would change from jungle greens to lightweight slacks and open-necked white shirts (long sleeves buttoned at the wrist after dark—strict discipline against the malarial mosquitoes.) Then it was time for a couple of stiff drinks before dinner.

Civilian clothes and alcohol helped but could not demilitarise our leisure hours. Every night the twin-engined Mohawks, the 'purple people-seekers', roared overhead to probe the countryside with their amazingly sensitive heat detectors. The remote possibility of a rocket or mortar attack on 1ALSG could never be completely pushed into the background. The artillery rumbled in the distance, the Mess tent trembled when B-52s dropped their loads. If a warship shelled the Long Hais we would watch the yellow flashes, then steady our drinks against the coming reverberations. We were akin to the onlookers in the Crimea who safely picnicked while men were being killed; it was an uncomfortable feeling and the solution was another gin and tonic.

ASCO supplied cans of spirit plus mixer which were convenient but lacked power. Mick and I, the great G&T drinkers, would take a mouthful then top the can up from the gin bottle at the bar. For most of us, drinking and smoking came almost as naturally as breathing. Though the Mess treasurer might be a teetotal non-smoker, his monthly accounts always showed a flourishing trade at the bar. Is it possible our consumption may have been less had the cigarettes and drinks not been duty-free? I don't think so.

It is astounding how attitudes have changed in a quarter century. I gave up smoking three years after Viet Nam when our first child was born. By then I was concerned at the influence my thirty-a-day consumption must exert, not only on family but on friends, colleagues and patients. In 1967 we were smoking much as the soldiers did in World War I. I relied heavily on nicotine as a calmer of nerves and I enjoyed almost every cigarette. I loved everything about smoking—the style and the smoothness of a fresh pack, the rituals before lighting, the sensuous feel and taste between the lips, the long, satisfying inhalation, the misty smoke patterns blown from nose and mouth. It never crossed my mind that I was setting a bad example. Today I loathe the smell of cigarettes; I despise the manufacturers, and particularly the politicians who fail to control the consumption of such a destroyer of people's health.

Happily I have not suffered a similar transformation regarding alcohol. The taste for gin and tonic is still there, although the intake is but a fraction of the frightening peaks in Viet Nam. With medical science now offering good reasons to have a tipple, even Morrie Peacock has developed a taste for good wine.

In mid-1967, had there been no military, clinical or administrative stresses, the 8 Field Ambulance officers would still have been heavy drinkers. We were a small, confined community. Once the old guard of 2 Field Ambulance were all gone, and the nurses settled in, the company seldom varied. At 1ALSG's Mess there were enough officers to allow some diversity and the twelve-month rotations were sufficiently staggered that Mess members could usually find someone new to talk to. We were stuck with each other. Most of us came to Vung Tau together and would leave together. This prospect lost much of its appeal as the months slowly passed. No wonder we enjoyed the occasional visit from the Australians at Le Loi, from the Americans, or from anyone else who cared to brave our sand. There is no doubt that the tension was eased by booze, either a steady intake or an occasional binge. Even the youthful, quiet and industrious John Purser sometimes took to rum and Coke, while Pete Grainger spectacularly hit the vodka, orange and Benedictine one memorable Saturday night.

For a while, well-lubricated conversation provided a good defence against boredom. Many differing backgrounds and interests had been brought together in our small Mess. Every Australian State was represented. Mick, John Frewen and Morrie had all been in different parts of New Guinea. The CO and the adjutant shared a collector's passion for medals, John Kelly tried to persuade us to read Tolkien, the nurses had tales from their training hospitals. But the stories were good only once. Since Mess rules forbade any discussion involving politics, religion, swearing or sex, the opportunities for new topics were limited. On the other hand there were few arguments and the rules allowed the padres to be fully integrated. They were good value, especially the Catholic chaplains Eugene Harley and his successor Frank Doolan. Frank brought Edam cheese and smoked oysters as a present to the Mess, a very welcome titillation of the taste buds. I thank Frank for that brief delight, and also for two quotations which still torment me: I cannot find where they came from.

Here's the first—someone may know its source. On leaving the Mess the padre would observe, 'Time for a hirondelle', which he defined as leaving formation gracefully. The word is the French for 'swallow': was it a phrase used by World War I aviators? The second quotation is more irritating, since it must be findable. We were talking about growing old, about mortality and similar philosophical matters, when he suddenly said: 'Kissing the golden girls who soon will be toothless crones.' Right on, Frank; not bad for a celibate priest, but where did it come from?

As well as doing their share of the drinking and talking, the padres joined in our word games. The puerility of these gives an indication of the depths we were reaching. Would you believe 'I Spy', with abstract nouns permitted (a for annoyance), or outlandish versions of stinky-pinky (a melodramatic yellow fanatic)? The padres usually declined another literary contest: composing scurrilous limericks about our fellows. My least libellous effort ran:

An industrious dentist named Kentwell,
For his lovely young patient he meant well.
At the end of the filling,
Which proved long and willing,
His drill which was straight is now bent well.

This got around and was published in the unit's irregular broadsheet *The Sandpaper (It's Rough).* Peter, always genial and even-tempered, accepted it with remarkably good grace. I hope he does so again.

Routine Orders forbade gambling in the Mess, so we played for innocent multicoloured chips. If a few dollars changed hands outside the Mess that was no concern of the Committee. The amounts were not crippling (usually 10 cents blind poker): it was pride that was at stake. The padres were into cribbage and our poker school too. As I have previously observed, Jack Gardiner, the Anglican chaplain, seemed to have God on his side when the poker hands were dealt; he was a lousy player whose runs of luck with full houses and four of a kind were quite uncanny.

Mick the semi-professional played only rarely. I had learned from him, at some financial cost, to play a serious game. I knew the mathematical probabilities of improving a hand, and I studied the psychology of the opposition. Despite this tuition, like most of the company I would get bored with bad hands and have a go. To Mick it was taking candy from babies, playing with those who preferred a flutter rather than working with the odds. He never lowered his standards; for Mick there was no such thing as a friendly game of poker.

We did not have enough players for bridge. There was chess and there was Scrabble, which Amy played with a humiliating virtuosity: in those days you didn't like to be beaten by a woman. But the basic difficulty remained: you were always playing the same opponents, and they were often people you had been working with all day.

The movies offered our major escape. If we were lucky, 8 Field Ambulance could get a show up to five times a week. The films came from both Australian and American sources and their quality varied. Many were good, such as *Barefoot in the Park* or *Combat* with Vic Morrow, which our patients from Nui Dat deemed to be a pretty good representation of infantry activity. There were also some truly terrible oldies.

The reels of film were soon worn by repeated showings around the units and our projector was prone to breakdown. Commentary from the Diggers was often better value than the on-screen entertainment. Sitting on a hard bench in a sandstorm waiting for the projectionist to repair the second break to a reel, we heard from the rear a loud voice: 'What a c__t of a drive-in!' During the wet season, a star-studded movie was just visible in the teeming rain. At a tender romantic moment someone gave vent to his feelings: 'What I like about the f___ing Army is waking up in the f___ing morning saying here goes another f___ing day, working all day in the f___ing sand then sitting in the f___ing rain watching f___ing lovely sheilas I can't f___ing f__k.'

All this is by way of explanation that a Dining-In Night was worth pursuing. The stimulus was the announcement of a visit by two medical VIPs, our Brigadier Gurner and Air Vice-Marshal Trudinger of the RAAF. Such visitations have their uses. The Tamworth Triangular Toilet was suddenly replaced by an establishment of higher plumbing standards, more shelter and greater privacy. A serious search for the cause of an odd smell in the Mess revealed a tray of curdled milk and maggots under the fridge. John Kelly and Ron Gregg did some carpentry repairs to floor, wall panels and bar. The Mess was not remotely smart, but its appearance was improved and it didn't stink.

The VIPs arrived on a Monday, earlier than expected. The Great Batman, despite repeated pleas for a special effort, had not cleared up the empty drink tins scattered about from the Sunday night excesses. Private Pettifer was truly amazing. To be in the presence of the heads of both the Army and the Air Force's medical services meant nothing to him. Blank of expression, bare-chested, he stood behind the bar stolidly cracking ice, while a flustered CO and PMC tried to cover up the most glaring of the deficiencies in the Mess.

It was a fortunate coincidence that the day our VIPs arrived was the first time 8 Field Ambulance got a visit from an Australian concert party. What a great way to keep the top brass happy—watching the show and afterwards mingling with the performers instead of snooping around the untidy corners of the Mess. The cast were not all greatly talented, but they didn't need to be. Their show brought a reminder of home, music with a solid beat, some colourful jokes, plus singing and dancing girls in revealing gear—they had to be a roaring success.

I didn't realise at the time that these Australian entertainers were unpaid volunteers doing their bit to cheer the troops. They deserved more recognition and more thanks. The Twilighters singing group had a very good grasp of the local idiom. 'Sorry 'bout that'; 'Number One'; 'Would you believe? Never happen'; 'Massage parlour short time'—the in-phrases were all slotted into the lyrics and the patter. Valmai Johnston, Maria Blanch and John Stoddart are names in my diary, the faces sadly unrecalled; but for the lads and for me the star turn that night was Cathy Wayne, blonde, curvaceous and sexy in bell-bottom pants. I read in the paper that she was killed on stage in Da Nang in 1969, murdered by some mad American.

The itinerary of the VIPs' brief Viet Nam tour was demanding. They wanted to visit the Nam Binh clinic on the Wednesday afternoon and Thursday was their only night free for the Dining-In. This let me off the hook; the final burst of organisation would need to be on the Wednesday and I undoubtedly had to be at Nam Binh. For this occasion, Mick would have his rightful role of PMC.

The Mess Committee and its co-opted helpers, spurred on by Maggie, rose to the challenge. The unit's outside work party under Sergeant 'Dusty' Miller cursed all officers as they put boards down to cover the sand floor of our dining marquee. We coaxed and cajoled ASCO and the PX to obtain some drinkable wines. The sergeant cook was given a sizeable budget and instructed to buy fish, prawns and vegetables in the local market. The nurses arranged occupational therapy for their patients: cutting out and decorating menu cards. We cadged cutlery, crockery and extra tables from the ALSG Mess. By some miracle the Ordnance Sergeants Mess had two port decanters. Even more miraculously they were willing to lend them to officers of another unit. (Did we have a grateful patient or two in the Advanced Ordnance Depot?)

John Frewen assembled an unlikely collection of volunteer stewards, including a couple of grinning representatives from the theatre team. Maggie, the Great Shopper, returned from Vung Tau market with two dozen red candles. In lieu of silver candelabra she set them in small glass bowls filled with plaster of Paris. On her instructions, Padre Pres Sullivan returned from Saigon bearing huge bunches of fresh red roses purchased that morning in the city's flower market.

The evening was a triumph. The men wore tropical dress of light khaki shirt and trousers. The girls looked wonderful in their ward uniform with red capes and white veils. Maggie knew what she was about, getting red roses and candles. The softness of the candlelight and the flowers transformed our ugly dining tent; the adjutant's well-drilled volunteer stewards performed like professionals. The cooks, given fresh ingredients and time for preparation, produced dishes they could be proud of, artistically presented and unbelievably tasty. Under Mick's direction the rituals of passing the port and the speeches went without a hitch.

Afterwards, with the coffee and liqueurs in the Mess, our high-ranking guests were profuse in their congratulations. Colonel Siebert and Major Jacoby, his chief nurse, were dumbfounded. Nothing like this happened in the US Army. Normally they were not garrulous. Now they had a few stories about the Medical Corps. The best of them concerned a friend who was heading for home leave from Japan. He was about to board the night flight to San Francisco when a service policeman tapped him on the shoulder: 'All Medical Corps officers on this other aircraft, please sir'. He was a bit surprised, and then disturbed when the plane landed after a very brief flight. He disembarked to be told he was in Seoul, Korea, and at war, and was bundled into a convoy heading north. At dawn the convoy found itself surrounded and for three and a half years he was a prisoner of war. There was no military record of his whereabouts; his family and the Army labelled him as a deserter. Despite all this he was still happily married, still in the Army and was commanding a medical unit in Viet Nam.

The Americans wanted tales confirming their belief that all Australians were unsophisticated rugged individualists. By this time there were many stories about Jack Blomley. Jack had made the transition from Tumbarumba ('he's at Tumba-bloody-rumba shooting kanga-bloody-roos'—they loved that) to 'Jack the Quack from Nui Dat', the favourite doc of the boys at the sharp end. When Jack's small hospital became overcrowded he would do a swift ward-round.

'What's the matter with *you*, son?'

'Diarrhoea, Sir.'

'Had a crap today?'

'No, Sir.'

'Well piss off.'

When things began to wind down, I asked Jane Jacoby if they had transport organised for the return to 36 Evac. The chief nurse was a big girl with a booming voice. 'Sure we do. It's an A-frame and I carry Colonel Siebert.' Disappointingly they departed by pre-arranged jeep. The brigadier and the AVM retired. The Mess Committee lingered over a self-congratulatory nightcap.

You could argue that the Dining-In had been a waste of time and resources. It had been a more grandiose and transient exercise than Bruce Turnbull's current hate—Diggers planting gum trees to decorate the quadrangle, while the theatre and wards were understaffed. We thought it had been worthwhile. The VIPs and our American guests had been impressed. A fresh interest and pride had been put back in the unit. The volunteer stewards, still clearing up, were happy; during the evening several bottles had been slipped under the tent flaps to mates outside. Inside, it was apparent that too many bottles had been uncorked. They didn't like to see booze wasted.

Mick and I plodded unsteadily to our tent. He carefully shook out the sand from his sheets, stripped off and collapsed on the bed, leaping out again immediately with a roar of rage. He had forgotten a fundamental rule: shake the mosquito net before clearing off the pillow and sheet. As he towelled the sand from face, hair, torso and limbs his stream of obscenities was like a lullaby. I fell into a dreamless sleep.

Nineteen

ONE OF THE main reasons our VIPs had made this particular trip to Viet Nam was to personally look at the medevac system and to accompany a group of patients on their journey home. Until recently the casualties had been evacuated on freight and courier flights by old model Hercules aircraft. A scathing report on the inadequacies of this service was published in the *Medical Journal of Australia* and picked up as headline news by the Australian press in March 1967, just as we were heading for Viet Nam. Much of the reporting was as inaccurate as it was sensational. Nevertheless the government was stung into making improvements. The newer, quieter Hercules C130-E had already been introduced into RAAF service and only this version was used when the fortnightly service dedicated to medical evacuation began in May.

The press, however, would not drop a good story. Any lack of news and the front pages returned to the dreadful way Aussie wounded soldiers were being treated. Western Australia's Paul Rigby captured the public mood with his witty but unfair cartoons in the *Daily Mirror*, contrasting the politicians' luxury jets with the standards of comfort in the service aircraft. The top brass could not simply ignore this adverse publicity. Thus our brigadier and the RAAF's air vice-marshal, having inspected the medical setup in Nui Dat and Vung Tau, and having survived our Dining-In, departed for Australia the following Monday with the patients on the medevac flight.

Whether the suggestion was made to Ralph Meyer that other medical officers should have personal experience of the flight I don't know. Our CO, to his great credit, decided that we all should be given the opportunity. The decision was easily defensible. If the journalistic attacks persisted, the more medical officers who had actually made the flight (which the *MJA*'s critical commentator had not) the better. Our opinions could then be called upon in support of the medical evacuation system. By making the flight we would also better understand the RAAF's problems and we could liaise with the medical officers at Butterworth on the best management of the patients moving from our care to theirs. Perhaps, too, it would give our more seriously wounded Diggers some reassurance to have doctors they knew on the first leg of their journey home.

Of course, the real benefit would be for us—a few days of rest, comfort, and freedom from the strain which by now was affecting us all. In short, as our non-medical colleagues were quick to point out, what we were being offered was a swan or boondoggle.

The RAAF were completely co-operative. They would be delighted to have an extra MO on board and there was no problem with accommodation at the Butterworth Officers Mess. A slight difficulty was the return journey. The only available transport back to Vung Tau was a courier aircraft which made the Butterworth–Vung Tau hop on the alternate Monday. This sad circumstance meant that the Field Ambulance MO would have to spend a full week in Malaysia. Familiarisation with the RAAF Hospital and liaison with its staff would occupy 48 hours at the most; Penang was just a ferry ride away: as swans go, this one was a beauty. I would not say that negotiations were furtive, but the scheme to lose an MO from Viet Nam for a full week every fortnight was not widely advertised.

Dependent on fluctuations in workload and availability of cover, the doctors of 8 Field Ambulance began to make the Butterworth trip. Mick went before me and came back such a different man that the benefits of the break were obvious to all. Bob McLean, the chief surgeon of 36 Evac, made some comment on how much better Mick was looking. Bob had become a frequent visitor, checking up on a succession of Australian patients being transferred back after surgery in his unit. He was a tired man. His operating theatres, like ours, had been very busy; also he was 'getting short' and he was twitchy because there was no news of a replacement surgeon. His trips to 8 Field Ambulance were a respite. He enjoyed the different company, having a beer in the Mess, attending our boozy barbecues. He and I were becoming good buddies. When it was my turn for Butterworth I said he should come too.

At first Bob thought I was joking, which I certainly was not. The 36 Evac surgeons had done a great deal of work on Australian wounded. It was perfectly reasonable that their chief should see how we organised their follow-up and evacuation. Mick's transformation from irritability to grinning cheerfulness was clear evidence that the

US surgical service would benefit in the long term if Major McLean took this chance of a week's break. Paul Siebert saw the logic of the argument. 'OK,' said Bob's commanding officer, 'just make sure he comes back on time.' The RAAF didn't mind; they teed up the arrangements for two Major boondogglers.

On Medevac Monday 14 August I happily did both the RAP and the VD clinic for a grateful Mick, who was involved in organising the patient transfers. The least happy homegoer was Padre Pres Sullivan, who was being evacuated because of his coronary, a decision he regarded as totally unjustified.

Bob and I met at the airfield to observe the loading of the stretcher patients on to the 130-E. They had all been sedated before leaving 8 Field Ambulance; the most severely wounded came by chopper, the rest by ambulance, driven most carefully: the bumpy road through the dunes to the airfield might well be the worst part of their journey. A team of Army and RAAF ORs hand-carried the litters on to the aircraft, their occupants euphoric or in a state of uncaring drowsiness. The Hercules crew supervised the positioning of the stretchers along the centre of the fuselage, secured by straps and stanchions. It was all done gently and with impressive efficiency. There was no shortage of helpers; ours was not to be a heavily loaded flight, just 23 patients and ten healthy passengers.

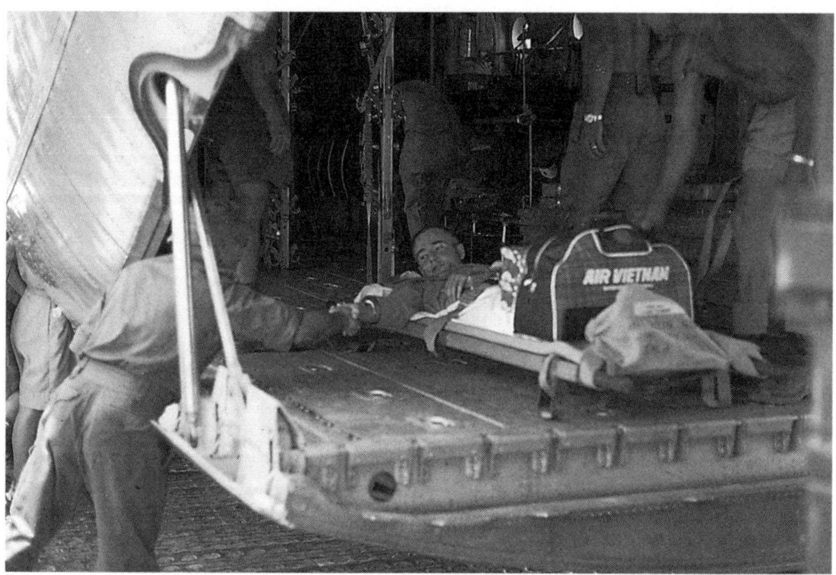

Loading the 'silver bird' with patients on their way back to Australia.

When the litters were fixed and checked, the ambulant patients waiting in their RAAF bus were called aboard. Bob and I followed them up the rear ramp, out of the glare and heat of the afternoon sun into a cavern of air-conditioned coolness. The loadmaster motioned us ahead; we passed alongside the central tiers of stretchers giving a thumbs-up to the boys who were still awake. For'ard of the litter patients, our group were settled into two facing rows. The seating was the standard Air Force foldable bench: your weight was taken on aluminium-framed nylon, your back rested against a wall-high lattice-work of nylon straps; a few inches behind this net was the bare fuselage. It sounds very basic but was in fact quite comfortable. The huge loading door closed; everyone was issued with earplugs; the RAAF sisters and flight lieutenant medical officer made final checks of the litter patients, and we were away. Bob and I sat together, grinning companionably, still scarcely believing our good fortune.

The Air Force again provided a splendid package lunch, as they had done on our flight from Darwin to Vung Tau (my God, that was a long time ago). On this more relaxed journey the mobile patients and the passengers were invited to visit the flight deck one at a time. The flight crew looked ridiculously young to be in charge of such a huge machine, but they exuded professional confidence, and displayed much charity, allowing me the luxury of a post-prandial cigarette.

The flight time to Butterworth was just over two hours, smooth and noise-free with the benefit of earplugs. Many of the stretcher patients slept the entire journey. From the air Malaysia looked wonderful—green coconut palms, orderly fields, macadam roads—well-regulated, peaceful. Butterworth airfield belonged to a different category from Vung Tau or Tan Son Nhut. The runways were carefully maintained, the surrounding grass was manicured, aircraft movements were infrequent, the ground staff unhurried. We were indeed in another country.

The RAAF ambulances were waiting on the tarmac to transfer the patients for their overnight hospital stay. Bob and I saw them aboard, then hitched a ride with the Australian Red Cross to Butterworth Officers Mess. This establishment stunned us both into silence. The contrast with our miserable accommodation could not have been more complete. A Malay servant in spotless white escorted us deferentially to the Senior Officers Wing. We traversed cool elegant corridors past a panelled dining hall, luxurious bar, palm-fringed patio. Our rooms were immaculate; high-ceilinged, airy, a fan gently turning overhead. From somewhere nearby came the soothing unhurried click of billiard balls.

Showered and changed, we investigated our happy situation further. The Mess, surrounded by acres of green lawn, looked over the Malacca Straits. The island of Penang, 'Pearl of the Orient', gleamed in the evening sunshine a few miles across the water. We wandered somewhat dazedly into the bar and sank a few Tiger beers in the tolerant company of Wing Commander Ron Plowright, our guide for a tour of the RAAF Hospital in the morning. Ron had served in Vung Tau and must have been aware of the culture shock we were going through.

It is difficult to convey how good I felt and how privileged. Never before out of Australia, I already had seen more of Viet Nam than most servicemen and experienced the unique colonial atmosphere of old Saigon. Now I was a guest in a pukka Mess, a last bastion of the British Empire. In Viet Nam you had the sense of being part of history in the making, in Butterworth we were sampling its past.

Our Air Force companions had travelled the world, with fascinating stories to tell. The talk flowed, as did the wine during dinner. Five courses were served with old-world graciousness, each dish a new stimulation to jaded taste-buds. And this was just a routine meal! Our primitive attempt at a Dining-In on the sand at Vung Tau had been a joke. The thought was cast rapidly aside. We were here to forget Vung Tau.

Much fortified by the food and wine, Bob and I changed into civilian gear and took the ferry across to Georgetown, Penang. Mick had instructed us on two places we must visit. First the Runnymede—colonial architecture, lawns down to the sea, beer in pewter pots, round-eyed girls but all regrettably under close escort. Next a tri-shaw to the town centre and the Ambassadors Hotel. As Mick had promised, Robert Tan was playing in the Chopsticks Room. This delightful schoolteacher cum pianist jumped up from his piano, genuinely pleased to meet Mick's friend. 'He plays beautiful jazz piano. You tell Mick job waiting in Chopsticks.' But the key information we wanted, Robert could not provide. 'Very quiet tonight. Best you try the E&O.' By now it was 11.30. The Eastern and Oriental Hotel was a mausoleum, no one in the bar and not a round-eyed girl in sight. Probably just as well, it had been a long day. We retreated to the ferry, a boatful of boozed servicemen, and back to the Senior Officers Wing for a dreamless sleep between ironed sheets.

We woke to the sound of jets screaming in a mock attack on the airfield, which was definitely not on the agenda of our restful boondoggle. We got down much strong coffee and a little tropical fruit, cold, fresh, delicious. Mercifully the din stopped by the time we stepped out into the bright sunshine.

In the hospital we found our patients in good shape. They were being fussed over by RAAF nurses; the fitter ones were sampling almost forgotten delicacies; there were plenty of admiring listeners for their tales of heroic exploits. They were having a whale of a time. The stopover at Butterworth was an excellent concept. We were just beginning to cope with the transition from Vung Tau; they would undoubtedly benefit from this bit of adjustment time before hitting Australia. The walking wounded were not available to make any comment. They had already left to go shopping and sightseeing in Penang, courtesy of the Australian Red Cross.

Bob and I did our liaison stuff with Ron and the hospital staff, admiring their facilities, mindblown by the comfortable environment they worked in. It was impossible to adjust to their slow, easy pace in the wards and operating theatre; throughout the day a sense of urgency and tension stayed with me. While I was in the hospital environment my mind just wouldn't accept that I was not on duty, that there would be no Dustoffs. By late afternoon Bob agreed we had decently fulfilled our official duties and we could do a Frank Doolan hirondelle. We peeled off gracefully, headed to the Mess and phoned for a 'teksi'. Fifteen minutes later we were in civilian garb but still far from relaxed. We cringed, eyes shut, in the rear seat of a diesel Mercedes as a fatalistic Chinese hurtled us once more to the Penang ferry.

In any circumstances Penang must be a beautiful island. After five months in Vung Tau (and for Bob many more) it was paradise. Last night we had not been in the best state to appreciate it; now sober and in daylight we could properly take it in. Georgetown basked in well-ordered prosperity. The main streets were wide and clean. The colourful traffic flowed smoothly, directed by smartly uniformed native policemen. Graceful colonial buildings relieved the sameness of modern glass-fronted hotels, shops and offices. Dominating the island's centre, Penang Hill concealed the setting sun behind a riot of tropical greenery. In these Elysian surroundings we lacked only one thing.

Bob was sceptical when I announced that the great Australian girlfinder would not fail. An RAAF pilot officer, who I hope is now at least an air commodore, had told me where a group of Australian schoolteachers were accommodated. I led the doubting American back to the E&O, which had to be worth a proper visit anyway.

The Eastern and Oriental, beloved by Somerset Maugham, had been a classical part of colonial history. It was now well past its glory days; the grandiose architecture and cane furnishings seemed haunted by ghosts of a bygone age. There was, though, a distant sound of tinkling laughter; we passed through the dim, echoing foyer to emerge on a modern patio overlooking the sea. Here was a tiny swimming pool; here, lazily using up the last half hour of daylight, were a man and *four girls.*

Apart from a bored waiter, the patio itself was deserted. We ordered a beer and listened to the swimmers' casual conversation. The man was definitely German, the girls unmistakably Australian. I hailed them as a fellow countryman. How surprised I was to find Australian girls in this unlikely spot! Their encouragingly friendly response switched at once to wariness when I introduced Bob. My goodnatured friend had already met this cautious attitude towards Americans and was puzzled and hurt by it. Fortunately the girls were soon convinced that Bob was neither a loudmouthed dollar-waving tourist nor a drunken GI on R&R. They accepted our offer of drinks, sat on the pool edge sipping their Gunners and asked sensible questions about the war. We had another question: who would like to have dinner with us? Alvys and Dawn would. Bob's eyes met mine with a flicker of new respect.

The girls went inside to change and we chatted on with the German. Gunther was a pianist/singer currently entertaining in the hotel dining room. He was unimpressed by the E&O: 'Such stateliness and now it is a bordello.' Not referring to the schoolteachers, he hastened to add. 'They are very nice, intelligent girls.' He was not concerned about our moving in on his private harem. He was about to depart on the next stage of his journeying, to Bangkok by bicycle. What a lifestyle! Nowadays the world is covered with backpackers. Then, a solo wandering in the Far East was an entirely novel concept as far as I was concerned. Again I felt the sense of uplift that my experience was broadening so fast.

The girls reappeared, glamorous in evening makeup and bright dresses. They led us to the hotel courtyard and to Dawn's brand new Fiat 1500 saloon. It was a miraculous moment. Our boondoggle's twin deficiencies, female company and transportation, had been solved in one magnificent coup. We dedicated ourselves to these two ladies. Our evening and preferably the next few days were completely in their hands.

For dinner, they drove us to the Penang Sports Club. A tree-lined drive led to a stately entrance of tall white columns and potted greenery. Inside, the colonial atmosphere had gone. Unlike the E&O, clinging to past memories, the Sports Club had moved with the times. A jukebox blared pop music, poker machines rattled, garish posters advertised bingo and Hawaiian nights, a multiracial crowd thronged the bar. It was brash and tasteless but the place was very much alive. In dignified contrast, the dining room was calm and quiet, the food and wine (a '62 Burgundy, says my diary) magnificent.

Afterwards we drove to the Runnymede, where we left our drinks on the green terrace and strolled arm in arm in the moonlight by the sea. This was therapy of the highest order. Nobody was going to shoot at us, there would be no sudden demand for hours of exhausting concentration over shattered bodies. Viet Nam for a while was ceasing to exist.

Our foursome had drifted easily into two pairs. Mick and I would by now have discussed objectives and tactics. I did not know Bob well enough to share thoughts on personal matters; he was a quietly reserved man who was pretty obviously happily married, wanting nothing more than some pleasant round-eyed female company. I tended more towards Xuan's Number 35, the randy old goat. The pleasure of Australian female company was in itself great, fantastic. There was not much time to convert it to something more, but it would be fun trying.

All pretence of work was discarded. We paid our ridiculously low bills at the Butterworth Mess and moved into the Ambassadors Hotel. During the day we toured the town and did some idle shopping for things like pewter and clothes. I did all the talking to avoid the special charges associated with Bob's American accent. He had the US male's appalling taste in holiday wear, gaudy shirt, baggy Bermuda shorts and tiny black socks. Now of course it is all the fashion; I refused then to associate with him in this attire. I bought him a pair of Australian-style long white socks, which he wore a bit self-consciously. But I had arranged his boondoggle, I had produced girls with a car. At this stage he would probably have done whatever I told him.

Alvys and Dawn, after their day's schoolteaching, were delighted to help us explore and enjoy Penang Island. We had been so lucky. These were genuinely nice girls who were not out to spend all our money. We four all clicked and simply had a very good time together. Bob and I were made temporary honorary members of the Penang Club. We danced in the Chopsticks Room while Robert played our requests: 'As Time Goes By', 'Lara's Theme', 'Stardust'. We drove at night through the rain forests. We had late curries, cheap and wonderful, at Poshni's Pakistani Restaurant.

We rode on the tilted toy-train to the top of Penang Hill and disapproved of the electric clock in the mosque on the highest point of the island. We stood on the balcony of the Penang Hill Hotel in a gathering mist, watching the lights of Georgetown flicker on. In the darkening straits ghostly ships rode at anchor, the brightly lit ferries threading between them like lazy fireflies. On the terrace below us, British officers of a Gurkha regiment were having a farewell party. The regiment was being transferred to deal with troubles in Hong Kong. The men were lean, tanned and upright, their womenfolk gleamed and rustled in silken evening gowns. It was a scene from John Masters, moving and poignant and just a little too close to home. We snuggled together in the mist, and hurried back to the little railway and to the bright lights of Georgetown.

On Friday morning Bob and I reported in at Butterworth to visit the RAAF Air Movements Office and remind them we would be on the Monday courier flight. The flight lieutenant calmly announced that there had been a change of schedule. The Monday plane would henceforth fly direct from Darwin to Vung Tau, no longer calling at Butterworth. 'Sorry about that.' No other planes were flying to Vung Tau or Saigon; there were no seats available on the DC3s scheduled for Bangkok, Ubon and Phan Ranh.

Only those with a service background can comprehend the gravity of our situation. Two senior officers, we were absent from the war on our own unit's authorisation only; all arrangements had been made on the 'old boy' network, with no confirmatory documentation. Now we were stranded, hundreds of miles away in a peaceful country, where we had no right to be. If we could not get back this was the stuff of a court martial, for us and for our commanders. A firing squad for desertion was probably unlikely, but it was in feverish haste that we combed the civilian airline timetables. The earliest possibility was a Pan Am jet which called at Singapore, then Saigon on Tuesday morning; we could fly from Penang to Singapore on Monday. We booked the flights, then sent messages to 8 Field Ambulance and 36 Evac via the RAAF Signals Office. Our return would be a day late. Perhaps no-one would notice.

Panic at least somewhat abated, we still had the weekend, two full days with our schoolteachers and their car. The entire island was available for our enjoyment and we would make the most of it. Bob bribed plaster gods in the Temple of the Reclining Buddha. I photographed indelicate monkeys in Waterfall Gardens. We had a very British afternoon tea at the Sports Club, watching the finals of a tennis competition. We climbed the pathway from the village of Ayer Itam to a gold-topped Chinese temple. Our future prosperity was assured by feeding the sacred turtles. We hoped their influence extended to military tribunals.

On Sunday afternoon we drove to the Penang racecourse to see a 'broadcast race day'. The grandstand was packed with well-dressed racegoers, everyone with their back to the track which was completely deserted. They were listening to speakers at the rear of the stand blasting out descriptions of the Singapore races and they were milling about placing bets on the Tote. The scene was bizarre to the point of being disquieting, like viewing the behaviour of the inmates of a gigantic madhouse. We would not spend time there on our last afternoon.

At sunset we came to Lone Pine. This was more like it: gentle waves on a sandy beach, tall drinks under tall palms. Then to the Swimming Club for lobster and champagne on the dining balcony built out over the water. Back to the E&O and final farewells, a mixture of jokes and tears. It had been a wonderful time—and it had been fun trying.

A Fokker Friendship of Malaysia Singapore Airways flew us to Singapore via Ipoh and Kuala Lumpur. The diabolical RAAF Movements officer had booked us into Changi Creek Hotel, twelve miles out and designed for service families on leave. The place swarmed with children, the dining room was like a mess hall and the bar didn't open until six. For our last night before the war and retribution? Never happen! We bolted to the city and to Raffles Hotel.

I was sadly impoverished by the unexpected cost of our return journey. Bob now came to the rescue. Like a knight in shining armour he wielded two magic weapons—Diners Club and American Express. He booked us into Room 7. This was actually a suite of Edwardian opulence, the bathroom bigger than most bedrooms, and a fully furnished sitting room looking out over Raffles' tropical garden. There was no sign of the grandeur decaying at Raffles, nor of modernisation wrecking the elegance. For once a legend lived up to its reputation.

Down the marble staircase we descended, determined to have a meal suitable for the occasion. We ordered drinks in the ornate cocktail lounge next to the Elizabethan Grill Room and asked for the menu. There was a frisson of discomfiture. Without a jacket I could not be admitted to the dining room. OK, said Bob, could we be served in the Cocktail Lounge? 'Certainly, sir.' We were directed to a low settee in a corner, and cutlery and condiments were set on a marble-topped coffee table. We ordered oyster soup followed by Tournedos Parisienne and a very expensive champagne. The manager appeared. He apologised profusely that we could not enter the dining room. Instead, he said, the mountain must come to Mahommed. He had a table and two chairs from the Grill placed in the centre of the lounge. A white damask cloth and gleaming silver accoutrements followed. When the table was to his satisfaction we were invited to take our places; a waiter was stationed a respectful distance behind us.

Normally I would have been mildly embarrassed at this ostentatious display. Casual drinkers at the bar and around the wall tables were openly gaping. The uniqueness of the occasion and of our situation overrode any such qualms; Bob and I ignored the onlookers and continued down the menu and wine list with huge enjoyment. The cost in Malay dollars, from aperitifs to Benedictine and Havana cigars, was spectacular. The evening was worth every cent.

Twelve hours later Pan Am deposited us in Saigon, probably the only two medical officers ever to pay for the privilege of returning to a war. The civilian terminal at Tan Son Nhut was a grubby, dilapidated bedlam after the efficiency and modern facilities of Penang and Singapore. The delays over customs and immigration became alarming; I had no passport, just a military certificate of identity. Explaining the situation was not very easy. Finally we were cleared. We tore across to Rebel Ramp and found the afternoon Caribou still being loaded. At least the RAAF would transport us the last 50 miles of our return journey.

Our reception at Vung Tau was distinctly chilly. Colonel Siebert personally met the Caribou, deposited his chief surgeon at 36 Evac and drove me back to 8 Field Ambulance. I was clearly not flavour of the month. Why hadn't I sent my message only to the RAAF in Vung Tau and asked them to quietly inform our two units? Copies of my signals from Butterworth through the Army network had gone as a matter of routine to 1ALSG headquarters, where senior staff officers had asked some very embarrassing questions.

Any further trips to Malaysia were strictly forbidden.

Those next in line cursed me in a most inventive and colourful manner. They wasted their breath—diversion of the return courier flight had destroyed the system anyway. The Butterworth swan was fini. Sorry about that. *Xin loi!* Bob and I went back to work.

Twenty

RON GREGG, THE Great Surgeon, was 'getting short'; some of our Nashos were too, because they were coming to the end of their two years. Those with a departure date had a morning chant: 'Would you believe twenty-three days and a wake-up?' Each day the phrase became more confident as the number decreased. Those staying had a bleaker outlook. Trusted buddies would be replaced by unknown newcomers and they still had months to serve.

Once again we were being heavily pressed by casualties from mine injuries and ambushes. Ron and Morrie worked flat out, Mick had to be called in as second anaesthetist. More amputations, more massive debridements, one nasty surprise—a soldier brought in with multiple shrapnel wounds was found also to have a bullet in the back of the

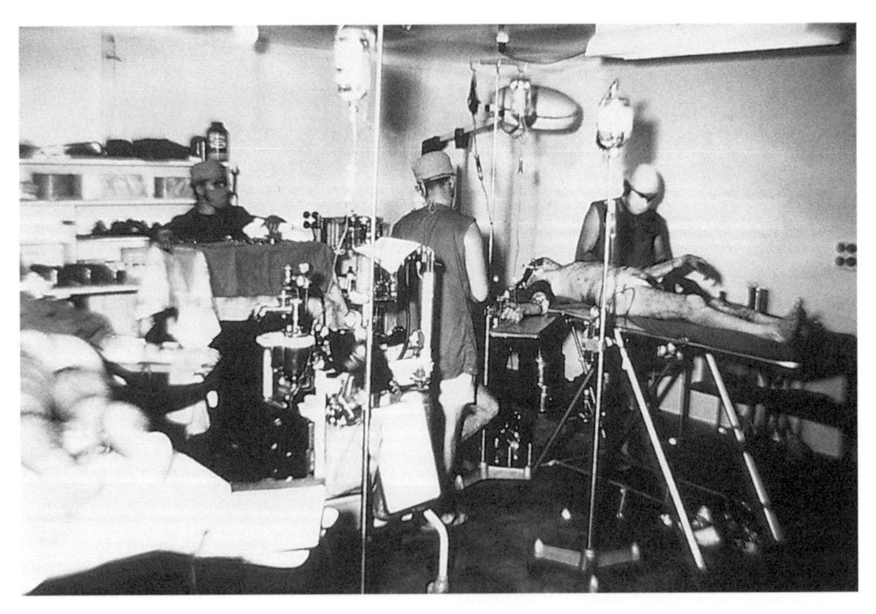

Both tables in action in the operating theatre. (Photo: M. Peacock)

head. Ron did a first class craniotomy; with his experience of almost every type of surgery he was going to be a hard act to follow.

Our darkest time was the day the National Serviceman was rushed in, fearfully mangled by a mine and pronounced dead on arrival. The word spread at once through a scarcely believing 8 Field Ambulance. Our patients simply did not die.

This was a period of stress for the whole unit. The increase in casualties meant pressure on everyone. And now there were rumours of an impending VC attack. More sandbagging was ordered, with all ranks required to help protect their work areas. Filling the sandbags and building up the walls was heavy work on top of the fatiguing hours in resus and theatre. The strain was beginning to show. Our boys were getting just a little slower in responding to emergencies and slower to relax when all went well.

The CO made another good decision. He gave permission for a Sunday beach barbecue, a farewell for Major Gregg which the whole team could attend. All casualties would be diverted to 36 Evac while we had an afternoon of partying and a night to recover. In truth it was a Great Decision.

The minor ops and DPCs were finished by Sunday midday; all hands helped load a trailerful of beer, ice and food. To get a supply of thick American steaks all it took was a carton of Australian beer. (Trading was brisk for Australian products. Outnumbered by the Americans 100 to 1, our rarity gave anything Australian an inflated value. A bush hat was worth at least 10 greenbacks. One Yank down from the Central Highlands gave up his prized Montagnard bow and arrow for a slouch hat; Wally Williams was offered a jeep for his 9mm pistol.)

The ALSG's most popular barbecue site lay between the road along our seafront and the beach beyond. It was an ideal spot, a natural hollow, roughly grassed and shaded by scrub and small trees. There was plenty of wood to fire up the two barbecues fashioned from 44 gallon drums. For once the weather gods smiled on us. It was a beautiful day, not too hot, the sunny sky fluffed with cloud. Instead of the usual sand-hurling wind, a pleasant breeze disturbed only the leaves.

We drank Victoria Bitter cold from the trailer; we ate huge steaks and Hygiene-approved noggie rolls; we swam and played childish games on the sand, like kids enjoying a day off from school. The traumas of recent days receded and were forgotten at least for a while. We laughed at the poor bloody workers across the road, sweating Diggers loading ammunition slings on St Kilda Pad ready for the helicopters. Chinooks clattered in and out and we waved cheerfully at the crews. There was no dwelling on the lethal cargoes going to Nui Dat on a Sunday or on the combats and casualties certain to come.

Swimming and exuberant horseplay gradually succumbed to the food and drink. Towards evening we gathered around the fire and started singing. We had a new song, composed, it was said, by a couple of lieutenants in the Education Unit, although probably it just evolved. The tune was 'This Old Man', the title possibly was 'The Bar Girl's Lament'.

Uc Dai Loi, cheap Charlie,
He no buy me Saigon tea.
Saigon tea cost many, many P,
Uc Dai Loi he cheap Charlie.
Uc Dai Loi, cheap Charlie,
He no give me MPC.
MPC worth many, many P,
Uc Dai Loi he cheap Charlie.
Uc Dai Loi, cheap Charlie,
He no go to bed with me.
Go to bed cost many, many P,
Uc Dai Loi he cheap Charlie.
Uc Dai Loi, cheap Charlie,
He make me give one for free.
Mama-san go crook at me,
Uc Dai Loi he cheap Charlie.
Uc Dai Loi, cheap Charlie,
He give baby-san to me.
Baby-san cost many, many P,
Uc Dai Loi he cheap Charlie.
Uc Dai Loi, cheap Charlie,
He go home across the sea.
He leave baby-san with me,
Uc Dai Loi he cheap Charlie.

Again, not very politically correct, nor were we very tuneful. Bob Burgess and Ken Youngson brought out their guitars and shut the discordant choristers up. For an hour or so we listened in silence, apart from the opening of cans of VB, as they played and sang bitter-sweet songs of love, of war and of home.

Many beers later the mood again became riotous. Ron accepted a farewell ducking in the ice-cold water of the now empty trailer; he was by now sufficiently anaesthetised and barely noticed it. Sergeant Bruce Turnbull, the model of military correctness, decided on a close inspection of shoes and sandals. His crawling progress brought him to Maggie's feet. Recognising the footwear as female and therefore belonging to an officer, Bruce staggered upright. His eyes briefly focused on her flaming red hair. 'Whacko, Blue, you bloody beauty,' he shouted, and collapsed back on the sand. Cisco became paranoid, prepared to fight any rotten bastard who said he was too drunk to go for a swim. It was clearly time for the party to end.

I never again experienced the degree of unity and unselfconscious enjoyment shared by the officers, NCOs and soldiers at that barbecue. With no outsiders involved and many beers consumed, the differences in age and rank had been reduced almost to insignificance. There may have been more orthodox or more sober ways of restoring stability to an exhausted team, but they could not have been more effective.

Major Gregg's departure also gave the excuse for another candle-lit Dining-In, or in this case, a Dining-Out which we held on Saturday 2 September. The organisation was relatively easy now that we knew the ropes. I said a few inadequate words and presented Ron with a unit plaque (an order for these having been on the CO's shopping list in Malaysia). It was small recognition for all the work our irascible surgeon had done.

The dinner was graced by some welcome guests: two RAAF nurses, Gwen Ely and Jean Liddicott, and a group from the Australian Civilian Team at Bien Hoa. The RAAF nurses came with a special medevac flight to cope with our increased number of patients; the Bien Hoa bunch came for a weekend break. They enjoyed it so much they sent a second lot down a week later.

It seemed extraordinary that they should wish to come to the sands of Vung Tau, the place we kept trying to escape from. A change though is a holiday. We did have the sea and a lot of new people for them to talk to and to drink with. What was also extraordinary was the immediate affinity I felt for the Bien Hoa people who came to visit. They were from Adelaide, home of my old medical school. Tom Allen was a topnotch anaesthetist from the Adelaide Children's Hospital whose pioneering work has never been properly recognised; he and I shared several anaesthetic research interests, and as a young man he had been a Spitfire pilot! But the rapport was not simply a shared background or common enthusiasms. This group were something special. They got on well together, they worked hard and they played hard. Tom, Doug, Margaret, Peter, Rodney, Jo, Beth—they were a great crew. Come and see Bien Hoa, Tom said.

Another welcome female at the Dining-In was Margaret Torrey, recently arrived as our first New Zealand Army nursing sister, a girl of exuberant high spirits and no small size. Late that night she entertained the stayers in the Mess with a Maori war dance executed on a bar stool with a balance and precision which, all factors considered, were quite remarkable. No one could follow that act and we boozily dispersed. Since Mick was getting along well with one of the visitors I spent the night on a trolley in the operating theatre.

We met up in the Mess at about 0900, half a dozen conscientious officers including a subdued Kiwi, cleaning up after the party. There were two pieces of news. Bob MacLean had his posting: he was soon to go to Germany. On our surgical front there was to be a delay in the arrival of Ron's replacement. The theatre therefore was to be closed for repairs and improvements. Once more I was temporarily redundant.

Ralph Meyer suggested another trip to Nui Dat to relieve Jack the Quack for a couple of days. Why not? I owed the unit a few favours. I flew up on the Caribou accompanying Major Ken Bladen, yet another friend from Perth schooldays, who was returning to his company after a sojourn with 8 Field Ambulance.

Nui Dat was depressingly soggy. The fine red dust was now a sea of mud. Rain intermittently pelted down; between the cloudbursts the rubber trees dripped continuously on tents and iron roofs. Security was tight. Several infantry companies were out and VC night attacks were expected on the weakened perimeter. A grateful Jack flew off with his US Dustoff friends to their base at Long Binh, his visit there coinciding with a concert by a Japanese twenty-girl orchestra! He grinned lasciviously, but we knew he was all bluff. Jack was really a straitlaced, God-fearing Catholic.

Even I was well behaved that night. Because of the security alert the Messes all closed at 1830. I squelched through the mud, the earliest to bed since arriving in Viet Nam, and was kept awake half the night by the guns.

Next morning there were 40 patients to be seen in the humid RAP. I was much strengthened by thoughts of lunch, since the most inventive cook in 8 Field Ambulance had been transferred to the forward detachment. With only a few to cook for, Moggie was turning out spectacularly appetising meals. Many people found it necessary to visit the forward detachment at mealtime. They were all welcome, particularly the Americans, whose unattended vehicle or helicopter always left with a red kangaroo emblem. Surreptitious decoration of US property with Australian insignia was the Diggers' latest craze.

I don't believe in paranormal manifestations, but there can be odd coincidences. In the MO's tent that night I had a vivid nightmare that an aircraft was crashing. During the night an FAC (forward air controller) on a familiarisation flight had crashed into a hillside in the pouring rain. The new pilot died instantly, his veteran companion had broken a leg and was rescued at dawn by the Dustoff chopper. At 1400 I saw a young lieutenant, a pilot of 161 Reconnaissance Flight, who had been convalescing from a helicopter crash. I certified him fit to fly and two hours later he crashed on landing, fortunately with no damage to himself. Jack returned in the late afternoon and I took the Dustoff to Vung Tau, not quite as happy as usual to be in a chopper. There were no letters waiting for me because the mail plane had crashed.

I was back in time for the Vietnamese class. Monty and I went along, and no teacher turned up. We repaired to the USO (United Services Organisation) for some coffee from the doughnut dollies, then changed our minds. We called on the way home for a drink at Marie's Bar, and then the Starlight Bar where voluptuous Mai made the great proposition. I be her full-time husband for free. Never happen! Why couldn't Xuan make an offer like that?

After the recent frantic activity 8 Field Ambulance was now boringly quiet. I gave a couple of dental GAs for Peter and a brachial block for broken fingers following a drunken brawl. I took Ken Youngson as an observer to Nam Binh, and Ziggy the photographer, but the light was poor with a black sky and the patients were nearly all 'hot and cough'. No diseases in real need of medical attention, no interesting marks from alternative treatments for Ziggy to record.

At 36 Evac I said farewell to Bob Watson and met the new anesthesiologist, Bill Hein. Bob MacLean invited me for drinks at the Villa du Bois. This was the accommodation for the officers of the US Medical and Nursing Corps, the American Red Cross and USO, and for our Red Cross girls. The Americans' equivalent of our Officers Mess was an annexe called The Gazebo erected in the Villa's front courtyard. It was rather a twee establishment, with a parachute canopy as the ceiling. Despite the number and variety of the Villa residents, the Gazebo did not have much atmosphere. Small groups kept apart. There were undercurrents of racial tension which had not been evident at work in 36 Evac or at Tay Ninh. On this night a cheery nurse called Rosie Hernandez was trying without any success to brighten things up. No wonder Bob had so liked our Mess, which always sparked up when visitors arrived. But even Bob was quiet tonight, as was his colleague Dave Nahrwald, also shipping out. Both were classically 'switched off'.

The Villa du Bois, despite its uninspiring Gazebo, had plenty of visitors. They were checked in by an armed guard at the gate. Another, stationed in the entrance hall, did a round a few minutes before midnight, knocking on doors to politely remind residents that all visitors must be out by twelve. The curfew did not seem to seriously restrict activities. The plumbing, seldom reliable, one day failed completely. The cause was a blockage due to 180 contraceptives. My Red Cross informant was disgusted: 'It isn't that surprising, but what sort of mind bothered to count them?'

A volleyball competition was started, I think by John Purser, who was himself no mean player. Two courts were marked out in the sandy hollow beside the causeway to Vampire Pad. There were matches between officers and NCOs and, more importantly, between different sections of the Field Ambulance for a black Buddha trophy. All were taken fairly seriously—good occupational therapy while things were quiet, and useful fitness-training too: it was hard work leaping up from the clinging sand. As a fairly incompetent member of the theatre team I rose at the net against John, both of us trying to 'spike' the ball vertically downwards. Somehow my bare toes became jammed around his achilles tendon; I felt a snap followed by the pain of a broken bone.

I hobbled to theatre and gave myself a metatarsal block; would you believe injecting 'buku' local anaesthetic? My assistant was Private Bruno (Peter) Davis, who had been working in X-ray and was keen as mustard to do more in triage and theatre. When the deformed toe was completely numb I invited Bruno to do his first manipulation of a fracture. He gave a tentative, then vigorous pull. The toe was nicely straight but Bruno wanted a picture. His X-ray showed perfect reduction of the fracture and no orthopaedic surgeon could have been more satisfied with his handiwork.

After the local wore off the toe hurt like hell. Sod's law applied once more: for the next couple of days I had to cope as PMC with some genuinely important VIPs—Lieutenant General Sir John Wilton; Major General D Vincent, Commander AFV; consulting physician Colonel J E Clarke; and consulting surgeon Colonel D Leslie. Also, blowing in like a breath of fresh air, came John Dunn, recently appointed as senior medical officer to the Force and based in Saigon. I limped about in hospitable mode, sustained by alcohol and codeine. We got shot of the big boys at last and Mick and I took John Dunn on a memorable tour of the Vung Tau bars. Xuan was flirtatious but still unwilling for any assignation. 'You will drive me crazy,' I said. She smiled. 'Many men are crazy.'

My toe still hurt; our tent was full of water again; Mick was getting all moony over Red Cross Marie; the new surgeon was about to arrive, but now the theatre would not be ready for him. They had run out of glue for the floor tiling and white ants had been found in the woodwork. One frustration after another. It was mid-September, over five months in-country; time for another swan. I teed up a visit to my new friends at Bien Hoa.

Twenty-one

I MET TOM ALLEN on Saturday morning at the Free World Building where he had driven in to collect the Bien Hoa team's mail. We headed back at once, the white Kombi van weaving through Saigon's congested streets and then on to a heart-stopping four-lane racetrack. This was the highway northeast towards Bien Hoa, 30 terrifying miles of it. Vehicles of every description from military transports to Lambrettas travelled this route at maximum possible speed, switching from lane to lane wherever a tiny gap appeared. Nobody bothered to signal. The hell with dreams of crashing aircraft, where was my chopper?

I relaxed a little when we turned on to a less congested secondary road, which crossed the Dong Hai River by way of an elongated, fertile island. A narrow one-way bridge took us on to the island, with another connecting to the far bank. Tom pointed to a group of Vietnamese soldiers standing upstream of the bridges. Their job, he said, was to shoot at bundles of leaves and debris floating down the river. The VC had tried several times to destroy the bridges with camouflaged mines.

Bien Hoa was a bustling river market town of about 50 000 people. The surgical team lived on a busy road not far from the river, in the upper two floors of a modern three-storey building, protected by a high wall and with a guard at the gate. Across the road were smaller villas. To the left and the rear was a large complex of American aviators' quarters. Bien Hoa airbase was said to be the busiest in the world. The airmen's buildings were fronted by sandbagged pillboxes. Behind, they half concealed a tiny chopper pad oddly called the Honor Smith Compound. The view to the right of the team's quarters was open and peaceful—contented ducks in a vegetable patch, green paddy fields, and in the distance red-tiled houses clustered among palm trees.

Tom had to get straight back to the hospital. This was a work ethic I warmed to. I dumped my bag and drove with him to the hospital, still in uniform. The Bien Hoa Provincial Hospital was similar in appearance to its counterpart in Vung Tau, but the scene of much greater activity. The area was seldom free from VC rocket and mortar attacks or allied counteroffensives and civilian victims of the war (and of traffic accidents) flooded into the Surgical Suite. In the previous month the Australians had performed or supervised over 500 operations, a phenomenal workload.

The many patients known to be VC were locked up after their surgery in a dismal ward behind iron bars. Probably at least as many remained undetected in the open hospital. The Australians made no enquiries; they were not concerned with politics, but with illness and injury, and making the best of severe shortages of facilities and staff. Between the two operating theatres a wide passageway was littered with instruments and equipment for which there was no storage space. The same corridor also held patients, on trolleys, propped against the wall or lying on the floor. Some were waiting for surgery, some recovering from their anaesthetic.

In theatre, a Vietnamese nurse was giving an ether anaesthetic, using ingenious apparatus devised by my guide and his predecessors. Tom was training two of these anaesthetic nurses, using mostly mime and sign language although an interpreter was available. The big smiles and the bustle of activity were evidence of the cooperation between the Australians and the local staff. It was all very different from Le Loi. On this Saturday the Bien Hoa operating team did not get home until dark.

I was given a high-ceilinged room with its own shower and toilet (and this lot came to 8 Field Ambulance for a holiday!). Tom urged me to get upstairs in time for a pre-dinner drink. 'Upstairs' was the flat roof. A large section had been enclosed and furnished as bar, lounge and dining room. The remainder formed an open patio, cool in the evening breeze, with comfortable cane chairs and outdoor cushions. We had an excellent view of the surroundings, and notably of the adjacent roof where muscular young Americans were working out with gymnastic equipment, obviously for the benefit of the females among us. It was flattering that they appeared more interested in their Australian visitor. They were as surprised that I should come to Bien Hoa as I had been by their enthusiasm for Vung Tau. I seemed to represent many different things—a new face, someone from home, even, with my uniform and pistol, some extra security! They freely admitted being scared at the level of VC activity.

Dinner was a festive occasion. The food was good, the beer and the wine likewise. We talked non-stop, recalling old friends, good times and good places.

Afterwards we played erratic table tennis, sang and danced on the patio. Twice the duty team were called to the hospital and twice they hurried back to the impromptu party. 'The Seekers' on LP kept the mood nostalgic—and romantic. In the early hours I gratefully accepted a generous but puzzled invitation. How was it Mick and I were so alike, she wanted to know.

On Sunday morning four of us went on a tour. In the vast military enclosure called Chain Compound, two attended Mass in the US Army chapel while Tom and I walked about the pool and its surroundings. Clear blue water, lazy swimmers, sunbathers on the lawns. It was all very suburban and peaceful except for the machine-gun post on top of the bathing pavilion.

Mass over, we drove the few miles to Long Binh, which was even more impressive from the road than from the air. This was US military might on a gigantic scale, extending way across a barren, dusty plain. Buildings of all sizes, tents, shelters, ammunition dumps, water tanks, helipads, gun sites, vehicles, stores, machinery—somewhere in there were the 24th and 93rd Evac Hospitals and the 45th Medical Evacuation Company whose Dustoff helicopters covered our triangle, Long Binh, Nui Dat and Vung Tau. They were my hope for a passage home; but we were not thinking about that quite yet.

We turned westwards, past a huge prison camp for VC where I took illegal photographs from the moving Kombi van. It was a grim place of wire enclosures, low huts and watchtowers; the only people in view were guards. A bit further on we gave a lift to a dejected-looking GI walking alone to Bien Hoa. 'I don't mind Viet Nam,' he said, 'I just can't stand being in the Army.'

Back in town Tom took me to a pottery works hidden in a cul-de-sac behind a dilapidated school. Inside it was cool and dark. Some unfinished pieces stood on rough wooden tables. There were shelf-loads of inferior products awaiting delivery to the souvenir shops. The white-haired Vietnamese foreman saw me searching for something better. Speaking a slow, schoolboy French he showed me, almost lost among the trashy bowls and cheaply moulded animals, a few samples of beautiful workmanship. Why so few? I asked and he nodded sadly: 'C'est la guerre.'

In the afternoon we visited the market, then took a swim at the airbase, gazing up as the planes roared relentlessly overhead. The surgical team had an open invitation to this Olympic-size pool, not unconnected with their complement of six attractive females. This probably helped also with my travel arrangements. We got ready access through the US telephone system to the 45th Medical Evacuation Company. They would be happy to deviate the morning Dustoff to Vung Tau. The noble physician Peter Last offered his alarm clock and a promise to drive me to Long Binh at 0600 hours.

We had dinner at the Blue Diamond, says my diary, although I cannot remember where or what that was. I do remember many fond farewells to a magnificent bunch of people, plus a long chat with Tom about flying. The Yanks gave him a try with a helicopter, which he could not control at all. Another therapeutic late night; Peter's alarm clock played 'Oh what a beautiful morning', and it was, even at 0530.

Back into uniform and there was time for a three-egg omelette, toast, pineapple juice and coffee. The roads were full of traffic even at this hour, and the drive was straight into the rising sun. Thank you, Peter, the Great Provider.

The 45th's Dustoff was going to Vung Tau anyway: they already had two extra tasks, a passenger for Saigon and oxygen and nitrous oxide cylinders urgently needed by 36 Evac. Oh, oh! That meant an unexpected drain on the anaesthesia supplies. I was back into work mode. With the four massive cylinders strapped horizontally across the aircraft floor there was no fancy flying, certainly no steep turns. A slow and steady takeoff, a gentle climb over the Dong Hai River to Tan Son Nhut heliport, then at 2000 feet along the Saigon River south-east to Vung Tau. The 36 Evac medics were waiting, and had the cylinders unloaded as soon as we set down on Cotton Gauze. The chopper danced across to Vampire Pad in more carefree fashion, swinging with a flourish to deposit me close to the causeway. I waved my thanks, strode past the still inactive theatre and reported to the Orderly Room. It was not yet 0800.

Twenty-two

MY TWO-DAY ABSENCE had worked wonders. Our tent was dry but no longer needed. The wooden huts for our new officers' lines were ready for occupation. Mick had already moved my stuff—the end of an era: we were now in adjacent partitioned cubicles. In theatre the tiling was almost finished; malathion had killed the white ants. And we had a surgeon.

Arthur Crawford was a specialist from Brisbane who had volunteered for six months CMF full-time duty. He was a very tall man, with a pompous manner curiously at odds with his awkwardness in unfamiliar boots and jungle greens. He exuded confidence, though, and was happy to pontificate on matters military about which he knew little. Although eyebrows were raised, none of this was of real importance. The brashness was probably covering an understandable nervousness: the poor bloke had been tossed in to our strange world without any handover or period of familiarisation. The key question was how he would perform as a surgeon.

On the big Theatre Reopening Day, Arthur took things steadily and sensibly, working through a backlog of elective cases. He coped easily with operations as diverse as transposing a nerve, repair of a hernia and the usual plantar warts and circumcisions. Next day we got our first shrapnel injuries, a nasty appendix and a DPC which had reopened and bled profusely. That was seventeen cases in two days without problems, curses or tantrums. Inevitably he did some things differently; just as predictably Morrie voiced a few disagreements. No one was seriously worried, though. We knew after 48 hours that the new operating team was going to be OK.

On that second night, finishing fairly late, we found that some Americans had turned up and a spontaneous party had developed in the Mess. Wally had brought Dom Ingrando, pharmacist from 36 Evac, who was expressing his opinion that the only good thing in South Viet Nam was meeting Australians. A group of Mohawk pilots led by

Lieutenant Colonels Jonah B Davis Jr and Eckols L Sheddon had the same view but it seemed more focused on the Australian nurses. These American aviators with their outlandish names had new songs ('Tiny Bubbles . . . in the Wine', 'Hello, Mother, I Knew it was You'), new catchphrases ('Take my picture!') and phenomenal thirsts. But Arthur was not a party animal. He stayed for a few polite minutes, had one drink and disappeared. A change from Ron; this was a private man we were not going to know really well.

Another Australian show came to Vung Tau a week after Arthur's arrival. They were staying at the downtown Grand Hotel Annexe, where I was called to see the lovely Pattie who had a severe tummy upset. (Why me? I think it may have been due to our mate Brian Kelleher of the Education Corps—he had the tough task of looking after Australian concert parties. Brian would have wanted Mick or me, and Mick was on his way to Nui Dat.) The patient was determined to do the hospital show that night and against my strong advice she did. She sang and danced, radiating a sex appeal from our tilted stage that had the Diggers yelling and even staid Arthur smiling. I saw her in the sisters' quarters during the interval, near to collapse; she didn't need more medicine, what she wanted was for me to hold her hand. I would still be holding it while she performed, she said. Freshened makeup hid her pallor; she went on again and even got John Kelly up for a sexy go-go. I was the only one who knew how ill she was. It was a privilege to have helped her.

Arthur had his first sight of the enemy when a 30-year-old Vietnamese woman was brought in under guard, shot in the shoulder by a 7RAR patrol. She admitted via the interpreter to being a VC, a member of the Women's Committee. This was rare; most prisoners claimed, not surprisingly, that they had been coerced into working with the Viet Cong. She understood some of my halting Vietnamese and I felt very pleased with myself. That was until I made a hash of the resuscitation, pouring in far too much IV fluid and overdosing her with pethidine. I was so used by now to managing battle trauma in fit soldiers, I had simply misjudged how small, undernourished and anaemic this frightened little woman was. It was not disastrous; her condition stabilised, Arthur did a good job and she recovered well. But I was badly shaken by such a poor performance.

Then it suddenly seemed my normal anaesthetics were becoming less smooth. I was having trouble with veins, Arthur complained about poor relaxation, there was more than the usual coughing and spluttering. This was no time for me to start giving bad anaesthetics. Apart from the welfare of the patients, the new surgeon needed to have confidence in me. I would hate for Ken Youngson to leave when things were going badly; it would be worse for replacement OTTs to find themselves stuck with a technically incompetent clown. The period of anxiety coincided with one of my many gut-rot episodes, which perhaps was a factor. I led a very abstemious lifestyle for at least a week and the bad patch was soon over.

Now we had other worries. Cisco the autoclave expert contracted pneumonia. For a few days he was desperately ill. We had to transfer him to 36 Evac where more facilities were available. Then we put him, pale and thin, on the medevac flight home. Theatre would not be the same; Cisco was the one doing his ironing in minor ops when General Vincent made his hospital inspection.

Ken Youngson, my support in times of trouble, got severe sinusitis followed by another pneumonia. Fortunately his responded rapidly to treatment. Ken was now at the end of his tour. I took him to town for a farewell dinner, badgering him to get a university degree and so avoiding any of the emotional stuff.

There were more changes. Extrovert Bob Burgess disappeared for home. The X-raying was taken over by a quiet West Australian, Peter de Worboies, and that jack of all trades, Peter (Bruno) Davis. I had the pleasure of training two new MAAs—Magnificent Anaesthetic Assistants—one of the many phrases coined by Privates Peter Davis and Bob Manning.

Bruno (Regular Army) had come to Viet Nam doing general duties. He had worked and talked hard to get into the theatre team. Besides manipulating broken toes he made model aeroplanes, which flew spectacularly then tended to crash in the South China Sea. More significantly, he was one projectionist who could coax our movie projector and the worn reels into reasonably continuous function. He also liked to watch a good movie. When he was called away to X-ray a shrapnel case, Bruno stopped the film, hid the sound valve and blandly announced there would be a twenty-minute delay due to projector problems.

Bruno was tall and angular; no uniform fitted his gangling frame. In unironed theatre T-shirt, impossibly long baggy shorts, huge boots and rolled-down socks he was a sight to behold. He was solid and dependable in triage and theatre, seemingly unflappable. But after Viet Nam, Bruno was never the same.

Bob Manning, except in cheerfulness, was almost the complete opposite. He was a short, freckle-faced, red-headed rogue, seldom out of trouble with authority on account of his disrespect for military conventions. With his swift brain, ready wit and infectious good humour Bob was maddeningly impudent and impossible to dislike.

On mornings when no Dustoffs came, we would all sit on the resus trolleys during coffee break, munching biscuits wheedled from the Red Cross and exchanging idle chit-chat. Occasionally the talk may have been serious and work-related; I remember it more as sounding each other out, prying none too discreetly into people's background in Australia and social activities in Viet Nam. This was Bob's time for jokes and slanderous witticisms. Arthur and Maggie in particular showed amazing tolerance; many times Private Manning must have been close to being put on a charge, but he was used to that.

The MAAs brought a touch of the Crazy Gang to their work. They had the anaesthetist's facility to be serious when it mattered and at the same time fun-loving pranksters. Wheeling an unsuspecting patient in for a minor operation, Bob would transmit a sign message to surgeon and anaesthetist—'RIP'. Between them, each time a patient showed signs of lightness under the anaesthetic, they built up a verse based on the Uc Dai Loi, cheap Charlie tune:

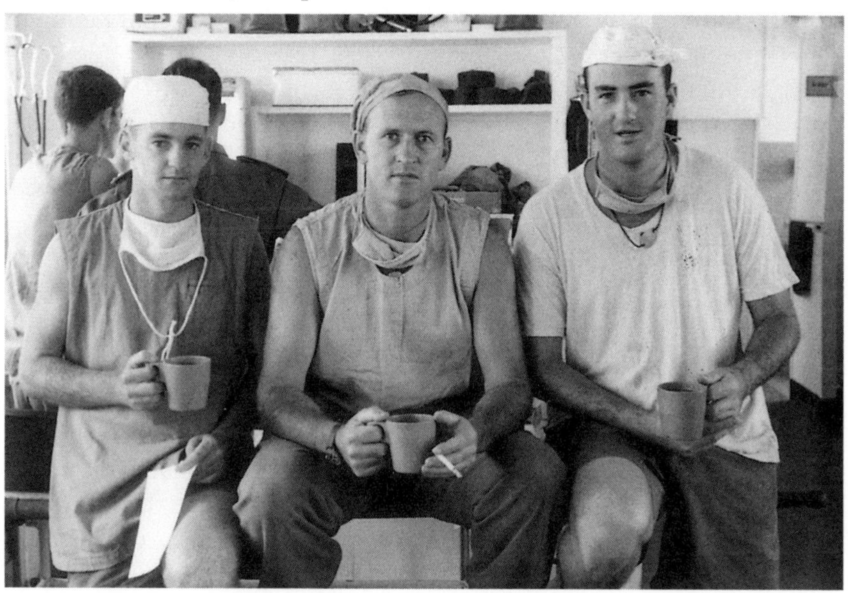

Three unwise monkeys? Bob Manning, the author and Bruno Davis between cases. (Photo: P. Davis)

Troi Duc Oi! What you do?
I think anaesthetist Number Two.
Pentothal cost many, many P,
Why you not give more to me?

Many soldiers recovering from my anaesthetic (only ever mine) would leave theatre with an arm raised, fist clenched and index finger pointed upwards; I have no idea why this happened but it was surprisingly common. Bob and Bruno called this the Barr Finger Sign; they would mimic it as they transported the patient to Recovery, chanting obscurely: 'Neg-lig-ible-huh!', thrusting their own pointed fingers skywards on the final grunt. The frightening thing was that we accepted this as normal behaviour. Arthur probably thought we were all mad.

The surgeon had plenty to occupy him without worrying about eccentricities among his team. He was soon faced with a succession of very serious injuries which culminated in an ambush victim with shrapnel in his chest, his belly and both legs. While we were sweating over his resuscitation, Frank Doolan insisted on giving the last rites. I was none too happy about this. For my money, the lad did not need to know how desperate his condition was, and I did not like being interrupted, even for just a minute. But it was certainly true that he might die on the operating table.

We got him into theatre and everything went right. Morrie was away at the sharp end, so Maggie acted as assistant surgeon. Mick scouted, keeping up the supply of equipment, drugs and blood. After about three hours he relieved me for a much needed coffee and cigarette. Arthur operated superbly, no time off for him, dealing with a stack of complications including bleeding from a torn liver. At the finish, we kept the patient in theatre until we were sure his condition was stable, then I spent the night sleeping beside him in the ICU. Come the morning, he was in remarkably good shape. I asked if the last rites had upset him. No, he had appreciated the priest being there for him. The Great Atheist wrong again!

More Vietnamese patients were coming in, better managed now I had learned my lesson. Soon I was taught two more. For another wounded VC woman we opened a new box of Intracaths only to find they were not size 14 gauge, but size 17, inadequate for the flow-rates needed in resuscitation. Sod's law for once in reverse: this small patient again was better off with less fluid pumped in. What I learned, however, was to check newly arrived equipment in every detail and never fully to trust computers. The US Medical Depot computer delivered the next nearest thing if an item was unavailable. For IV lines the programmer had gone for the same name rather than a different device of the right size.

The next Vietnamese admitted was a male named Mot. He may have been a terrorist, but he was only about nine years old. Mot had been used as an ammunition carrier and abandoned by a VC group during a surprise Australian attack. He was in an appalling condition. He was too weak to walk, filthy, emaciated and anaemic. The laboratory said his haemoglobin was 2G/100ml which was barely compatible with life. He had malaria and he had intestinal parasites—medical problems, not surgical. All he needed from us was an IV cannula for his blood transfusion.

It was astonishing how rapidly Mot recovered under medical and nursing care. The malaria and worms were eradicated, he began to eat like a horse. Each day saw more flesh on his scarecrow limbs. After a week he was chirpy and active, prancing around the unit with a slight limp from a deformed foot. He was spoiled rotten by the nurses

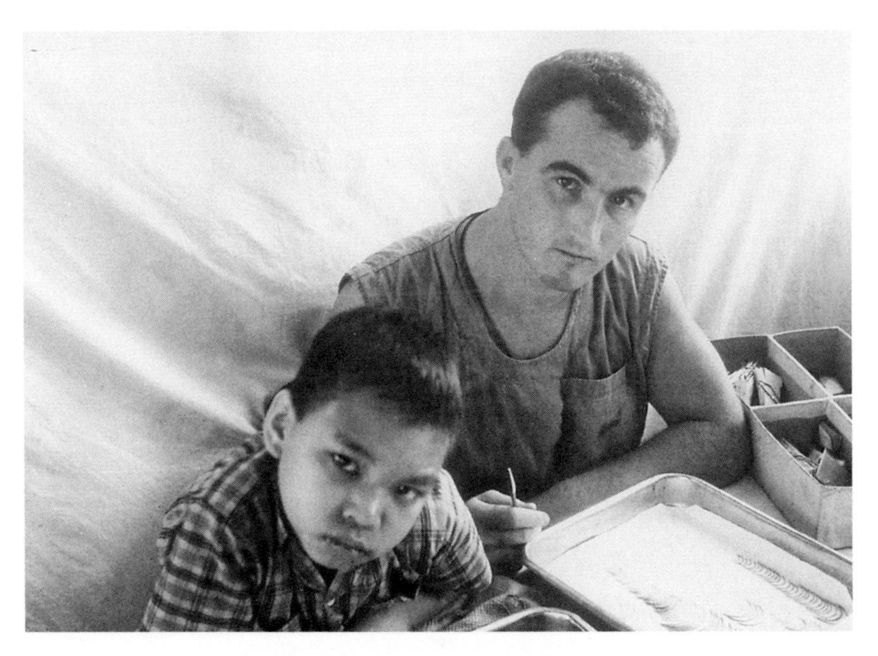

More unit mascot than dangerous enemy, Mot helps Brian Connelly sort suture needles. (Photo: P. Davis)

and the Red Cross girls, he was taught the worst Australian slang by the Diggers and he became a sort of unit mascot, our keenest supporter at inter-unit volleyball matches.

VC patients on recovery were expected to be handed over to the government authorities for internment in a prison camp, such as I had seen near Long Binh. The darling of the sisters and the Red Cross was most certainly not going there. Ever more inventive nursing and medical pretexts were found for him to stay 'in hospital'. He became more and more outrageously spoilt. Eventually he was sent off to school each day. His manner with the other children then decided the issue. Mot did not mix; he was better than them. *He* lived with the Uc Dai Loi and travelled to school by Army truck!

Continuing this unnatural life was obviously disastrous. The military authorities by now had probably forgotten about him. Mot was packed off in rage and tears to the local orphanage. How did he cope? Where is the middle-aged man today?

Twenty-three

THE ONLY TENT now remaining on the hill was the Mess, and a new Mess hut was promised before Christmas. The Vietnamese building contractors made up in workforce numbers what they lacked in modern equipment. To create each hut in the new officers' lines they poured a foundation of concrete, raised a timber building and roofed it with corrugated iron, all within 48 hours. There were no windows, just hinged wooden panels opening upwards and outwards; there was a ventilation gap between wall and roof, the overhang protecting us from even the most violent downpours. Our partitioned cubicles might be hot, but they were dry.

The nights of relative comfort proved to be shortlived. As the calendar edged from October into November and the rainy season ended, back came the strong southeasterly. When it blew, the swirling sand came through the gaps to settle again on everything, table, chair, trunk, mosquito net, bed. Inches of it covered the floor. With no handy cracks between floorboards the stuff had to be shovelled out, not easy when drifts built up against the walls and outside the door. You could halt the incursion by closing the under-roof gap with sheeting and keeping the 'window' closed; that is, if you preferred a Turkish bath to an oven. Or you could spend more time in the old Mess tent with cold gin and tonics.

During its last weeks the battered Mess welcomed many different visitors. Matron Doig arrived, our nurses' colonel in chief, bringing a trio of American nurse VIPs, Colonels Jamieson and Morgan from the 93rd and 24th at Long Binh and Caylor from Saigon. I did my PMC stuff, chatting up the women and plying them with alcohol while Amy and her team stayed on their best behaviour. A potentially difficult evening turned into an enjoyable party. The middle-aged colonels liked a drink and they had a stack of interesting stories; I was sorry when they departed. Not so the nurses; now they could let their hair down. They wheeled in colleagues from 36 Evac plus aviators and other assorted boyfriends. The party had just begun.

For the early morning cleanup next day the nurses were not in evidence, nor were many other revellers. Only Mick, John Kelly and I showed, and I did my back in, lifting a block of ice. War injuries don't come much more heroic.

Would you believe that in 1967 the International Control Commission, formed by the Geneva Agreements of 1954, was still engaged in its watchdog role on both sides of the 17th parallel? We met two of the members. The Canadian acknowledged that inspecting and reporting on the massive military installations in South Viet Nam was ridiculous; in North Viet Nam, their visits were so restricted as to be a total waste of time. The other ICC man was an Indian colonel, a turbanned Sikh. He lamented the futility of this war—so many unnecessary conflicts. Why couldn't the Vietnamese, the Koreans, the Arabs and Israelis all come to a peaceful understanding. I thought it reasonable to ask about India and Pakistan. The bearded face suffused with anger. Pakistan! That was different. The treachery, the atrocities! How could America give aid to such a depraved country? His ludicrous stance was almost laughable, but world peace seemed a long way off that day in the Mess.

More Australians appeared, members of the new civilian teams. Michael Bookalil was now anaesthetising at Le Loi. The team he was with seemed a bit more active, or perhaps there were just more patients coming to the hospital. Visitors came too from Long Xuyen in the Delta. Among them was Jan Rayner, very young, very lovely and completely dedicated to her work as advisor in the School of Nursing. She was almost as scathing as Harry Dangerfield on mess-ups by USAID. New faces arrived from Bien Hoa, Queenslanders this time, with Margaret Howitt their anaesthetist. Again they were a go-go sort of bunch. Again I got an invitation back to Bien Hoa.

The most extraordinary visitors we ever had were a young Australian missionary couple who appeared completely out of the blue. John was a doctor working alone in a clinic near the Cambodian border. He had no X-ray, no IV equipment and few drugs. The nearest hospital was 40 kilometres away through VC-infested jungle. He and Elsie had tried to get to Saigon for a few days' break and had ended up at Vung Tau airfield. Somebody sensible had delivered them to 8 Field Ambulance.

John had been treating a lot of war injuries, no questions asked. He was worried about how to drain chest wounds and keep them drained during the rough journey to hospital. A one-way system is needed, to let blood out and stop air getting in. He had none of the usual equipment, which would not survive the journey anyway. A simpler device, less liable to damage, was the Heimlich flutter valve, but he had none of those either.

I tried some experiments, helped by intrigued OTTs. We showed that a decapitated condom attached to a short piece of tubing made a very serviceable valve. Blood flowed out, the collapsed rubber stopped air getting in. We donated to the missionary doctor a gross of contraceptives.

John and Elsie went back to their mission all gratitude, if a little embarrassed by the large box added to their baggage. They assured us they would be safe at their isolated clinic, although Elsie was pregnant and they had not decided what to do about her confinement. We never saw or heard of them again.

On Sunday 5 November the Peter Badcoe Club at the Back Beach was opened by Ambassador Border. Attendance by all officers was compulsory. On general principle, this went against the grain. In practice, of course, it was a worthwhile occasion. The ambassador kept it brief, the R&C facilities, particularly the pool, were excellent and we trooped back to 1ALSG Mess for a magnificent celebratory lunch.

Melbourne Cup Eve was not so successful. The nurses organised a pre-Cup party in our Mess, one of those good ideas that don't work out. There was plenty of interest in the two sweeps; after that the enthusiasm waned. I drew Red Handed in both, then Arthur and I were called away to do an appendix. They held another sweep on the time we would get back (it was 2220 hours), but the spark was simply not there. We were the same old crowd (by now this included the Mohawk pilots), it was Monday night, workloads were heavy and no one was really in the mood for partying. No one except Amy, who most uncharacteristically got tight and threw ice over everyone to liven things up.

Red Handed won the 1967 Melbourne Cup. You little beauty! Thirty dollars richer, I took Janice Webb with Mick and Marie for dinner at Cyrno's on the Front Beach. Cyrno's was conveniently close to safe parking at the Pacific and unlike most of the eating joints maintained a high standard of French cuisine along with some decent wines. It was a beautiful, still evening. We ate under the stars on a patio with gaily coloured umbrellas and decorative palms. We could have been on the Riviera except for the high protective fence of wire-netting, a precaution against grenade attack. Even that was not too obtrusive because Madame Anna had festooned the fence with coloured lights. She liked things to be chic.

Anna was a French-speaking Vietnamese of great charm who had introduced me to a new drink. If I remember rightly, a Nicolaski is cognac drunk in one gulp through a lemon slice coated in sugar and coffee, held deep in the mouth. That night Mick played some Beethoven for Anna and we got a free round of Nicolaskis. Afterwards we drank champagne at the Villa du Bois. It was a great night, even if the Red Cross commandant kept me at a distance. My suggestion, she observed, lacked originality.

Having established the boundaries, Janice became a very good friend, although she was shocked by my drinking. On the last Saturday in November we both attended the opening of the RAAF's new Officers Mess. Cocktails and champagne flowed. The more she disapproved, the more I put away. John Purser and I returned to our Mess and kept on boozing. There were deep matters to discuss. We both had our eyes on Bangkok for R&R.

Perhaps Janice thought she might reform me. She certainly gave me many opportunities for a more sensible lifestyle. She knew the Vung Tau area well, Red Cross activities taking her all around the peninsula. On Sunday afternoons she would drive me in the VW wagon to some of her favourite places—a fishing village untouched by Western depredations, the bunkers of old fortifications, the winding road to the summit of Radar Hill. Where the hill's green slopes flattened to meet the dusty streets of Vung Tau she stopped one Sunday beside a park. We had come to a small French war cemetery. Well-tended graves in neat rows each carried an identical headstone: a faded tricolour in the corner and the inscription: 'Inconnu. Mort pour la France.' Who maintained those graves, I wondered. It was a place of almost unbearable sadness.

Vung Tau was changing. Many of the seedier bars had temporarily closed. The signs 'Copacabana', 'Starlight'and 'Hollywood' suddenly vanished, replaced by Vietnamese names. This was the work of major Tinh, newly appointed mayor of Vung Tau, who was determined to clean up local corruption.

I met the new mayor when he was a guest at 1ALSG, a very earnest unsmiling man. He had been born and educated in North Viet Nam and urged me to speak with a northern accent! He also told me the VC were stepping up activities against civilians because they were losing militarily in Phuoc Tuy Province. Baria and Hoa Long had been mortared. There were rumours of ammunition coming into Vung Tau in vegetable carts. This was disturbing news. We had all believed that the VC, like the Americans and Australians, used Vung Tau as an R&C centre and were unlikely to stir the town up. Now people were not quite so sure.

Sinister edicts began to come from 1ALSG. Security was to be tightened, unit defences improved, everyone had to sharpen up. The new commander decided that Sunday a.m. was to be a normal working morning. He also banned the use of any military vehicle except when driven by an official Army driver.

Sunday did not worry me. Arthur and I worked when there was work to be done. If there was none, we would sleep in on Sunday morning. The driving ban was something else, though. Now after many months of active service my hard-won G11 was to be of no further use. Even driving the ambulance to Nam Binh was *verboten*. Fortunately, the 'hearts and minds' policy had a high priority despite the security scare. We could go to Nam Binh in a convoy of at least two fully armed vehicles.

On our first trip under the new regulations, John Purser rode in the escort vehicle. Fifty VC had been reported a mile north of the village and Nam Binh was strangely quiet. The patients waiting were nearly all children; there were almost no adults to be seen. As we dismounted in this eerie stillness there came a sudden report. John spun round with his carbine to see a giggling five-year-old who had just let off a firework, blissfully unaware of how close he had been to oblivion.

We would not go to Nam Binh if current military operations meant a high likelihood of casualties and we were only once called back. On the last day of November I had just seen the first patient when a Landrover plus Provost escort screeched to a halt at the door. Severe casualties from 2RAR were on their way.

Normally the journey back took 35 minutes; with the military police siren clearing the way we made it in twelve, just as the Dustoff arrived. The first soldier had Claymore fragments in his chest, belly and all four limbs. He had objected to being the first winched up to the chopper. Now he was complaining again: 'I'm all right. Look after the others first.' But their injuries were relatively minor, and he was going downhill rapidly despite two transfusions running flat out. There must be major internal bleeding. Arthur and I were agreed he had to go straight to theatre.

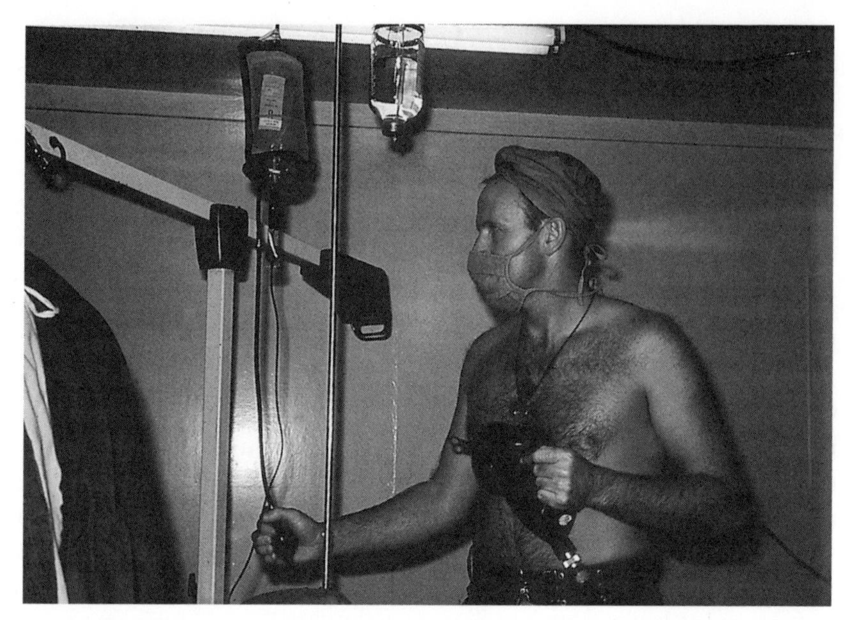

The hairy anaesthetist—the author 'squeezing the bag' and pumping in blood.

Anaesthetising a patient in haemorrhagic shock is about as sweat-inducing as it gets. We drained more blood from his chest, then Arthur slashed open the abdomen and clamped the pumping artery. At last I could catch up with the blood loss. Next a ruptured spleen had to be removed, then a segment of wrecked bowel; some lesser perforations of the intestine had to be closed, followed by debridement of the wounds in arms and legs. After six hours on the table our patient woke and enquired about a beer. We put him in ICU and started on the next case.

At the finish I had a beer with the OTTs, then crashed in theatre, too tired to move. Terrie in ICU had to wake me three times to deal with chest and drip problems. We operated next day till mid-afternoon. Arthur headed for bed. Maggie, pale and unsteady, took me to the Birds Nest for a couple of medicinal Mai Tais, the potent brew she had been taught to drink by the Mohawk pilots.

Amy and Colleen came off duty, bringing with them the CO, and a huge meal was produced on the electric frypan. The theatre sister and anaesthetist were being looked after. Somehow an Otter pilot called Art Walters also appeared, then John Kelly after his carol practice. A private little party in the sisters' quarters was a rare privilege. Many more Mai Tais, some impromptu singing and I fell asleep on Maggie's lap.

We made up that lost Nam Binh visit, as we always tried to do. Monty was soon to go home and other interpreters had to be found. For one trip I took a Vietnamese Army interpreter from the post-operative ward. On the way Sergeant Tai told me the sad story of his military career.

Young Tai had been called up from university and given a choice: infantry, airborne or languages school. He very happily chose languages, completed a course in English and was given another choice, whether to join an American or an Australian unit. Under the impression that all Australians were basking on the beach at Vung Tau, he picked a battalion of the Royal Australian Regiment. Within a week he was sweating on jungle patrols with a group of huge, mad, bush-hatted soldiers whose language bore no resemblance to that he had learned. His wounds were almost healed, but he was not desperately keen to return.

Co (Miss) Nha was a very different interpreter. She was a slim, sophisticated young lady who came to work in the Orderly Room, very conscious of her social position as the daughter of a colonel. The family also owned one of the most lucrative bars in town. Nha often chose to ride her Lambretta to Nam Binh, emphasising her superiority over the villagers. She was a good interpreter, but not a sympathetic one.

Much more likeable was Co Hong, affectionately known as 'Bubs' or 'Bubba'. She had started in 8 Field Ambulance as a kitchen hand while she went to night school to learn English and typing. Wally Williams soon snaffled her for his Medical Depot and we stole her from the pharmacists on Thursday afternoons. Bubs loved to come to Nam Binh. The patients were her sort of people. She would be full of sympathy while translating symptoms and delighted when the sick ones got better. A practising Buddhist, she showed an interest in the trappings of Catholicism but was very timid in talking with white-veiled Sister Mary. The nun in her turn was shaken by some of Miss Hong's English. Her vocabulary had been expanded by the Diggers with words most unsuited to religious ears.

The Mess Committee decided we also should employ a local girl. We would have a barmaid in the new Mess to work from 1700 to 2200 each evening. John Frewen, as adjutant, was given the job of finding the right person, weeks in advance—it would take time to get the necessary permits. He came up with Thuy, a friend of Xuan at the Thunderbird. 'I spy for Xuan,' she said. Not that I'd had time to see much of Xuan recently.

For the new Mess the contractors put up the usual basic construction of timber and corrugated iron. Extensions, architectural refinements and internal decor for the Mess would depend on the labour and the skills of the members. Corporal Miles of the Q Store was recruited as expert advisor. A surprisingly proficient team of officer artisans laid more concrete, installed glass windows and put in decorative shelving and plywood panelling. The bar, partitioning off one end of the hut, was John Frewen's *pièce de résistance*. He gave it a facade of padded imitation leather embossed with brass buttons of the Medical Corps and fashioned a centrepiece feature of multi-coloured stones in concrete. With a row of red-topped bar stools in front it was perhaps a bit flashy, but the bar was the clincher in transforming a hut into an Officers Mess.

Carpet on the floor, spanking new cane furniture installed, we opened two weeks before Christmas. Thuy was a huge success. Visiting officers admired her bartending skills and lusted after the ample curves of her body. She wisely distrusted all males—members or guests, Australian or American. She trusted her countrymen even less (several of the local policemen had suggested she 'be girlfriend to them' to speed up the employment paperwork).

We had some new officers to go with the new Mess: Paul Grainger-Smith, a psychiatrist doing a stint mainly as a general duties medical officer (we had very few acute psychiatric problems); David Kidd, also general duties; Colin Twelftree, a dentist (we called him Sevenoaks); and Geoff Barlow, a second pharmacist to assist the beleaguered Wally. The old order was changing. Morrie Peacock was temporarily back from the war, having been involved in some hairy episodes with the infantry and the gunners. He told me his 'warries', but I think no one else. He was glad to have been tested and glad to be out of it. Also back and on his way home was Jack the Quack from Nui Dat.

Before he left, Jack wanted to see and photograph a bit of Vung Tau. I gave him the scenic tour and he snapped away happily until we reached the French war cemetery. Jack read aloud the epitaph to long dead soldiers sacrificed for an Empire which no longer existed. 'A fat lot of good that did them,' I muttered. Jack was strangely moved, as I had been on my visit there with Janice. My flippant remark expressed a deeply felt sentiment. We drove home in silence, except that under his breath he twice repeated: 'A fat lot of good that did them. Yeah, a fat lot of good.' Jack the Quack, among our varied assortment, was the doctor with the common touch, a fatherly GP to the ordinary soldier fighting for a cause he didn't understand.

A few days later, on the Vung Tau tarmac, we shook hands for the last time. Jack's smile was rueful; a sweep of his head encompassed more than the activity on the airfield and the massive conglomeration of buildings and equipment. 'A fat lot of good this will do them,' he said.

Twenty-four

IN MID-DECEMBER ARTHUR was summoned to treat a VIP in Saigon. Morrie was back at the war, there was no other deputy surgeon; no surgery meant no anaesthesia. *Troi oi!* A chance for Bien Hoa!

Arthur and I took the Caribou to Tan Son Nhut where a car was waiting to whisk surgeon to patient. I headed for the US heliport. Had they any choppers flying to Bien Hoa? 'No, sir,' said the lieutenant on the desk, 'but we have a gunship leaving for Long Binh in ten minutes. Where exactly is your destination?'

'The Australian Team quarters next to Honor Smith Compound.'

'No trouble at all, sir.' Even for the generous Americans this seemed remarkably co-operative.

As we flew over Bien Hoa's red tiled roofs the pilot radioed Long Binh and I heard him explaining his delayed arrival: 'We have aboard an Australian general requiring transportation to Honor Smith.' Light dawned. With the badge of the Medical Corps centred on my cap and a single crown on each shoulder, the Movements lieutenant had mistaken me for a one-star general. I saw no point in correcting the error at this stage.

The Queenslanders were suitably impressed when I stepped into their backyard from my private chopper. They were also relieved, having watched a bit twitchily the arrival of a gunship; there had been a firefight down the street and VC had been caught setting up a mortar in the school ground. The relaxed atmosphere of my last visit was no more.

Despite the tension, Vicki and Tom Sale were perfect hosts and again I was made welcome by all the team. I talked shop with Margaret and some of her colleagues; I chatted up wives and nurses, Hazel, Vivienne, Tracy, Beth, Sue, Judy—a positive bevy of beauty. At dusk on the rooftop, flares lit the horizon and small-arms fire crackled in the distance. Once more I had girls saying how happy they were to have me and my gun on the premises. The Great Protector! Maybe they just liked me to think so.

Arthur arrived next day on the Australian Army minibus doing its courier run to Long Binh. His visit was brief in the extreme: a quick lunch rustled up by Vivienne, a chat with some fellow Queenslanders, and the minibus reappeared to take us back to Saigon.

The road swarmed with military traffic, Vietnamese soldiers guarded every major intersection, ambushes were on everyone's mind and our driver was very keen to get home. Once more I fervently wished I were travelling by air. At Rebel Ramp I was less sure: the Caribou's pilot looked to be fifteen years old and he was sprawled across the seats in the cockpit reading a Superman comic! We did reach Vung Tau safely, though, and Arthur was in time for carol practice.

Carols by Candlelight was held in the hospital's open air theatre a week before Christmas. Arthur, Neddy Kelly and the rest of the ALSG choir sang well. However, they were well and truly outshone by a choir of schoolgirls from Nam Binh, triumphantly presented by Frank Doolan and Father Paul. Singing their carols in Vietnamese, long black hair shining, white *ao dais* gleaming in the moonlight, those five- to fourteen-year-olds were as close to angelic as you could wish. Afterwards the padres hosted a supper for the girls. We filled them up with cakes, ice cream and lemonade while Frank counted the kitty, a couple of hundred dollars contributed towards a scholarship fund for a Nam Binh school child.

The schoolgirl choir from Nam Binh was the hit at Carols by Candlelight.

Our Mess pre-Christmas party might easily have been another flop: Prime Minister Harold Holt's mysterious drowning had affected everybody. He was a popular prime minister ('Shoot your bolt for Harold Holt', as they said) and conspiracy theories abounded. His death was almost the only topic of conversation in our confined community. What really got to us, I think, was the reminder that disasters can strike at any time and we were all a long way from home.

The party actually turned out to be a perfect dispeller of the gloom. This time people wanted an excuse for a rave-up. By inviting selected nurses from 36 Evac and Le Loi we raised the proportion of females to a respectable one in three and we brought in the best musicians from 1ALSG. The YMCA officer was there, not a party-pooper but a much admired entertainer with his banjo. John Thornton proved expert at diverting choristers from the bawdy to songs acceptable in the presence of the ladies, three padres and the ALSG commander. We had a lot of fun, good food and alcohol. Tony Mooy was among those who got as high as a kite. He pranced about the floor with one of the new bar stools. 'Ma Chairie,' he called her, 'the only four-legged redhead in Viet Nam.' Arthur was one of the last to leave—the evening was a great success.

Mick departed on Christmas Eve for R&R in Australia. I went for drinks in the commander's 'flat'. Lieutenant Colonel Ian Gilmore—he who had stopped me driving, who had been staid and formal at our party—was now relaxed and jovial in hosting a big assembly of military and civilian dignitaries.

Jan was there and afterwards we drove into Vung Tau. The unclosed bars and the souvenir shops were not doing much business although all had sprouted coloured lights, tinsel and garish signs wishing their customers Merry Christmas. The Catholic church was a little less flamboyant. The hundreds of decorative lights were all yellow and the illumination was concentrated on a giant tableau of Mother and Child. The square was crowded with Vietnamese families who had come to see the tableau and to worship. In Vung Tau on Christmas Eve, the church was the liveliest place in town.

A few blocks away Jan parked in the driveway of a large villa hidden behind a high stone wall. This was one colonial dwelling still maintained in the grand style. The friends she had brought me to meet were Charles Clayton, an American businessman, and his wife Hien who was matron of a nearby maternity home. The interior of their villa blended the technology and the elegance of two different worlds:

cocktail bar and delicately wrought furniture; radiogram and lacquered paintings. A Christmas tree dominated the living room and they had other guests.

Jan and I were introduced to a French family who had driven from Saigon for their Christmas holiday. In my terrible French I conveyed surprise that Jacques would risk their being ambushed on a notorious road. Civilians were only stopped to pay 'road taxes', he said. French nationals sometimes got a lecture on their country's past misdeeds, otherwise they were never harmed.

We drove back in time to beat the curfew and to attend Midnight Mass in the ALSG chapel. I was strongly against attending church just on special occasions, excepting of course to please a female companion. There were many other hypocrites who must have wished they had my excuse. The chapel was overflowing to welcome Christmas 1967.

The Army has set traditions for Christmas Day. At 0700 hours the regimental sergeant major, klaxon blaring, led his sergeants in the ritual rousing of all officers with mugs of coffee heavily laced with rum. Breakfast of pork sausages was followed by a Mess 'family Christmas tree', with John Kelly a suitably benign and tubby Santa Claus. Everyone got a present, including Buddhist Thuy, party-dressed for the occasion in shimmering silk.

At midday we were invited to the ORs' canteen for a drink with the Diggers; many, among them Bob Manning and Bruno, were already well primed. (Next day Bob recalled he had addressed his commanding officer as 'Ralphie Baby' and was surprised he was not again in trouble.)

Christmas dinner was served in strict order of precedence: patients, ORs, sergeants, then officers. The ward doctors and sisters dished out turkey, ham, roast vegetables, fruit salad and ice cream to those patients fit enough to cope with Christmas fare. Officers and sergeants then joined forces to serve the Diggers—a cheering, unruly rabble taking every advantage of this reversal of roles. Then we had a recovery drink in the Snake Pit (Sergeants Mess) and finally our own gargantuan meal.

There was no Morrie; so I had to stay sober, as did the unfortunate OTTs on call: we could scarcely ask 36 Evac to provide cover on Christmas Day. And in the afternoon we did have an emergency, Arthur having to operate on a leg threatened by gangrene.

I was fresh enough therefore on Christmas night to face the ALSG party, which had been apparently catered on the assumption that no one had eaten or imbibed all day. The ABC Concert Party were there: Jim Gussey, Lucky Starr, the delectable Lorrae Desmond dazzling everyone, well supported by tiny Bev ('What am I doing here with you?') Harrell. Many of these consummate professionals were spending their second Christmas in Viet Nam; on Boxing Night they would give us a magnificent show. I hope they have some idea how much they were all appreciated.

The commander left the ALSG party at its zenith to go to Cyrno's, taking Jan and me in his air-conditioned staff car. What a lovely man! Anna had invited her favourites to a champagne supper. She was enchanted at our arrival; but where was my great friend? Mick would have enjoyed her Gallic concern. The Claytons were there, and some anaesthetist buddies from 36 Evac, Bill Hein, Jim Rich and Bob Kyle. One of the Americans was just back from R&R in Sydney and loud in its praise. He had gone there, though, believing that New South Wales was an island off the east coast of Australia, like New Zealand!

Between Christmas and New Year the weather was beautiful. There was plenty of operating work and Arthur also gained a new non-surgical patient. When Thuy became ill the only doctor she would trust was 'Poppa-san' Crawford. The Great Observer had us all sussed out from behind her bar. You could not fault her logic in going for maturity and sobriety.

Between operating lists I got in a bit of swimming and volleyball to help remove the excess pounds from Christmas overeating, but New Years Eve was still to come. On Sunday 31 December, the officers of 4 Field Regiment held a luncheon at Nui Dat. They were too polite to invite only our female members and asked the 8 Field Ambulance Officers en masse. Somebody knew a Chinook pilot who was happy to provide transport from St Kilda.

Those who had to return early went by Landrover. The pre-Christmas security alert had died down. There had been no incidents over the holiday period and though the rumour now was of a VC attack over New Year, we were given permission to drive without a convoy. I rode as shotgun, with John Kelly, Janice and Margaret Torrey. We all wore jungle greens and flak jackets and we scanned the road and the countryside very closely for what turned out to be a peaceful Sunday drive.

The rice paddies had already dried out on the peninsula, while north of Baria the last of the harvest was still being brought in. From the speeding vehicle we could see the stages of this slow process in a series of passing vignettes—hand-gathering in the fields, clumsy wooden carts being loaded, yoked buffalo plodding the laden carts along the roadside, women and children outside their small houses threshing bundles of grain with straw brooms. Closer to Nui Dat the scrub and the plantations had completely dried out; we were back to the choking red dust.

The PMC at the Officers Mess was Gerry Salom, my schoolfellow from Wesley College in Perth. What a way to meet again—in a dusty rubber plantation on New Years Eve, at a party in the middle of a war. The gunners' medical officer was the dedicated, serious David Bradford, who had been on our Healesville course. (His RAP was decorated with sober Vietnamese paintings, very different from the pin-ups favoured by the staff of the infantry medical posts.)

Formalities done, our girls vanished as usual into an amorphous green mass of eager young gunners. John and I drank Castlemaine XXXX in moderation, ate vast quantities of scallops, curry and cold chicken, and enjoyed the vicarious pleasure of talking with officers who were really in the war.

The journey back was uneventful, there were no emergencies waiting or expected; it was time to party again at 1ALSG's Hippie Night. Our parent Mess on New Years Eve was an extraordinary sight. Most of the officers were unrecognisable with flower-decked hair and garishly painted faces. Flickering lights played on huge placards: 'Westmoreland is a pacifist'; 'Stamp out all officers'; 'Happiness is a warm Co'; 'Make love <u>and</u> war'. It was incredibly noisy—yelled insults and laughter, foot-stamping, singing and clapping, the music boosted by sitters-in from the Jim Gussey Orchestra. At midnight there was champagne, Auld Lang Syne and a kiss for every officer from Lorrae Desmond—what a fantastic woman! It was a moment of rare happiness. 1968 was the year we would all go home.

Twenty-five

THE WIND CAME back in the new year with a new ferocity. Arthur invented a way to watch the movies in a sandstorm: when it blew at night we wore brown paper bags with slit eyeholes. The concrete foundations of our new huts began to be undermined. The drifts and shifting sandheaps grew higher and the Christmas euphoria dwindled to pessimism. We were back to debridements and DPCs, and our patients from Nui Dat were gloomy about the future.

A wounded infantry captain asserted that Phuoc Tuy Province still only had daytime security. Terrorist activity and political executions were going on in the villages. He was sure the main force units had withdrawn only to regroup and rearm. He spelt out the frustration of fighting an enemy who could disappear across a border then return when rested and at full strength. I re-read *Street Without Joy* and *Hell in a Very Small Place*. My mind was just beginning to grasp the contrast between oriental and Western concepts of time. We were counting off the days to the end of our twelve months. The Vietnamese had been fighting foreign invaders for a thousand years, always with patience, always with eventual success. We would not have another Dien Bien Phu; aggressive Australian patrolling almost guaranteed there would be no surprise build-up of massive VC forces in Phuoc Tuy. On the other hand, as the captain said, the guerillas were always there and the larger units always threatening. It was hard to see a permanent solution to the current military stalemate.

On 10 January we Dined-Out the commanding officer. It was not only his departure that made this a milestone. There were many new faces. Major 'Digger' James had just arrived, a genuine hero from the Korean War who had turned to medicine after losing one and a half legs and gaining a Military Cross. Our first specialist physician was resplendently present, the debonair Lieutenant Colonel Keith Fleming. The colonel replacing Paul E Siebert had obviously not been fully briefed. He accepted the invitation that specified 'summer dress' and turned up in a Hawaiian floral shirt, accepting his gaffe with no apparent embarrassment and showing great interest in our traditional rituals. Mr Vice, my Dining Vice-President, was no longer John Purser. Lieutenant Geoff Barlow was now our most junior officer. The port circulated. We gave Ralph Meyer his farewell present. Maggie and I had scoured Vung Tau and chosen a lacquered painting, not one of the prettified, cheap products on sale everywhere but a beachscape study, with two bowed fishermen, capturing something of the patience and endurance of Viet Nam. The presentation address went down well enough. Our departing colonel had worked in a very difficult job, not made easier by the motley collection of CMF amateurs diluting and disrupting professional military routine. He had given me strong support, but he was not a commander for whom 'the troops and horses' necessarily came first. Even we had been surprised when he made himself the first member of the unit to take R&R in Australia. Only Mick appreciated the subtler points of my carefully prepared speech.

The organisation of his replacement was a complete shambles. Mick had been functioning as senior medical officer to the Task Force at Nui Dat. Digger James had come to take that role and Mick was told he would be acting CO of 8 Field Ambulance. Keith Fleming then arrived with a posting order saying he was to be the CO! Someone had blundered in spectacular fashion. The lower ranked Mick was confirmed in the acting post. Our new physician was understandably furious. Fortunately he was a man who liked a good time.

On Saturday night Mick and I took Keith to the Soai Kin Lam. Shark fin soup, stuffed crab claws to start, then heftier dishes to cope with the 1963 Coonawarra red brought from ASCO. On the second floor landing, as we descended, a Chinese girl suggested a brief commercial dalliance. 'Fifteen minutes! You must be joking,' said Mick. At the Starlight Bar too many Saigon teas were demanded and Mai swiped my Zippo. Then to Cyrno's to raise the tone of the evening. Madame Anna was enchanted by the handsome young colonel. At about 2000 hours we crossed the road to the Pacific, which was jammed to capacity, smoke-filled and deafeningly noisy. We showed Keith the drill. Mick rugby-forwarded his way to the bar to load a tray with three rounds of gin and tonic. I led Keith to the rear patio where some seats were concealed in the darkness. With the authority of their possession we worked our way back and wedged the chairs in a tiny space beside the stage.

The floor show was spectacularly good jazz—Pamela Hird on trumpet, Laurie Gooding from Sydney on clarinet. The gins were potent. Antagonism mellowed towards friendship.

I had done my bit towards peace and stability in 8 Field Ambulance. In the morning John Purser and I were off to Bangkok.

The R&R system was one of many miracles of American organisation. Over half a million troops were entitled to five days 'out of country' rest and recreation leave during their twelve-month tour in Viet Nam. This meant that on any given day transport and accommodation were required for several thousand soldiers travelling to or from their units. R&R could be taken in Hawaii, Manila, Tokyo, Hong Kong, Penang, Singapore, Bangkok, Taipei or Sydney, a ration of bookings for each centre being allotted to units on a monthly basis. Although there were inevitable moans about a particular destination being unavailable, I never heard a complaint about an unsatisfactory leave or fouled-up travel arrangements.

John and I, having chosen to go together to Bangkok, were booked for a flight leaving Tan Son Nhut at 1800 hours on Sunday 14 January. The Pay Office would only issue American dollars on the day of departure for R&R, to prevent black marketeering in greenbacks. Since our sole means of transport to Saigon was the 0700 Caribou, this necessitated a Sunday dawn appointment with a grumbling pay clerk, who filled our wallets for five days of extravagance.

The early start also meant an all day wait confined in the transit camp at Tan Son Nhut. This was without any doubt the most dismal camp I had ever seen: rows of dusty, dreary huts squeezed behind prison-like wire, no open spaces, nothing to do. It was entirely under US control and so were we; no old school mate here to let us into Saigon for the day. Officially this was Camp Alpha, unofficially it was called Endsville.

After wearisome hours of heat and boredom, the well-oiled R&R machinery went smoothly into action at 1600 hours. The 60 passengers on our flight were assembled in a briefing room to be 'processed'. We were sorted into groups based on nationality, rank and gender (several US nurses were on the flight). Identity cards were checked, we completed international travel documents, declared our hoards of US dollars and were told the customs regulations between Thailand and Viet Nam.

A bus drove us onto the apron of the civilian air terminal and up to a chartered Pan Am DC6B, its engines running. As the aircraft doors closed, we began to taxi for takeoff. It was exactly 1800 hours. The civilian cabin crew, a purser and three hostesses, handled with experienced efficiency their planeload of warriors scenting freedom. They served a good meal during the two-hour flight, but no alcohol. At least when we arrived we would all be sober.

At Bangkok Airport, Master Sergeant Hooker of the local R&R staff came aboard before the propellers had stopped turning. He introduced himself on the aircraft's public address system, stating precisely the programme for the next two hours. If we kept to the system we would be free in Bangkok that evening. Any premature merrymakers would find themselves on the next flight back to Viet Nam. We followed him like lambs onto the airport bus and thence to a large tourist coach outside the terminal.

On the 25-minute run into the city, Sergeant Hooker continued his briefing. He described local manners and customs, the Thai monetary system, how to use public transport, how to avoid being fleeced by taxi drivers. We were issued with a card carrying the R&R Centre's phone number. In the event of any difficulty, altercation or emergency we were to disengage, step back smartly, reach for the card and phone the number. We were given a list of the R&R hotels, all modern, all air-conditioned, all with swimming pool; the rates for R&R personnel were incredibly cheap. Sergeant Hooker gravely assured us that they all had a 'liberal guest policy'.

The bus halted outside the reception office of 'Tommy's Tours'. Here we were separated for more detailed briefing, Hooker taking the ORs into another room while Captain Martinez addressed the officers. The diminutive captain, like his sergeant, had a chest full of combat ribbons. How unfair it was, he said, that they should be forced to do this hardship tour in Bangkok. He was a mine of information about hotels, restaurants, churches, temples and sightseeing tours. He was also available for more private and personal discussions. John and I suspected Hooker's talk to the GIs would have been even more interesting.

The whole group now reassembled. Tommy's hostesses distributed free Singer beer and coffee while slides of Bangkok's tourist attractions were flashed on a screen. We were invited to sign up for any number of Tommy's tours. This commercial monopoly, with Tommy's Tours appearing to be the R&R Centre, seemed to our Australian minds unfair play. John and I decided to compare other tours before signing up. The Thai hostesses were disappointed. No one had ever not signed up for a single tour.

They were more amazed when our choice of hotel was not one on their list, but the Oriental. I had done the E&O in Penang and Raffles in Singapore. Now I wanted to experience the classic hotel of Bangkok, the only one actually on the river. John, on his lieutenant's pay, had been dubious but agreed to give it a try.

The Oriental was indeed worth sampling—traditional colonial architecture, wide verandahs overlooking the broad stream of the Chao Phaya River, luxurious fitments, Gert Steffen's Combo in the Bamboo Room, magnificent food. It was also ridiculously expensive. We booked for two nights only, rang the R&R Centre and asked them to arrange a transfer to one of their establishments.

I had two contacts, Phil Russell from WRAIR and an Australian businessman with the unlikely name of Digby Mackintosh. How I knew the latter I cannot recall. Between them they produced a key list of places we had to visit—bars, restaurants, clubs; also, should we require the information, where to go for girls who were guaranteed clean and safe.

We began to whittle the list down. Our rate was one restaurant, two bars and two nightclubs each night . . . Chao Phaya Officers Club, Normandie Grill, Dew Drop Inn, Ginza, the Yard of Ale!, Carlton, C'est si Bon, New Orleans Cat House (more innocent than its name suggested), Fireplace Grill, Café de Paris. Phil Russell also confirmed that Tommy's Tours indeed gave troops on R&R the best value for money. We signed up for trips during the day to temples, Thai boxing, the floating market . . .

When body and spirit flagged, we attended as instructed the Chevala Turkish Bath, where political correctness had never been heard of. The place was factory large. You selected your masseuse by looking through glass panels at a 'stable' of girls. Number 24, about eighteen I would guess, took me upstairs in a lift, into one of many cubicles. Under soft lights and with music playing, she filled a bath and undressed me. She was in a demure blouse and shorts. I was now naked and pleased to sit in the bath. She played the shower hose all over me following the spray with much enthusiastic soaping. There were no provocative movements or suggestions and my exhaustion plus a little self-hypnosis kept me docile. Next a huge drying towel and onto a low couch for a very efficient massage. Number 24 worked over every joint then walked barefoot up and down my spine (she was very small). The whole process was remarkably comforting and relaxing. It was only at this stage that I was offered a special massage. Further delights were possible, but would have to be arranged when she finished work.

I preferred to beat a retreat in my invigorated state.

The R&R clerks, with only a suggestion of 'we told you so', said we were booked into the United Hotel. It was quiet, secluded and very comfortable. It was also run on the assumption that every guest would have a girl in his room. Our bellboy was surprised when we arrived unescorted and almost unbelieving when we refused his offer to remedy the deficiency.

The hotel was full of American servicemen with their Thai girlfriends. Most had come to the standard arrangement of five days' continuous company for about $60. In this way the atmosphere of the United was not in the least sordid or licentious. There was no soliciting, the couples were a fixture. The girls were affectionate and faithful; by day they escorted their soldier on sightseeing and shopping trips, protecting him from racketeers. They would return arm in arm in the evening, high-spirited and laughing, seldom drunk. The bar and the lobby were never crowded; it was very much like a honeymoon hotel. Not quite the Oriental, the United was conveniently central and it was certainly cheap enough to allow our continued assault on Bangkok.

In the basement of another hotel, the President, was a cosy little den called the Cat's Eye where Thai kittens in miniskirts and long tails were gladdening the eyes of late night drinkers. It was our second last night and I was strangely discontented. Enough of oriental concupiscence. 'Find me a beautiful round-eye,' I commanded my junior. John began to wave an invisible wand and a stunningly attractive blonde appeared in the doorway.

Of course, she had a male companion. He was Australian, talking loudly and behaving like a drongo; she looked bored, he was smaller than me. When he went to the gents, I made for her table. She was amused by the lightning attack and obviously enjoyed my very sincere flattery. Tonight was out, tomorrow night she also had a date, but lunch would be fine. I scribbled Dorrit van Haven and her hotel on a cigarette packet and rejoined Lieutenant Purser. 'Sorry, no sister,' I said.

Next morning I was happy even at 6 a.m. Our guide on Tommy's Early Morning Floating Market Tour was charming, informative and particularly helpful with advice on purchases of Thai silk and jewellery. She had much admired one little brooch. I bought it and presented it to her: 'A small thank you for helping an ignorant male shopper.'

Later in the morning I explained I would have to leave the tour early to keep a luncheon appointment. The guide disembarked John and the other passengers, bleary GIs and their girls (no extra charge on

Tommy's Tours), to inspect the Temple of the Dawn. She directed the boatman to a landing on the city side of the river, hopped ashore and called me a taxi. As the cab began to move away, she gave the graceful Thai gesture of farewell, upturned fingertips touching, and dropped a parcel through the window. It was a set of delicate bronze forks which she must have bought after accepting my gift of the brooch. Are tourist guides in modern Bangkok still as gracious?

Green-eyed, flaxen-haired Dorrit looked even more glorious in the midday sunshine. I took her to the Oriental's Riverside Restaurant. We ate lunch watching river cowboys racing their long craft with extended outboards and the more leisurely traffic rocking in their wash. Dorrit was an advertising designer from Copenhagen, making a round the world journey home after a year in the States. She had just spent two months in Hong Kong and had been handed every possible line by troops on R&R there. Not propitious, but I talked hard, took her on a boat ride to see the Royal Barges, and she agreed to readjust her plans for the evening.

That last night was going to be memorable. We ate Kobe steaks with a bottle of Chateauneuf du Pape at Nick's No. 1 Inn, a marvellous eatery kept for some reason in a state of cobwebbed scunginess. Then to the Tropicana Room of the Rama Hotel; we drank Irish coffee and watched the floor show; danced cheek to cheek when the orchestra played slow, romantic music. At the Oriental, the Gert Steffens Combo greeted me with Waltzing Matilda, then switched to Wonderful Copenhagen when they saw Dorrit. She had obviously got around! Much later in a fashionable dive called the Balcony, Dorrit had the Filipino musicians cheering her wild go-go, her blonde hair flying.

We said goodbye at dawn on the seedy stairway of her tenth rate suburban Chinese Hotel. She would live here cheaply, she said, until she found a job. We arranged to meet in Copenhagen on New Years Eve, 1968. (I had already decided I would not be going back from Viet Nam to Perth. There was a whole world out there!) How would I find her? 'Easily. We are the only van Havens in the telephone book.'

Five months later in London the heading of a small paragraph in *The Times* caught my eye. 'Murder Trial in Thailand.' Dorrit van Haven had been brutally killed less than a week after I left Bangkok. I should have made some effort to contact her family to say how well and happy she had been. I took the weasel way out and did nothing.

Part IV

Tet '68 and all that

Twenty-six

THE R&R BUS arrived promptly at 1130 hours. John and I hauled ourselves in with the others from our hotel, stumbling over luggage, exchanging sympathetic nods with those who had already been collected. Sergeant Hooker ticked our names on his list; the pick-up round continued until the whole flight was aboard. It astonished me that no-one was missing, late or drunk. No-one was cheerful either and some were very shaky.

Again we were assembled in Tommy's reception hall. Tommy's uniformed girls circulated with badly needed coffee, while we checked in our gear and changed Thai currency to greenbacks. I kept one baht note as a souvenir, perhaps a talisman. As part of our final debriefing the R&R staff gave us a detailed pro forma with sections for comment on the hotels, the tours, shopping facilities, restaurants, bars and girls. Provision was made for the notification and tracing of any venereal disease contracted in Bangkok. Suggestions were requested for improvements to the R&R service. It was difficult to think of any.

I remember very little of the return trip to Saigon; mostly I slept. His Thai Majesty and President Marcos passed us in a flashy motorcade on the road to Bangkok airport. A moment of shock at the middle-aged homeliness of the air stewardesses. Easy job this trip, everyone asleep. John nudged me awake on the descent towards Tan Son Nhut. 'Air strike.' He pointed to the south, in the delta; unseen planes glinted, turning in the sunlight, there were flashes from rockets and ugly puffs of smoke rising from lush greenness . . . back to the war.

Saigon was hot and sticky. There were no customs checks. All that was needed was to change our few remaining US dollars to MPCs. It was too late for the Caribou run to Vung Tau, so we hitched a ride and reported in at the Free World. The staff at headquarters were very quick to agree that we spend the night at WRAIR—two less accommodation problems for them.

Although Harry Dangerfield and most of the old gang had gone there were one or two familiar faces at the Cong Ly Hilton. The new chief, Lieutenant Colonel Leeroy Jones, who didn't know us from a bargepole, was warm in his welcome. The operating theatre seemed to be even more crowded. It was astonishing how readily they accepted two foreigner blow-ins. Pathologist 'Bubba' Brown cleared two bunks ('They're up at Da Nang till Wednesday') and introduced us to Fred Fried and Jim Farrell, the two rather bewildered-looking dental officers perched alongside us. They too had just arrived, to spend a weekend away from Pleiku. Since their base was being hammered by the VC they were mighty pleased to be in Saigon.

We had a few cans of beer, then Bubba and I dragged a weary John Purser and an enthusiastic pair of dentists out on the town. La Pagode, the Caravelle, Tu Do Night Club . . . Fred and Jim thought it was just great. After Bangkok, though, Saigon seemed tawdry and soulless. The nightspots were cheaply and hideously decorated, unmusical bands massacred five-year-old pop songs, prices were extortionate (210 piastres for a small beer), small boys offered us marijuana, dirty postcards or their sister, very clean. I was relieved, and John surely was more so, when Bubba reined in the dentists and drove us unsteadily back.

At 0800, with a few comments about junior officers doing all the work, John headed for the Caribou and the sand at Vung Tau. I reported back to the Free World for an appointment with the senior medical officer. It was Saturday 20 January. The guards at the entrance had a mirror on a long pole, looking under all vehicles for explosives. Someone here was taking seriously the rumours of trouble to come at Tet, the Chinese New Year.

Lieutenant Colonel John Dunn, aggressively Australian in speech and manner, was now the SMO to the Army component of the Australian Force in Viet Nam. We had got on well together at Healesville and on his several visits to Vung Tau, he being a surgeon as well as an administrator and passionate in his concern for the Medical Corps. We had sunk many a beer together; now he wanted the dinkum oil on how the unit was functioning.

I gave my biased opinion on a few key figures and some less subjective thoughts on the future. After two years 8 Field Ambulance was still just a surgically equipped cottage hospital. With more troops being committed more staff and facilities were essential; we must get a better pathology service; new medical and nursing officers must get proper handovers; the training of new medics must be improved. Of course the SMO knew all this and he had no instant solutions. However there were big plans, he assured me, for expansion to a proper Field Hospital.

Dunn did have one immediate piece of good news. The theatre was undergoing more maintenance work and I had another two free days. During lunch, steak and ice cream at the Five Oceans BOQ, I concocted a schedule to visit within 48 hours the British Surgical Team at the Childrens Hospital in Saigon and the Australian Civilian Team (including Jan Rayner) at Long Xuyen. I also wanted to talk to someone at the Australian Embassy. The SMO had no objections to any of this. Circumstances, though, conspired against me.

I failed to contact the Brits due to telephone communication problems. It took an hour to get connected, then a non-English, non-French speaker answered. The US transport system could get me to Long Xuyen, but there was no guaranteed flight back. It would be pushing my luck too far to risk another delayed return to duty. The embassy of course was closed till Monday. Defeated, I walked in the late afternoon from the Free World back to WRAIR. It occurred to me as I strolled along the broad pavements that there were fewer servicemen than usual on the streets. Come to think of it, mine was the only uniform to be seen. I felt suddenly very exposed. The city activities and the clutter of traffic seemed completely normal, nonetheless my pace became very brisk. A gang of workmen were erecting barbed wire in front of the building next door to WRAIR, which housed the Nationalist Chinese Embassy. The lone walk had probably not been a good idea.

At No. 179 the inhabitants were apparently unconcerned. We were having the ritual evening drinks on the roof when there was a rattle of small-arms fire. It sounded just a few blocks away and I wondered if the shooting was on the route I had walked. Now safely indoors, I was not particularly worried. All the pre-Christmas brouhaha at Vung Tau had come to nothing. Tet Nguyen Dan, New Year in the Vietnamese lunar calendar, was still over a week away. Time for another Budweiser.

On Sunday morning, over a stomach-soothing breakfast of milk and toast, Fred and Jim persuaded me to try for Pleiku, halfway to North Viet Nam and 'operationally interesting'. The suggestion was mad enough to attract my interest. Their flight was not full, but with no written orders I could not get on it, a Movements officer sticking to the rules. Anyway, there was again no guarantee of a return flight.

Once more I lugged my gear across to the heliport and 120th Flight Operations. My luck at last had changed: a chopper was about to depart for Bien Hoa. I jumped aboard, they cheerfully dropped me at Honor Smith Compound, and it was here that I dropped and smashed my trusty Mickey Mouse watch.

The Westmorlands were still there and nurses Beth and Vivienne were off duty, otherwise there was an almost completely new gaggle of Queenslanders: Ken Hogg, anaesthetist, John Nye, physician, and surgeons Peter Grant, Ron Aitken and John Lahrz. Bien Hoa seemed to attract the most friendly of people.

Security concerns here could not have been too bad, since that same day the team had a more important visitor. Labor politician Gough Whitlam, leader of the Opposition, arrived by road with his entourage. He and Mrs Whitlam, both towering over the nurses, were gracious, charming and keenly observant; they showed intelligent, informed interest in the team's activities and in mine at Vung Tau; but how and why, on this potentially hazardous enterprise, did they bring a long-haired gawky son?

With the VIPs' convoy gone, the Queenslanders took me for some table tennis and a swim at Bien Hoa airbase. At dinner I met Colonel Bob Deets, CO of the 145th Combat Aviation Battalion—200 'ships' and 1500 men. He was going to bed early because he was flying a first light mission. Could I come along? 'Sure,' said Bob, 'if you wear a uniform and don't mind being shot at.' John Scott lent me his alarm clock.

At 0700 the next morning, the Honor Smith Compound was dark and misty. As we waited for the chopper Bob described the mission. He was flying control and command for eight 'slicks' inserting a company of ARVN troops south of Tay Ninh, near the Cambodian border. Opposition was expected.

The gunship from Long Binh arrived and sank gently on to the tiny pad, navigation lights blinking in the semi-darkness. Bob explained me to his surprised crew, then settled with maps and orders in the co-pilot's seat. The Negro crew chief motioned me to the canvas seat next to the open port doorway, just rear of the gunner and his M60. He produced a mug of hot, black coffee for me from a large vacuum flask. The babyfaced gunner checked, quite unnecessarily, that I was firmly strapped in.

An hour later we were circling a bare and dusty airfield, while the slicks loaded soldiers in jungle camouflage; small men, ten to each aircraft. We flew on, above and ahead of the troop carriers. It was easy to recognise the area to be secured; even I could follow what was happening in the softening-up bombardment. A squadron of jets flew in to make a rocket strike; artillery shells whistled invisibly beneath us and erupted as dirty mushrooms rising from the brown fields and green stretch of forest. In a straggling line astern the slicks crept below us, swinging in one at a time to hover briefly in an open paddy. Green-brown ants tumbled out and scuttled towards a ditch and the trees beyond. Four other gunships had appeared; they were circling low, blazing away at the borders of the paddyfield. Bob yelled into his throat mike to concentrate the fire on the southern boundary. Some small bright lights twinkled at the edge of the trees. 'What are they?' I asked the crew chief. 'They don't like us,' he said, white teeth flashing in a grin. How stupid is it possible to feel? At last under fire and I had not even realised it.

In truth the shooting had probably all been at the now departing slicks. None of Bob's choppers appeared to be damaged and his face relaxed into a smile. After ten months in Viet Nam, from the relative safety of 2000 feet I had seen my first enemy action.

We flew on to Song Be to refuel. It was barely recognisable as the muddy, desolate stopping place on my wet season Otter trip. The airstrip was a blur of activity, everything half hidden in a pall of brownish red dust which swirled and deepened as each new plane tore at the surface of the dirt runway. Every vehicle, aircraft, animal and person was thickly coated. In a bizarre sideshow a young Vietnamese girl had set up a bamboo leaf shelter at the edge of the strip. She was selling bananas to the crews of combat planes and helicopters queued for refuelling.

No bananas for us; we flew on, patrolling within half a mile of the Cambodian border. The area below seemed lifeless and deserted in the afternoon sunshine. Bob and his airborne-liaison officer, Captain Tony Cummings, pointed out signs of trails running east–west through the forest. These, they said, were used all night to resupply the VC from depots across the frontier.

Back finally to Honor Smith and a long, long shower to remove the Song Be dust and sweat. The Queenslanders loved my 'warrie', already being refined and suitably expanded. We drank much beer. Later I found myself alone in agreeable female company, but she just wanted to pour out her soul to a stranger—the Great Catharsis at my expense. Nice, though, to be so close to a round-eye again.

After about two hours sleep I had breakfast with Tom Sale and we drove to Saigon in the team's Holden. The highway was much less congested. Did this mean the region was more or less secure? We had no way of knowing.

At the Australian Embassy, I talked my way past a French-speaking receptionist. What were the possibilities of coming back to Viet Nam in a civilian teaching role? Jan had persuaded me that formal postgraduate teaching was the most effective way of helping the Vietnamese. The official was interested only in my joining one of the Australian surgical teams. Back to the Free World, two hours kip on a tiny corridor couch, then Tan Son Nhut and a rough ride in the Caribou to Vung Tau.

Mick was being bullish in his command. He had put Arthur on the general duties roster while theatre was closed. The surgeon was apparently none too happy, but he was in Saigon on more VIP business. We must have just missed each other at the embassy.

After several catching-up G&Ts, Janice arrived in the Red Cross station wagon to take me to the Soai Kin Lam. The food was great, the dance music good, the emotions were running surprisingly high: she was leaving next day for Australia via a holiday in Cambodia. An early night was indicated—she drove me back well before curfew. I ignored the sand in the sheets and slept like a log.

I toured the hospital in the morning and found the unit transformed. There was a sense of guidance, a smartening-up, heads held higher. Mick was very much in charge. Good on you, mate. No worries about Keith pulling rank: lieutenant colonels in-country being few, he had been grabbed to participate in a court martial which would keep him occupied for some time.

Still no Arthur, so the holiday from Dustoffs continued. There had been no mail for ten days due to a postal strike and the mood in the Mess was ugly. Letters from home were of the utmost importance to morale. The action most talked about was killing the strikers. I gave Thuy her Thai silk and infuriated everyone with a colourful version of my 'combat' adventure. They were more interested in that than in the delights of Bangkok. Most still wanted to see more action than drunken brawls in Vung Tau.

Thursday was Nam Binh clinic day. No convoy was required, and there was no restriction on females making the trip. It appeared that the only security worries were in Saigon. I took both Colleen and Margaret Torrey. Father Paul was preparing for a special Mass, the conversion of St Paul, and was not available for long. Co Nha arrived on her Lambretta looking very smart and sexy. All the patients seemed to have 'hot and cough'. For the one or two who genuinely had cough and fever the girls doled out antibiotics; for the others, placebo aspirin or vitamins. While we were away Arthur arrived back and Mick took him to Cyrno's as a peace offering. All was sweetness between them on our return.

In the evening we were invited to a supper party at Thuy's home—Mick, myself, Keith Fleming, John Kelly, John Frewen and a US civilian called Jim. Why not Arthur? Perhaps because Thuy did not want to socialise with her medical adviser.

She lived in a tiny but well-furnished house tucked away in a Vung Tau alley. Her guests were seated in a circle, shoulder to shoulder. Thuy, Mama-san, cousin Jacqueline and two most attractive reserves (sadly not Xuan) began to ply us with drink and local delicacies. Diced vegetables, chicken liver soup fortified with chicken blood, noodles, prawns, fishcakes wrapped in lettuce . . . some were delicious, some totally repugnant in appearance and taste.

The favourite sauce in Viet Nam is Nuoc Mam (pronounced nook marm), a fish sauce which is aged to increase its flavour. A bowl of this truly nauseating concoction had been set before each of us; every new dish, rich or blessedly benign, had to be flavoured with Nuoc Mam. The girls and Mama-san hovered around us, urging their guests to enjoy a true Vietnamese feast. We did justice to the first plate-loads, murmuring appreciation to our beaming hostesses. But again and again they disappeared to return with new creations, oily and unidentifiable. My eyes began to glaze. I tried to avoid the Nuoc Mam ritual. Kneeling beside me, Jacqueline politely corrected my forgetfulness: generously dunking food with delicate movements of the chopsticks, she slipped morsel after morsel into my unresisting mouth. I was beyond resistance—the liquid continuously supplied to wash it down was a fiery bourbon, slightly diluted with orangeade; not good for the sinusitis I could feel coming on.

That was the only evening I recall being grateful for the curfew. Apart from the Claytons and Father Paul's kitchen, it was also the only time I was invited into a Vietnamese home.

On Friday 26 January, with a horrendous headache from the alcohol and the sinusitis, I eased myself back into work proper: four GAs for elective ops in the morning, then a Dustoff at 1400 hours. A Kiwi had been booby-trapped out at the Horseshoe. After the long break we were straight into multiple shrapnel wounds again. There were no hitches, the routines functioned smoothly, the operating went well. Very encouraging.

Peter Grant and John Nye appeared from Bien Hoa. Like their predecessors, they preferred the change of the Army environment to weekending with civilian counterparts. A neat sort of shuttle hospitality was developing. I took the visitors to ALSG for the Australia Day celebrations—free booze and a magnificent spread. J B Davis was there and he was well away. He had made the list for promotion and he insisted we go with him back to the US aviators' club, the Hawk's Nest.

The Americans were all in happiness mode. 'Tiny bubbles, in the wine'; 'Take my picture!' Our girls were there and a good scattering of US nurses. At least a quarter of the Americans wore slouch hats in celebration of our national day. It was a good feeling to know the Aussies were so popular, good to drink with friends. We got home at midnight, leaving 'Neddy' Kelly behind. He was working on getting a ride in a Mohawk.

Saturday morning was frustrating. An exploratory laparotomy for abdominal pain and nothing found, then my local anaesthetic failed on a Vietnamese girl with a badly cut hand. Damn! I had to switch to GA for Arthur to repair the severed tendon. We were both pleased to be finished in time when Mick called an urgent officers' briefing.

There was major enemy activity north of Long Binh. The Yanks were so far coping with the acute injuries, but would be referring their Australian wounded on to us for DPC. How many cases expected? Buku.

Peter Kentwell had organised a big afternoon barbecue. No reason yet to cancel. Keith Fleming produced some bottles of Chateauneuf du Pape he had found at the PX. Was this our ball before Waterloo? It felt that way and the boys from Bien Hoa were impressed with our panache. Afterwards everyone went to the movie *A Man For All Seasons:* we didn't get many as good as that. The night was surprisingly cold. I huddled under a rug with Mick and Marie, ignoring sotto voce comments from Private Davis in the projection box.

Sunday 28 January 1968 (Diary entries reduced to brief snatches.) Eight dead and 30 reported wounded north of Long Binh; a Tet attack now expected on Vung Tau. All elective operations and all leave cancelled. We hold an unusually sober lunchtime BBQ to farewell Bruno and Huck Thompson who start for home tomorrow morning.

Everyone is very subdued. Bob Manning is on stand-by to go as medic to one of the battalions. I play table tennis in the afternoon with Bruno and get thrashed, sweating like a pig: another way of avoiding emotional outpouring. 'Good luck, mate' . . . 'And you, sir' . . .

In the evening we farewell Tony Mooy too. Inevitably, he does get emotional. Tony should never have been here. He is too highly strung, too defenceless against adversity, but basically a nice man. Then two night Dustoffs; a gunshot wound to the right shoulder, fair enough, but the next chopper brings two advisers badly beaten up by the village locals. No explanation why. I crawl to bed at 0130 after a very loose crap. Oh, oh! Just as the sinusitis is recovering.

Monday 29 January

It is gastroenteritis. I have to get Dave to take over an anaesthetic while I retreat to the latrine. Big doses of codeine. No food, no grog. There is no question of time off. With Paul ill and Tony now gone we are desperately short of MOs. Sod's law again, a major attack due and for many units it is the twelve-month changeover period. There are hundreds of RTAs to be done. I front up to the RAP and do my bit throughout the afternoon.

Extra night picquets are mounted and we are issued with tin helmets. We sit in nervous groups outside the blacked-out Mess. Midnight, and it's on! To the north of the airfield we hear mortars and 50 cal. machine-guns. The sky is lit up, red and green signals, streams of tracer, illuminating flares. The first action is nearby and I have almost no interest. Still crook in the guts and groggy with codeine, I slink off to bed. They will wake me if it is necessary.

Tuesday 30 January

There have been no military developments; the collective unit nervousness has dissipated. I still have the colic, but get through nine anaesthetics. No booze, so in the evening I win at poker against less sober competition. I even get a few dollars off Mick. His mind is on keeping the unit going in a time of potential disaster. With 65 patients the hospital is already full.

Wednesday 31 January

My gut is still not right, but quiet enough for me to complete another eight GAs including a difficult emergency dental. Rumours abound—

heavy VC activity in Saigon, Long Binh, Bien Hoa, and at Cat Lo just up the road—but there are no hard facts.

Lunch time conference at 1ALSG; at last some definite information. There has been no enemy activity in or near Vung Tau, despite all the hoo-ha at midnight on Monday: nervous defenders to our north had been retaliating against shadows; the locals had just been celebrating their new year, civilians with fireworks, drunken soldiers with sky-pointed tracers; the flares had been put up by the Americans to see what was going on! Everybody's still buzzing about in tin hats, though.

Elsewhere the situation is less humorous. In the delta, and around Saigon, Bien Hoa and Long Binh, there is evidence of a concerted massive VC offensive. Many more of the Australians at Nui Dat have been moved northwest and are expecting plenty of action. After the false alarms there is now no doubt we are going to be busy.

At night the order is 'lights out'. To a mere medical officer, blazing lights everywhere would seem a more sensible defence against infiltration by guerillas. A 'twenty-five' set has been installed in our Orderly Room for radio communication if the phone lines are cut. Good thinking, but why the hell didn't they leave us the set we used to have for communicating with the Dustoffs? I abandon the poker game in the dimly lit Mess and go down to try and get some news. Our set is tuned to the same frequency as a US platoon commander somewhere in the delta. The radio operator and I listen to his urgent messages. His voice is clear, frighteningly close, describing a shambles in a riverside village. He is surrounded, under small-arms and rocket fire from the market place. He is talking to the pilot of a gunship overhead, trying to direct its fire onto the rocket launcher. Abruptly his transmission ceases. The chopper pilot, a faint voice blurred by interference, tries to regain contact. After ten minutes there is nothing but static. I hang around for another hour, then bypass the Mess. Card-playing has lost its appeal. I clean my pistol with some care, then go to bed.

Thursday 1 February

Now the war is not so far away. Our first direct Tet casualties arrive and they are American: two US Intelligence NCOs who were stationed at Baria, the province capital. Their civilian house was wrecked by grenades in a dawn attack. Wounded by shrapnel and pinned in the wreckage, they had lain very still while the VC used the less damaged front room as a machine-gun post. At about 1000 hours there were sounds of heavy retaliation. They peered cautiously through a shattered window and saw 'the greatest sight of our lives', Australian armoured personnel carriers and infantry from Nui Dat 'zapping Charlie'.

Late in the morning we get four Australian wounded. Many others have gone to 36 Evac. At 2200 three more arrive including Roger Tingley, a young Troop officer of 3 Cavalry Regiment who had been hit twelve hours before. We finish by midnight. With no replacements yet for the homegoers, the depleted theatre team has worked well. Arthur has coped all day without any medically qualified surgical assistant.

Outside, the area is fully blacked out. Bob Manning, still with us, describes an episode from his picquet duty with 'Chips', on the perimeter about this time last night. They heard a rustle in the bushes immediately ahead. 'Chips' had the answer: 'You go and investigate, Bob. I'll stand guard.'

I sleep in the ICU next to the seriously wounded.

Friday 2 February

Breakfast! At last my gut is settling down. General Westmoreland's press conference on Armed Forces Radio is sobering. We seem to be the only major centre that's not under attack so far. I ride shotgun for Mick, both of us in the obligatory helmets, down to the R&C Centre, now converted to a convalescent annexe to cope with our overload of patients. The regimental sergeant major in charge has things well organised. In the afternoon we deal with some minor shrapnel wounds and some more cases sent on from Long Binh.

I'm duty MO at night, must remember the password! I listen on the wireless net for a while, then sit alone outside the Mess gingerly nursing a weak gin and tonic. It is eerily beautiful. The stars shine brightly, the lighthouse beam flashes its regular course, a Mohawk circles overhead and its landing lights suddenly come on. There are flares going up from the airfield; in the Long Hai Hills, the flash and crump of guns. Below me, the darkened hospital is silent except for the background hum of the generator. Oddly, it seems very peaceful.

Saturday 3 February

The colic has nearly gone. Negative report from the path lab on my stool sample; probably a virus, as they say. The *Sydney* is in and a Sikorsky 'flying crane' is swapping new trucks for old. One forklift was dropped into the South China Sea. We get five more DPCs from Long Binh and a platoon commander from 3RAR with shrapnel in the neck; he is very proud of their action in Baria, shooting at anything that shot at them. The province chief has been wounded and refuses to be evacuated. Politics demand that Mick, in administrative charge of the unit, go to Baria to assess and treat him. He takes John Frewen on the chopper to help him gauge the local military situation. The chief's shrapnel damage is minor and he can continue to direct mopping-up operations. Baria has been badly damaged but is now fairly secure. Just as well, with the numbers of wounded coming in from further west.

Sunday 4 February

Unexpectedly, a day of rest! Just one shrapnel case and an appendix. Orders still demand that we wear only greens. No swimming. We sit around doing nothing. No one can give us any news of the war, except that our two battalions are extending their operation to catch the VC out of Baria. At night the order is for a semi-blackout! What's the point of that?

Monday 5 February

Five new cases from 93rd Evac, including our first American from Long Binh, have been sent because the Yank hospitals are being overwhelmed. Nice to help them out for a change. The Long Binh surgeons did not have time to chase the shrapnel that hit the man's sciatic nerve—they're getting something like eight multiple Dustoffs an hour. Arthur finds the metal fragment. It went right through the nerve. He also removes the blood clot in the nerve itself: big success, great improvement in sensation and movement of the leg. In post-op we have a very grateful American.

I do an afternoon spell in the RAP; another million RTAs and still no medical officers. Paul Grainger-Smith has been diagnosed: glandular fever, that's all we need.

At night there is unexpected mail. No thanks to the bastards on strike in Australia—this has been posted from Saigon. Tan Son Nhut has reopened and I have a double letter from Janice Webb. The first, warm and nostalgic, describes touring the ancient temples at Angkor. 'I wish you'd been there with me. It can't possibly last many more years, so do come before it's spoilt.' How right you were, Jan. The second note, hastily added, is written in Saigon, dated yesterday, 4 February. Instead of flying to Australia, she had been caught by

Tet, trapped in the Saigon Red Cross Villa in the middle of the street fighting. About a thousand refugees were camped in the building. 'All these wounded and homeless are potential VC unless the Viet Government is strong enough to provide adequate housing and jobs.' Astute, caring Janice Webb is at this moment on her way home.

Tuesday 6 February to Saturday 10 February

'Transfers in' arriving by the chopper-load from Long Binh; now they are coming from 36 Evac too. Twenty-three on Tuesday, make it 43 surgical patients in the hospital and 50 at the R&C Centre. One boy caught by a machine-gun burst is bitter. 'They had bunkers fourteen foot deep. The air strikes didn't touch them. If the Yanks had used defensive patrols Charlie wouldn't have been there. Bastards, bastards!'

'OK, son, you're with Aussies now, you'll be OK; breathe on the mask, just a needle prick . . .'

Arthur is handling his massive burden extraordinarily well. Everybody is edgy, though. For the nurses and the OTTs it's not just the operating—they have to do the sterilising, clearing up, paperwork. Voices are up a pitch. The jokes are slightly forced. Bob Manning has acquired an invisible pet monkey; we are all close to seeing it . . .

In the middle of chaos, too many patients and too few beds, we get an influx into the Mess! VC are still reported well down the peninsula. The Australian nurses from Le Loi have been sent to the only female quarters inside the 1ALSG perimeter. Their male colleagues have gone to the R&C Centre.

War is not all bad! Jan Rayner was visiting Le Loi so she is with us too, being forbidden to travel back to the delta. The Red Cross girls have been ordered to leave the Villa du Bois. All are squeezed into the sandswept sisters' quarters. 'Fort Petticoat' (the hessian wall now replaced by wooden palisades) is being called 'Xin Loi Villa'.

Would you believe another concert party? Naturally they are grounded, so again we score: more female guests, plus a great show with Eden Kane, the glamorous Maggie Joddrell and the Sisters Sullivan. I blow in and out from theatre doing my PMC hosting bit. Keith Fleming turns on the champagne and the charm.

More transfers in, more DPCs. As each chopper-load arrives, Arthur whips around them, assessing the priorities for theatre. At the end of each operating session he tours the surgical ward choosing post-op patients for transfer to R&C so their beds can be used for the new casualties. Each day a bus brings the post-operative cases back to the hospital. They wait, uncomplaining, outside the theatre while Arthur dashes in and out between cases to check their progress.

Our surgeon is getting very weary. He is cutting corners, his civilian experience defying the rules of military surgery. To save a second operation he sometimes sutures wounds that would be better left open. It is nonetheless a stupendous exhibition of prolonged efficiency and concentration. Not once does he grumble or falter. Only a bowing of the head and sagging of the facial muscles reveal the degree of his fatigue. Just once, he swears during an operation.

On Wednesday, at 2000 hours the call comes: Stand to! The first full alert since we have been in Vung Tau. A contact has been reported on our perimeter and there is a shot. The victim is a Digger, shot by a sentry while trying to sneak in after curfew. What a clown! His knee is smashed by the SLR, his belly full of beer. A spinal anaesthetic solves the problem: he mumbles happily while Arthur does his stuff.

In the Bird's Nest and in the Mess, not all is sweetness and light. The quota of females has risen from eight to seventeen; tempers fray, snappiness and bitching are frequent, particularly about inadequate ablutions and latrines. To relieve some of the tension, a party is called for. With so many girls it is in any case an opportunity not to be missed. Because of the situation of alert the ALSG Happy Hour on Friday is cancelled, much to the disgust of their Mess members, who were looking forward to having a crack at our abundance of females. Our Mess Committee, less Maggie and myself who are otherwise occupied, organise a party for the coming Saturday night. We plan to ignore the blackout and the ban on all Mess activities after 2100 hours. In our special circumstances, the commander graciously extends the entertainment curfew to 2130!

More casualties. More DPCs. Intelligence estimates that there are 200 VC in Vung Tau equipped with rocket-propelled grenades. On Thursday three boys from 3RAR are brought in, having been hit at Long Dien. 'Don't shoot, we're ARVN,' they heard. They stepped forward and were shot. One is unconscious, with a bullet through the frontal lobe. Endotracheal tube, IV drip and I send him off, with oxygen and suction, to the neurosurgeons at 24 Evac. We operate on the other two. Arthur at his best—a bullet tracking behind the peritoneum and a smashed-up leg and elbow. High velocity injuries all, shocking damage. At 0300 we hear that the first boy has died at Long Binh. Maggie sheds a tear. Bob Manning, the Great Joker, and Geoff Harris, who used to rely on Bruno for support, are both badly affected and again I am too slow in realising it. I don't think of my assistants as young.

We work on through the night and next morning, finishing at 1300. No Nam Binh this afternoon! (Only military convoys are permitted anyway.) Arthur and I take all the theatre team to the beach and the Peter Badcoe Club for beer and hamburgers. Morale is just holding up.

More DPCs of our own, more transfers in from Long Binh. The news is good. The Tet offensive is failing, casualties are much fewer. After a mammoth session on Saturday morning the backlog is cleared. 36 Evac have some spare capacity now and Mick decides we have had enough. He closes the theatre for the weekend.

In the Mess, Morrie Peacock and Nev O'Connor are back from the war. They have seen some terrible things. Morrie gives me the lowdown on his job with the infantry. If a second chopper was required, he went in. The bad injuries went off with the paramedics, his job was to stay and get the minor cases fighting again with their company. Nev, before he fell asleep on a cushion on the floor, said that teetotal Morrie had three beers when the infantry farewelled him. No beer now. Morrie is off to Australia tomorrow and we are both regretful that our paths may not cross again.

A young American Airborne lieutenant appears, searching for a nurse from the New Zealand Surgical Team at Qui Nhon, halfway up the coast. She had been on leave in Saigon when the Tet fighting began. Probably she is still there. He is full of stories about battles in the Qui Nhon area and the destructive capability of his tanks. The VC had occupied several French mansions on the outskirts of the town. 'I've blown up some lovely houses,' he says.

There is time now to work on tonight's party; Neddy Kelly and Colin Twelftree rallying around. We lean on Peter Richards, 1ALSG's new PMC, to borrow their piano. Professional birdwatcher Private Manning volunteers to be chef of the barbecue. We set it up, well screened from prying eyes, beside the Mess hut. Bob proves to be the Great Chef. We eat well, drink only moderately. I am exhausted, content just with the sense of some normal socialising. The carefully selected guests from 1ALSG and neighbouring units discreetly vanish at curfew time. Our party floats on in the blackout. Jan and I sit together in the dark. The extraordinary, dreamlike atmosphere has got to us both. We cuddle close, childlike; she is gorgeous. Melbourne is far away and the perfumed letters have been getting fewer. In the violence and bloodshed of Tet this could be more than friendly comfort.

Twenty-seven

SUNDAY WAS A shocking day with a howling gale. Jan and I went for a swim and nearly drowned in the rip. Back in the Mess we listened to the war news on Armed Forces Radio. Bien Hoa and Can Tho in the delta had been heavily hit. We could not get a phone connection to the team at Long Xuyen. I did get through to Bien Hoa. They reported business as usual despite heavy fighting in the town,

The American claims of enemy casualties seemed fantastic, but our patients had supplied first-hand confirmation of fearful VC losses. They described seeing literally hundreds of dead and wounded in the fields and on the roadside north of Long Binh. Many were young teenagers, all carrying in their field pack a clean uniform and flag ready for the victory march through Saigon. In this area the VC had undoubtedly suffered a major reverse. This sort of factual information was extraordinarily difficult to come by. All over Viet Nam people knew for certain only what was happening in their immediate vicinity.

It was weeks before we pieced together the full story of the abortive Tet offensive. Militarily the VC had suffered a huge defeat, which was not reported by the Western journalists. The world media by this time were totally against continuation of the war. What they reported was a VC triumph in mounting such an attack despite the well-equipped forces of the Saigon regime and the half million US servicemen in Viet Nam. Politically, it was a stunning victory. In the United States, confidence would never be restored; a war which had not been winnable was now undoubtedly lost.

None of this was obvious at the time, nor was it on our minds that Sunday afternoon as Jan and I sat in the Mess listening to Mick play on the unreturned piano. The wind died down. Good friends old and new wandered in and out. The danger period was over and conversation was lighthearted. I wrote some reassuring letters. The relief of knowing I would not be dragged back to work was like a soothing balm. No need for therapeutic doses of alcohol. After dinner Mick's Akai boomed the Choral Symphony into the night air—civilisation after the horrors of the last week. Jan stayed close. It was one of my happiest days in Viet Nam, and it showed. The poor girl, without justification and without even knowing it, was hopelessly compromised.

Next morning we got 36 of our wounded off on the Monday medevac flight. With so many serious cases to be loaded, their 'silver bird' did not depart till mid-afternoon. The influx of casualties had quietened down, but there was much surgical tidying up to be done. The drunken curfew-breaker requested another spinal for his DPC. A few hours later he had meningitis, undoubtedly caused by my needle: the only case of infection due to a spinal I ever had. In Viet Nam I had switched from autoclaved needles to the disposable pre-sterilised units being used by the Americans. We checked the remainder in our stock and found that in two of them the all-important seals were broken. Keith Fleming treated the meningitis and the patient made a good recovery. I never again gave a spinal without checking that the needle had been fully autoclaved.

The 1ALSG commander gave permission for the women to return to their own quarters. Marie, now in charge of the Red Cross contingent, was pleased to take Robin and Margaret Young, who had arrived in the middle of the chaos, back to the Villa du Bois. The Le Loi nurses, plus of course Jan, moved back to the Grand. Colonel Gilmore thought he was doing us a favour and doubtless Amy and her nurses were happy about it. I was less happy. Jan was furious that she was still being kept away from her work.

It was another five days before Jan was permitted to get back to the Nursing School in Long Xuyen. The day before flying back to the delta she came on a goodbye visit. Sod's law again: I was duty MO and had to send her off to the beach with the least lascivious officers I could find. In the evening we had some Mumm champagne with Mick and Marie before I was called yet again to the wards. I would get down to see her soon, I promised.

The lovely Jan was the only one of our enforced guests who thought to thank Mick for the hospitality of 8 Field Ambulance. She wrote a letter to the Mess thanking us, and reporting that the Australian team and the Nursing School were unharmed although several of her student nurses from outlying districts had lost their homes. At Long Xuyen things were returning to normal.

On the Vung Tau peninsula, too, normality was slowly returning. We got permission for a 'recce only' visit to Nam Binh. The driver and I took helmets, flak jackets and two extra magazines with our F1s. The village was deathly quiet; the school was closed, the church sealed up. Father Paul peered through his small window before admitting us. The village he said was 'maintenant tranquil'. A few VC had prowled around at night but they had not attacked. Night fishing had ceased and rice was rationed. Still, there was no great hardship. He comprehended the impossibility of holding a clinic. I promised to return as soon as it was permitted.

Our operating lists settled to a more reasonable schedule. Bob went on R&R and I recruited a keen new assistant in Roy Sprake. There was still plenty of work in the RAP. I specialised in forging entries on International Health Certificates which had been stuffed up by now absent colleagues. For my money (and possibly for my career, now I think about it) a minor technicality was not going to delay any Digger's homecoming.

On our first clinic run to Nam Binh after Tet, Bubs came very reluctantly. Bob Manning, back from R&R and sporting a brand new pump-action shotgun, came eagerly. How he got permission to tote the gun I have no idea. From then on, he seemed to spend all his spare time lovingly polishing it, apart from the considerable effort he put into reblocking my slouch hat. He hated military discipline, but he liked us to look like soldiers.

Not surprisingly we had 'buku' patients, still mostly 'hot-and-cough'. There was no sign of any trouble; to his evident disappointment the only shots required of Bob were injections of penicillin. We had a couple of *dau rangs* and just one 'war casualty', an old lady who had gashed her leg two nights before, fleeing from a VC patrol. Father Paul confirmed the story. The enemy were still around.

Intelligence, admittedly not wholly reliable (what happened to all the RPGs in Vung Tau?), were confident that many VC had stayed in Phuoc Tuy Province; the dispersed Australians were back in Nui Dat and penetrating widely into the surrounding countryside. Again we were on the receiving end of direct patrol–to–Vampire Pad Dustoffs. Of the original theatre team only Bruce Turnbull, Geoff Harris and I remained. Arthur was pale and drawn but still uncomplaining. *I* felt absolutely shattered.

The truth was that the entire unit had been shattered by Tet. The unrelenting workload had pushed every section of 8 Field Ambulance to the limit. And we were being messed about: there was no word on the new CO; replacement MOs had not arrived; nor medics, and those who did appear were inadequately trained. The promised pathologist had arrived and he was a prize. Colonel D C Cowling, an eminent pathologist from the Royal Melbourne Hospital, was with us for only three months CMF full-time duty and no improvements had yet been made to our makeshift little laboratory. A skilled workman deprived of his tools! All around the unit and in the Mess there was grumbling and sniping. Mick was being left to run a sinking ship. And I was no support to him at all.

Digger James did me a big favour by suggesting I spend Saturday with him at Nui Dat. He wanted to talk about improving the resuscitation facilities at the sharp end. There were no frights on the way. A few blown-up houses were visible from the road going through Baria; we took a detour around the village of Hoa Long because it was deemed 'unsafe', even in daylight. Not exactly evidence that we were winning . . .

Digger, fresh and chirpy compared with our burnt-out bunch in Vung Tau, was like a tonic. He was brimming with enthusiasm and commonsense and he had already done much to improve the medical setup at the forward detachment. I made a few suggestions on laryngoscopes, Intracaths (care with the sizes!) and suction apparatus, but basically Major James had it all organised. Even he was getting fed up, however, because he had no time to fulfil his SMO administrative duties. He needed another doctor. Didn't we all, mate.

I went back on the evening Dustoff. The co-pilot said he had had four choppers shot out from under him in the last fortnight. That shut up my whingeing for a while.

On Sunday things were still quiet. We held another theatre beach barbecue, this time for the team to farewell Arthur who was due to depart in a week. He had offered to stay on a few days to give his replacement a handover and was told by John Dunn that it would have to be for a month. What a monumentally stupid cock-up.

The BBQ was low key. We were all exhausted and casualties were expected. We got in some good steaks, a bit of nostalgic joking and a couple of drinks, and then were called back. At least this one was different: the wounded soldier was a dog-handler, his magnificent alsatian–kelpie cross waiting patiently outside until his master recovered from the anaesthetic.

That evening the Mess held a semi-formal dinner for two important visitors from the Directorate, Colonel McLellan and Brigadier Hanway, the assistant director general of Medical Services. Only one

Mess member had arrived at the appointed time for greeting the VIPs. Just another example of things going to pot. I kept my temper (morale and discipline in the Mess were, after all, my responsibility), everyone turned up and the evening went off well, with Bob Manning as barman and steward. No shop talk in the Mess, but the representatives of the Medical Directorate would be in for some flak when they toured round the unit next day.

And next day I did lose my cool. The pay clerk announced that he had received a PVA (Pay Variation Authority): Major Barr is reduced in rank to captain as from 28/4/1967. Paybook docked $930.

The adjutant this time was quick off the mark: the pay rep had already asked, 'What's he done, sir?' I was threatening to resign and to sue the Army for defamation. John Frewen's signal demanded immediate clarification. The answer referred back to the time I had left the Field Ambulance in Fremantle without completing my captain's exams. Someone had now decided that without a confirmed captaincy I could not be even a temporary major. I was in no mood to tolerate the information or the manner in which it had been communicated. The military hierarchy got the message. The next signal arrived with, for a bureaucratic rethink, lightning speed. After 48 hours we were informed: 'The PVA has been adjusted.'

Mick got drunk as a skunk that night. He was commanding 'the biggest bag of shit in Viet Nam'. Our deficiencies were being exposed through the eyes of the VIPs, his questions were not being answered and he was feeling guilty as hell about what the Army had done to me. Having fired off my broadsides of rage, I could no longer be much bothered. The assistant director general on his inspection tour had demonstrated deep knowledge and perceptive insight about our surgical activities. If he had such a good grasp, who then were the incompetents?

Arthur's swansong was entirely appropriate. During his last few days Long Dien, Hoa Long and Dat Do were all hit. He was faced with major surgery on a lieutenant with a perforated liver from his own M79 (shotgun grenade launcher) and on a Digger blasted by shrapnel from the action at Dat Do. Then another mine blast and a multiple Dustoff: bilateral below-knee amputations, numerous bowel perforations, a compound fracture of the radius. The surgeon worked his way through them all without Bruce Turnbull, who was on R&R. The depleted team coped well, supported by Sergeant Graeme Chapman, and by Amy who came in after finishing her own duties to help with the clearing up. Unit morale had not entirely evaporated.

Next morning we dealt with a 60 per cent burn case (cleaning out a latrine with petrol was a standard, and dangerous, procedure). I got an IV line into the only unburnt limb, the right foot, poured in fluid and then a 'lytic cocktail'. How ironic that this potent mixture of analgesia and sedatives had first been used by the French Army doctors in Viet Nam. The beauty was we could have the patient conscious, cooperative and pain-free. Our 17 stone (108 kgs) patient happily turned himself from one side to the other as Mick cleaned up the burns. I got on with some elective cases—before the next Dustoff arrived.

One dead, eleven injured by another mine . . . we rattled them through theatre, with Mick assisting both anaesthetist and surgeon. He was pleased to escape from admin to do some useful doctoring. Twenty-three cases in two days. It was 0130 on Sunday morning and we were all wiped out again. Mick reverted to being an administrator. He notified 36 Evac that our theatre was closed for 24 hours.

Barbara Buchanan, Marie's newest Red Cross girl, had just arrived. After a morning ward-round to check on the post-op cases, Mick and I took Marie and Barbara to Cyrno's for Sunday lunch. I apologised to Barbara in advance. My plan was to get drunk, which I did: on wine, Nicolaskis, Biere 33 and some gins back in the Mess. What Barbara thought of her new posting, the Officers Mess and its PMC after this introduction I don't know. She never mentioned the episode again. From the little I remember, instead of being appalled, she was concerned and caring. I do vaguely recall that she got me to bed . . . I woke fully clothed.

Twenty-eight

ARTHUR LEFT US on Monday 4 March without fuss or fanfare, his farewells having been disrupted by the week's heavy casualties. I had said my inadequate piece at the theatre barbecue. How apt, I reflected, that on Arthur's last morning the anaesthetist was hung over.

While the surgeon got his gear and his documents organised, I did the surgical rounds, checked the IV drips and made some last-minute medevac decisions. The OTTs and I coped with a compound fracture and then were presented with a Vietnamese woman whose hand was badly burned. She was thought to be VC; we were told to wait for Intelligence to arrive. Their interpreter would listen for secrets as she went under anaesthesia. Bugger that! I got Bubs to interpret, gave a brachial block and debrided and dressed the hand. While we dealt with all this in theatre, Colonel Cowling, pathologist without laboratory, nobly did the RAP.

Within a few hours of Arthur's departure, the afternoon Wallaby brought both our new surgeon and a new physician! Colonel Don Beard had served as a regimental medical officer in Korea before specialising in surgery. Lieutenant Colonel Tom Beare was replacing Keith Fleming, who had suddenly been sent to a SEATO post in Bangkok. Both newcomers were from Adelaide and Tom was of my vintage at the Adelaide Medical School. It could have been another heavy night. Fortunately for my liver, they opted instead to go to bed early.

The first casualty Don Beard treated was a Viet Cong soldier, his femur shattered by the high velocity impact from an SLR. The theatre boys were nervous. This time they were working with a full colonel who knew the Army backwards. My spinal only half worked: what a great start! The surgeon waited patiently as I switched to full general anaesthesia. And hallelujah, he was a skilled operator. Three times lucky!

Don Beard brought to us something more important than his surgical abilities. He restored humanity to a hospital which was close to losing its way. He was deeply disturbed by the bitterness of our wounded Diggers towards the Vietnamese patients. Their callous attitude was painfully obvious to the newcomer with past experience of war. We had all been blinded by the dehumanising effect of Viet Nam, especially following Tet. A very nasty ditty was going the rounds:

> Viet Nam swings like a pendulum do,
> Ho Chi Minh and a B-52
> Nuoc Mam, napalm, Nam Tram Dong,
> The dying screams of the Viet Cong.

We would cheerfully sing at least the first two lines. Some of those who had suffered or had lost good mates made less attempt to hide their hatred. I had barely noticed the derogatory remarks, the thinly veiled threats, the gradual slide towards brutishness. Don Beard very quickly re-established the principle that all patients were equal and all would be treated with courtesy and kindness.

In the Officers Mess, too, where my PMC responsibilities had been so badly neglected, he brought new dignity and a degree of gentlemanly graciousness we had almost forgotten existed. I owe a great deal to this tall, kindly man. He did much to preserve my sanity during the last dragging weeks at Vung Tau.

His was no gentle reintroduction to war surgery. We still had the dual challenge of multiple transfers in, plus the acute trauma brought by our own Dustoffs. Our first big test together was a Kiwi with horrific mutilation of both legs and still with massive haemorrhage despite no recordable blood pressure. I got in three IV lines while Don clamped the pumping arteries. By the time we eventually got the man out of theatre we had transfused 25 units of blood. Mick was the Great Provider, organising fresh supplies from willing donors. The new surgeon was lavish in his praise of our resuscitation and theatre routines. His only demand was for us to be quieter while he operated. Another thing I had not noticed was how rowdy we had become.

The weekend revealed new talents. Don Beard was expert at volleyball and he could down a pint of beer faster than anyone in the unit. He was also a skilful physical and mental trainer. Between the bursts of surgical activity Don would take me to the beach and make me run and swim with him. I must have been an appalling companion.

I was edgy, irritable, plagued again with chronic diarrhoea and resorting to Amytal to help me sleep.

After exercising we would head for the Peter Badcoe Club for several thirst quenchers and a bit of conversational psychotherapy. It was Don Beard's tolerance, thoughtfulness and good humour that kept me from sinking into depression and self-pity. Mick, the Great Morale Booster, still had too many worries of his own. Apart from running the unit he was having to rethink his life: Marie's Red Cross tour of duty was finishing and they had become very close.

Physician Tom Beare showed an immediate interest in the clinic at Nam Binh. The situation had changed because a village nurse had set up shop a few doors from our clinic. This was a delicate matter: she could provide the continuity of care I had wanted, but our free clinic was a threat to her livelihood. We asked Father Paul to invite her to the clinic. She spoke no English and was very nervous in the presence of two Bac Si Uc Dai Loi. Through Bubs we asked if she would like to help us on Thursday afternoons and look after the patients between visits. We would be happy to see any of her patients giving cause for concern. If she had trouble with medical supplies we would try to help her out.

Bubs cottoned on at once, probably with a very free translation. The last suggestion in particular went down very well. Our nurse stayed and soon showed she was competent. I would leave Nam Binh to the better qualified physician and his new assistant.

The probing from Nui Dat continued: more disasters from mines in the Long Hais, more traumatic Dustoffs. I was training Dave Boyle as the next anaesthetic assistant, and just in time. Roy Sprake, fortified by a few beers, came up to Don and me at the Peter Badcoe Club to show us the infected hand he had been concealing. 'Can I have some antibiotics, please?' he asked. Perhaps he felt he was safe, being away from the theatre. *Xin loi*, Roy. In a few hours he was on the receiving end of the pentothal and the surgical knife.

Don himself at last got an assistant—a live, experienced general duties medical officer. Bruce Daniel arrived on 16 March. He said he'd been on one week's stand-by for Viet Nam since June!

The next to make a belated appearance was the new commanding officer, who appeared in the Mess on the night of 19 March. Colin Twelftree and I, being the duty officers, were commendably sober. Our colleagues had rolled in from a night at 1ALSG and were playing Moriarty. This involved two contestants on the floor, blindfolded, right hands clasped, left hands wielding rolled up newspaper to strike at the sound of a voice: 'Are you there, Moriarty?' 'I'm here.' Excellent entertainment for the onlookers, but ice-eyed Lieutenant Colonel Bill Watson was not amused.

Next morning—the timing could hardly have been less fair—the new CO had his unit inspected: Lieutenant General Wilton was back with Major General A L MacDonald, Commander of the Australian Armed Forces in Viet Nam. Mick was very despondent. He had known and greatly respected MacDonald in his New Guinea days. Now at the finish of his temporary command, all the glaring defects were being ruthlessly exposed. We were a run-down outfit and we looked it. Bill Watson quietly bided his time.

Problems and cares were temporarily forgotten when we Dined-In the new CO. I rambled through a speech of welcome, then one of farewell to Peter Kentwell, Neddy and Mick (our private farewell was at the Soai Kin Lam). Afterwards Moriarty reappeared in the Mess, this time with the commanding officer's blessing. The game is funnier when you are not completely sober.

Jan arrived for the weekend and our Friday night was wrecked by more mine injuries from the Long Hais. Neddy et al. took her to Happy Hour. We worked on in theatre until midnight. Saturday made up for it—a beautiful day, no Dustoffs. Don and I took Jan to the beach, to Cyrno's for lunch, then back to the beach. We ignored the OTTs giggling in the background and the Vietnamese, male and female, who invaded our area to inspect Jan in her swimsuit. For a few hours the three of us chatted, swam and soaked up the sun. We could have been in Australia.

Then, would you believe, on Sunday at 0830 Jan and I were at 102 Field Workshops (Sunday, remember, was a normal working morning). The men had contributed $170 to the Nursing School and she was giving a thank-you talk, describing the work the school was doing. I sat back, enjoying the twin pleasures of the engineers ogling their speaker and envying my good fortune.

Everybody (that is, bring all the girls) had an invitation to 161 Recce Flight's Sunday lunch party at Nui Dat. Don Beard elected to stay at 8 Field Ambulance, the women all went by Caribou, the token men by Landrover. Major George Constable, the CO of the Flight, met us with the news that a multiple Dustoff was on its way to Vung Tau. He had a Possum warmed up and waiting. Bruce Daniel and I jumped in and were given a hair-raising ride at 30 to 80 feet, straight across 'unsafe' Hoa Long which we had just driven around!

All the casualties except one went to 36 Evac and we had ours sorted out by 1330 hours. George Constable had been keeping tabs on the situation. He sent down another Possum to fly me back to the party. With the pilot's permission I brought a very pleased Dave Boyle along for the ride.

By now the party was in full swing. George was effusive in his welcome and plenty of food and drink was still left. Somehow he had got the Bien Hoa nurses there too. The girls, reassured by numbers, were in sparkling form, lit up by the flattering attentions of his jungle-clad airmen. George wandered from group to group, beaming his approval. It was a fine memory to have of this warm-hearted aviator, who was shot down and killed two months later.

Back at Vung Tau the night brought another Dustoff, followed by an appendix case. Jan joined me in theatre—the only way we were going to see each other before she left. In the morning Private Walker, the new batman, woke me twenty minutes late. I whizzed Jan to the airfield, me unshaven, she at 0630 looking superb. Master Sergeant Owen of the 536th Tactical Airlift Squadron fixed in an extra seat for her to Can Tho. 'No sweat,' he said. I went back to a shower, the morning list and the last-minute hassles of the medevac flight.

At 1500 the CO called his expected conference. The weighing-up period had finished. There was praise for what had been done, comment on observed inefficiencies and slovenliness. Military discipline was now to be restored. Everything was to be channelled through him. An Officers Location Board would be reintroduced and would be accurately maintained. Soon we would be a Field Hospital. The new commanding officer was obviously going to command.

Bill Watson knew what he was about. He had noted that smartness and military discipline were at their worst in theatre, where the workload was most taxing. He took me aside for some serious words. He understood our situation exactly. A succession of CMF medical officers, with myself the continuing factor and therefore the chief culprit, had organised the theatre team along the informal lines of our own civilian units. Under the pressure of work this was understandable, but it had to change. The CO feared we had created an elite clique whose return to strict discipline would be a difficult and painful process. I guaranteed that there would not be a problem.

With the CO's permission and that of Colonel Beard, I called the boys together for a last friendly chat. Christian names were out, salutes were in. The high standard of work had to be maintained while they demonstrated their ability to be regimentally perfect soldiers. To Sergeant Turnbull and his OTTs this came as no surprise. Although they had enjoyed working informally, military discipline was their natural environment. 'OK, sir. She'll be sweet,' they said.

A few days later Lieutenant Colonel Watson brought Lieutenant General Sir Thomas Daly, Chief of the General Staff, on an inspection tour of the hospital. Triage and theatre were immaculate, the OTTs stood ramrod stiff, Sergeant Turnbull's salute quivered in military deference. The general showed genuine interest when Roy and Dave explained the work they were doing. He complimented Colonel Beard on his team, the surgeon praised me and I praised the boys with a most deeply felt sincerity.

The big changeover parade was held on April Fools Day. Suddenly we were 1 Australian Field Hospital (1AFH) and Digger James's forward detachment was 8 Field Ambulance (Restricted). Other than the flag, nothing seemed to be different. The parent unit and its Nui Dat offshoot might soon be expanding; but that would not concern me. My replacement was due. As soon as he had been given a decent handover I would be gone, and I was negotiating to terminate my full-time duty outside Australia.

The insignificance of my discharge plans and the administrative changes in our one small unit were suddenly put into perspective by President Lyndon Baines Johnson's bombshell speech. Later that day we listened as the slow, dignified tones pronounced that he would freeze troop levels and seek a negotiated peace. 'With America's sons in the fields far away and with America's future under challenge . . . I do not believe I should devote an hour or a day of my time to any personal partisan causes . . . I shall not seek, and I will not accept, the nomination of my party for another term as your President.' Many times in the past year I had felt little kicks of pride that 'I am here', involved in places and events which were part of history in the making. On that first day of April 1968, seated around the radio in the Mess, the officers of 1 Australian Field Hospital were a tiny element of something truly momentous. The mighty United States was giving in. 'All the way with LBJ' had been the slogan that took us into the war. Now LBJ had publicly embarked on the task of getting out.

Next morning Mick, Peter Kentwell and John Kelly (whose honour was satisfied: he had wangled a Mohawk flight before he departed) all went off on the morning Caribou. I mooched around despondently.

From now on each day was going to drag by. Mick and I had not been able to communicate the degree of our real feelings. All we agreed was that we would meet again. Late the same afternoon Captain John Vonwiller walked in, unannounced, and declared himself to be my replacement. I had trouble taking this in. He was so young and he was only a registrar. This was where I had come in. Was 1AFH going backwards in its medical staffing? Well, not my problem. All I could do was pass on what I had learned. I rang Long Xuyen via the military Emu network. 'Tell Jan to expect me within the next two weeks,' I told them.

John Vonwiller proved to be a very switched-on young anaesthetist; it was soon obvious he would do a great job. He and I shared the anaesthetics for a day or two, I filled him in on the equipment, the work, and the idiosyncracies of staff both in and out of theatre. Between sessions I put time into writing a report on the year's activities and catching up on a year's sleep.

When the next mine injuries came, for the first time in many months I stood back and watched. The bloody SOPs were not being strictly followed. My surge of irritation soon died down. John and Don Beard could talk to the OTTs. Maybe they would be doing things differently—it was their show. The reality and the relief were still just beginning to sink in.

The handover extended further afield. At 36 Evac, they were no longer so busy and John got the 25 cent tour. We called at ASCO, where I noticed for the first time that they were selling shirts made in Red China! At the RAAF villa, Ron Plowright was cheerfully slumming it again away from Butterworth. The RAAF commander, Group Captain John Hubble, was definite that the VC in the Long Hais had plans for a Tet attack on Vung Tau. Perhaps Intelligence had been right after all. The nearby Thunderbird Bar I avoided. It was months since I had been there and Thuy thought Xuan had gone to Saigon. John could discover the bar system for himself.

The Happy Hour on Good Friday brought my standard farewell speech from the PMC. It seemed a bit pointless, as hardly any of the officers there knew who I was. Of the old crowd, Brian Kelleher seemed to be the only one left.

On Saturday I started making plans for Long Xuyen, my final swan. Jan rang that night, barely under control. Her mother had died, quite unexpectedly. She had to get home and was obviously not thinking clearly. I promised to be there next day.

The US Caribou to Can Tho was delayed half an hour while they tacked down the floor. A bad start to Easter Sunday. At Can Tho airfield I met Major Larry Joyce and Lieutenant Colonel Humphries and asked about getting to Long Xuyen. Definitely only by air. An Air America helicopter had a spare seat and they would deviate for me into LX. Thank you again, helpful Americans. We could not be winning the war, I commented, if air transport was needed for the short daylight journey. 'The situation's not all that favourable,' said the colonel, 'when I have to work on Easter Sunday.'

Air America's chopper flew us westwards along the Ba Sac River. It might have been a different country from the dreary wastelands of the Vung Tau peninsula. I was looking down on lush tropical riverside vegetation and mile after mile of neat square green fields crisscrossed by a network of canals. Long Xuyen floated into view, a beautiful town spreading gracefully along the south side of the river—green trees, wide streets, well-kept houses, majestic villas.

The pilot knew the Australians' villa. He circled it twice as a signal, then landed me on the local soccer field. The team's pick-up arrived immediately. Jan was more in control. She was being very well looked after by her fellow Australians and by Lois, her American co-adviser. Her immediate concern was the difficulty in getting a message home. The telephone system had become even less reliable after Tet. Some very helpful American civilians including Abel Vella, the district adviser to MACV, organised a direct phone link for me to Colonel Gilmore at 1ALSG. The commander, right on the ball, guaranteed that Jan's family would be told she was on her way home.

The best occupational therapy while waiting for the flights was sight-seeing, with Jan as an informed guide. The Australians lived in a magnificent white villa set in half an acre of lawns and palm trees. Lois had an air-conditioned trailer suite parked permanently in the grounds. The surgical team and the two nursing advisers apparently represented a sizeable proportion of all the round-eyes in Long Xuyen. There were fewer than 200 Westerners in the whole of An Giang Province. The contrast with Vung Tau could scarcely be greater. No soldiers in the streets, no bars, no brothels. The only soliciting was done by well-fed children eager to be photographed. Even the weather was different: the first refreshing rains had already come.

Long Xuyen's hospital was much less busy than those at Bien Hoa and Vung Tau. The most attractive maternity block was a separate building surrounded by gardens and lawns. The facilities were very well maintained; sometimes too well, Jan said: the brand new ambulance refused to carry bleeding patients during Tet. The wards were still congested, parents and children were sleeping on the floor and there was as usual a dismal, barred ward for prisoners.

The most impressive sight was the Nurses Training School. The classrooms were modern, uncluttered and equipped with comfortable desks, wall charts, anatomical models and other teaching aids. The students were enthusiastic young ladies in spotless white uniforms who greeted Jan with respect and affection. It could have been any first class nursing school in Australia, except for the guards. These were half a dozen heavily armed young Vietnamese soldiers who had been installed during Tet. They were enjoying the job, wandering along the verandah outside the classrooms in a manner more adolescent than military. The student nurses were more frightened of these beardless youths with their rifles and grenades than they were of the Viet Cong.

The School had its problems: shortage of interpreters, jealousy in administration, misuse of USAID funds, the oriental streak of corruption. But the basic quality was there, a well-equipped training centre run by Vietnamese with the assistance of Western finance and expertise. Despite her grief Jan could still enthuse on the good that she and Lois were able to do. Formal teaching, not just helping with hospital work, was the key. She would definitely be coming back.

It seemed to me that this School offered a pattern that should be widely repeated, if only the rest of South Viet Nam could become as stable as Long Xuyen. I was appalled by how little I knew of Viet Nam after a year in the country. Although I had seen more than most, the forays out of Vung Tau had been fragmentary episodes with no possibility of really understanding the local situation. My efforts with the language had dwindled to a few halting phrases. There had been no time or opportunity to develop any meaningful friendship with a Vietnamese. 'What was it like over there?', I would soon be asked—and how could I possibly answer?

Our departure from the delta was arranged by the staff at CORDS (Civil Operations and Revolutionary Development Support). On Tuesday morning they put Jan and me into a three-seat Helio with Abel Vella, who was flying to Can Tho. There we waited some miserable hours in the Alamo Lounge of the Special Forces Club before joining an Air America Beechcraft to Saigon. The pilot, we were delighted to hear, was a trainee. The plot to scare me to death was persisting to the end.

After Tet, Saigon seemed totally unchanged from the air and to my complete surprise it was the same on the streets. Newspaper accounts had pictured the capital as a wasteland of destruction. We drove about in the familiar little Renault taxis and nothing seemed different. The US Embassy, a large, confident-looking building opposite its small British counterpart, showed no sign of the damage inflicted during Tet.

I dropped Jan at Mondial to see the nurse education chief, and called in to talk to the people at USAID (sorry, Harry). They 'had no current scope for an anesthesiologist'. Mike Inman, the British liaison medical officer for the Free World Surgical Teams, again made the suggestion that I join one of the teams. But I was still only interested in a more formal teaching post. There were Vietnamese academic doctors to contact, but it would have to be in writing. At the Australian Embassy they were at least helpful in producing the passport I had requested. It was stamped 'Issued at Saigon' and 'Not valid for North Viet Nam'. How fortunate I was not contemplating a few days' stopover in Hanoi.

To pass the hours we went shopping at the Cholon PX, did some sightseeing on foot, had a drink at the Continental Palace. Still there was no evidence at all of war damage. The fighting had been confined to small areas. Even Tan Son Nhut, which had been heavily attacked, bore no scars on the civilian side of the airport.

The processing of tickets and luggage at Air Vietnam was mercifully rapid. Neither of us wanted this goodbye to be prolonged. Jan was in tears as she walked quickly to the aircraft. A typically Arthur Crawford remark flitted through my mind: 'I wouldn't fly in one of those things with some little Oriental fiddling with the doo-dads'.

I was totally drained, but there were two important appointments to be kept in Saigon. At the British Embassy a young and seemingly clueless acting vice-consul found the concept difficult to grasp that an Australian soldier would want to go to Britain from Viet Nam. Reluctantly he stamped my new passport with a visitor's entry visa. Then I went to the Army Pay Office, where a staff captain agreed that my full-time duty would terminate on 22 April.

At Vung Tau there were more farewells. On Saturday night I was given a party by 1 Australian Field Hospital Officers Mess (the name grated; in a bizarre way I still felt it was *my* 8 Field Ambulance Mess). They presented me with an engraved pewter mug. John Frewen, the professional, fixed on my Viet Nam service ribbons. There was an invitation to the Sergeants' Snake Pit; a last theatre beach barbecue. But I no longer belonged.

Don Beard, John Vonwiller and Bob Manning came to Vung Tau airfield to see me off. I shook their hands and climbed aboard the medevac Hercules. It was Monday 22 April 1968, a year and a week since I'd arrived in Viet Nam. It felt like a lifetime.

Postscript

MY TWELVE MONTHS in Viet Nam would be the envy of any combat soldier at Nui Dat or those drearily trapped in the Logistic Support Group. I had the privilege of rewarding work without any great danger; I had many opportunities to play and I got to see something of the country we were sent to defend. Compared to the experiences of servicemen in the two World Wars, it was a brief and mollycoddled tour.

Yet the year had its traumas and the crushing overload of work from the Tet offensive affected me more than I realised. It took months to get back to some sort of normality. Jan and I met up again in England, but she went back to Australia while I stayed and tried to discover what I wanted to do.

The war dragged through its last futile years, the situation in the South deteriorated and I never did get back with my highflown ideas of doing postgraduate teaching in Saigon. The grapevine said that 1 Australian Field Hospital was improving its facilities all the time, staffed almost entirely by CMF doctors on tours of just three months. I was tempted to offer my services again.

They could probably use a bit of experience; Nam Binh was heavily on my mind. But after all the emotional seesaws I had met my English rose and Mary and I were happily married with a family on the way. My military and adventure days were done.

By choosing to live and work in England in 1973, I was spared the disgraceful way Australian veterans were treated by their countrymen and their government. The British were not interested in Viet Nam and I was able to get on with my life. I was all right.

Mick and Marie had married and the four of us stayed very close despite separation by wide oceans. With each visit it became more apparent that Mick was not all right. The stress of fearful responsibility had got to him—experienced, mature, fun-loving Mick. The realisation took a long while and it really shook me. Bit by bit over the years, I also came to recognise my most indefensible shortcoming at Vung Tau. I had totally failed to appreciate the emotional trauma being inflicted on our young medics.

Doctors and nurses become hardened by training and experience; if they are lucky, it happens in a controlled process of gradual exposure. Thanks to Australia's appalling toll of road trauma we were used to dealing with shattered young bodies. Our operating theatre technicians, particularly the younger ones, had no comparable background and no opportunity for a period of gradual adjustment. Yet they responded so professionally to our training and performed so well when the casualties began to arrive that I accepted their apparent calmness without question.

Counselling has now become a trendy, overused business with professionals creating jobs for themselves and busybody amateurs taking the opportunity to impart their own prejudiced opinions. In 1967, I am sure, the boys would have laughed at some tame psychologist trying to explore their emotions. They might well have looked to *us,* though—their older, medically qualified colleagues. We should have provided support, and we failed them. The best I ever offered was the superficial jokeyness we shared together when the times were good.

The awful truth, I later discovered, is that they were all affected by their experiences, some very badly. They had seen men of their own age with limbs blown off and bodies ripped by shrapnel. They had taken part in desperate surgical battles with bellies full of blood. They had been handed amputated legs to be burned. Occasionally they had seen death. The ghastliness was worst when the injuries were caused by accidents with our own mines or by friendly fire. In retrospect it is astonishing that nobody broke down and that the work in resus and in theatre rarely faltered. But the memories were being stored up. And when they got home they were subjected to years of abuse and vilification for serving their country.

I was lucky. I had my privileged officer's war, then an escape from the national hostility. My psychological traumas were shortlived. Or perhaps not: while writing this account I began to have nightmares flashing back 30 years—terrifying scenes of soldiers horrifically injured and me unable to cope. I wonder if Captain Morrie Peacock, Major Arthur Crawford and Colonel Don Beard have been similarly disturbed. The Vietnam Wall of Remembrance in Canberra does not include the names of those who served as members of the Citizen Military Forces. Choy-Oy! Perhaps we expect too much. At least they did readjust my pay book.

Glossary and explanation of medical terms

1ALSG 1 Australian Logistic Support Group
2IC Second-in-command
A&D Admission and discharge
airway The passage for air from nose and mouth to the lungs via the back of the mouth, the larynx (voicebox) and trachea (windpipe). Airway obstruction, e.g. by the tongue falling back, vomit or blood, is a much-feared hazard of anaesthesia.
Amytal Amylobarbitone; a sedative barbiturate given as a tablet or by injection. Rarely used today.
anaesthetist, anesthetist, anesthesiologist In British-influenced medicine, an anaesthetist is a specialist doctor. In the US, the equivalent is an anesthesiologist, while an anesthetist is a nurse trained to give anaesthetics.
Angiocath Trademark name of a short plastic tube (cannula) used for giving fluid or drugs into a vein
anoxia (more correctly hypoxia) Lack of oxygen
ARVN Army of the Republic of Viet Nam
ASCO Australian Services Canteens Organisation
bag and mask A system of emergency assistance for breathing by squeezing air or oxygen from a rubber bag via an airtight mask over nose and mouth
bilateral Both sides, e.g. bilateral leg amputations
Bird; Bennett Two types of ventilator (machines which assist or replace the patient's own breathing)
block, nerve block Local anaesthetic injected to block transmission of impulses through a nerve, thus producing an area insensitive to pain
Boyle Machine For over 50 years the standard British type of anaesthetic apparatus. Delivers a mixture of oxygen, nitrous oxide and agents such as cyclopropane and halothane. Boyle was an anaesthetist at St Bartholomew's hospital in London.
brachial plexus block Injection of local anaesthetic behind the collar

bone into the nerves running from the spinal cord to the arm

cannula A short plastic tube inserted into a vein

casualty As well as a victim of trauma, the area where the victims receive immediate treatment

central venous pressure (CVP) The pressure in the large veins returning blood to the heart. A low CVP can mean inadequate fluid replacement; a high CVP can mean over-transfusion or failure of the heart to pump the blood on.

chlamydia An infection, commonly sexually transmitted, which was unrecognised in the 1960s

claymore Command-detonated anti-personnel mine

CMF Citizen Military Forces

colloid /crystalloid solutions Types of fluid given intravenously to replace blood loss

compound fracture A fracture where broken bone is exposed due to damage to the overlying tissue and skin. The great risk is infection.

cupping Ancient treatment whereby a heated, wide-mouthed glass container is applied to the skin, creating a partial vacuum which draws up the underlying tissues and blood. Similar in principle to applying leeches.

cutdown Inserting a cannula in a vein by cutting through the skin, exposing the vein and tying the cannula in place

cyclopropane Highly flammable anaesthetic gas. Rarely used today.

debridement Surgical removal of all foreign material and all severely damaged tissue following injury

delayed primary closure (DPC) A few days after debridement, if there is no sign of infection, the wound is closed by suturing

diathermy Electrical apparatus used in surgery for controlling bleeding by heat coagulation

EMO Apparatus devised in Oxford (Epstein, Macintosh, Oxford) for giving controlled concentrations of ether

endotracheal tube (ETT) Rubber or plastic tube passed via mouth or nose through larynx into trachea (windpipe). Usually overcomes the problem of obstruction to the airway.

ether The first successful anaesthetic agent (1846). Strong-smelling and highly flammable, it is still used in third world countries because it is simple, relatively safe and cheap.

external jugular vein Large vein just under the skin on each side of the neck. The vein visible when a singer hits a high note.

GA General anaesthetic. The patient is unconscious, as distinct from a local anaesthetic or nerve block, where the patient is usually awake.

halothane Non-flammable anaesthetic which largely replaced ether in the 1960s. Now itself out of fashion

hindquarter amputation The entire lower limb is removed at the hip joint

hoochie A personal shelter. Purpose-made or fashioned from e.g. waterproof capes.

Horseshoe An elevated feature to the east of Nui Dat

ICU Intensive Care Unit

induction The start of an anaesthetic: the change from awake to unconscious. Induction is usually by IV injection or inhalation of anaesthetic gas or vapour.

inflatable tourniquet Method of controlling bleeding from a limb. An encircling cuff is inflated to high pressure by a bicycle-style hand pump.

Intracath Trademark name of a long plastic tube (catheter) used for giving fluid or drugs into a vein

intubation Passing an endotracheal tube through the larynx into the trachea

IV Intravenous; fluid or medication given by direct injection into a vein or through an IV line

IV drip Apparatus for giving fluid intravenously. The clear plastic tubing of the 'giving set' has a drip chamber and a flow control which is set to give the required number of drops per minute.

IV line A plastic tube inserted through the skin into a vein. May be short (cannula) or long (catheter).

laryngoscope Specialised torch with metal blade passed over the back of the tongue to view the larynx. Used to correctly place an endotracheal tube.

larynx The 'voicebox'. Its framework of cartilage produces the male 'Adam's apple'. Within are the vocal cords which protect the entrance to the trachea (windpipe). An endotracheal tube is passed between the vocal cords and so into the trachea.

litter Stretcher for transporting patient

litter team Four men tasked with carrying a stretcher patient

low-titre O positive blood Blood collected from donors which is unlikely to cause severe reactions when transfused even without cross-matching

lytic cocktail Mixture of sedative and analgesic drugs. With the right dose, the patient is conscious, pain-free and calm.

LZ Landing zone for helicopters
maintenance Keeping the patient anaesthetised following induction. In the 1960s this was nearly always done by breathing a mixture of gases from an anaesthetic machine. Many modern anaesthetists use a continuous infusion of intravenous anaesthetics.
manometer A U-shaped tube for measuring the pressure of a liquid
metatarsal block Injection of local anaesthetic into the nerves of the foot to anaesthetise a toe
MO Medical officer
moxibustion Ancient treatment. Application of heat, usually by burning material, to specific areas of skin.
MUST Medical Unit Self-contained Transportable
NCO Non-commissioned officer
nitrous oxide (Laughing gas.) Widely used anaesthetic gas given with oxygen via a Boyle-type machine. With modern anaesthetics its popularity is diminishing.
NSU Non-specific urethritis. Inflammation of the urethra producing a discharge from which no infecting agent can be identified. (Gonorrhoea is a specific urethritis.)
OR Operating room (US terminology)
OTT Operating theatre technician
Pentothal Trade name for thiopentone. The most commonly used IV induction agent in the 1960s.
Pethidine (meperidine in the US) Powerful morphine-like pain relieving drug
picquet Guard or sentry
PMC President of the Mess Committee
pneumothorax Air in the chest between the lung and chest wall. Small volumes are of little significance; large volumes can threaten life by collapsing the lung.
pre op, post op Before and after operation. Applied to treatment given and also the hospital areas involved.
PUO Pyrexia (fever) of unknown origin
PX Post Exchange. US Army duty-free store.
RAAF Royal Australian Air Force
RAASC Royal Australian Army Service Corps
RAP Regimental Aid Post
R&C Rest and Convalescence leave. Taken in Viet Nam.
resus Resuscitation. Mainly ensuring a clear airway, adequate breathing, pain relief, and restoring blood volume by control of bleeding

and giving intravenous fluids. Also the hospital area where this is done.
RPG Rocket-propelled grenade
R&R Rest and Recreation leave. Taken out of country.
RTA Medical examination before return to Australia
slick, slick-ship Unarmed Huey helicopter used for transport of combat troops. Usually protected by gunships.
SOPs Standard operating procedures
squeezing the bag Hand squeezing the rubber bag of anaesthetic apparatus or emergency equipment to 'breathe' for the patient
stone (urinary) Solid material formed from sediment in the urine. Can cause problems in kidney, ureter or bladder.
sucker/suction Vital equipment in anaesthesia to rapidly clear the airway of secretions, blood or vomit
tracheotomy An incision in the front of the neck to open the windpipe. Also the tube inserted in the trachea to keep it open.
triage Assessing and sorting casualties into an order of priority for treatment. Also the name of the area where the assessment takes place.
UPAC Central power unit of MUST
ureter The narrow tube through which urine passes from the kidney to the bladder
USARV United States Army Viet Nam
venous pressure The pressure in a vein; during resuscitation the important measurement is central venous pressure (CVP). See above.
ventilator Machine which assists or replaces the patient's own breathing
Viet Cong (VC) Communist force or individual fighters
Warrie War story; usually highly embellished
WRAIR Walter Reed Army Institute of Research (US)

Index